SELF-DECEPTION AND MORALITY

SELF-DECEPTION

AND

MORALITY

Mike W. Martin

UNIVERSITY PRESS OF KANSAS

© 1986 by the University Press of Kansas

Published by the University Press of Kansas (Lawrence, Kansas 66045), which was organized by the Kansas Board of Regents and is operated and funded by Emporia State University, Fort Hays State University, Kansas State University, Pittsburg State University, the University of Kansas, and Wichita State University

Library of Congress Cataloging in Publication Data

Martin, Mike W., 1946–
    Self-deception and morality.
    Bibliography: p.
    Includes index.
    1. Self-deception—Moral and ethical aspects.
I. Title.
BJ1429.3.M37 1986   179'.8   86-5467
ISBN 0-7006-0297-6

Printed in the United States of America

10 9 8 7 6 5 4 3 2 1

For Shannon

Contents

Preface

Ancient wisdom, or at least faith, regarded self-understanding as the basis for morally significant life. As deeply as we desire this significance, however, we are prone to avoid the truth when it threatens our self-esteem or sense of well-being. Achieving genuine self-understanding is a task that requires confronting our own evasion of ourselves and the world. As part of that task we need to enrich our comprehension of self-deception: not just what it is and why we engage in it but what it implies from a moral point of view.

Yet how should the deeply rooted tendency to deceive ourselves be understood in moral terms? No simple answer will do, for self-deception arises in many forms and circumstances and can be viewed from contrasting moral perspectives. For existentialists like Kierkegaard, Nietzsche, and Sartre, self-deception was a fundamental concern in moral philosophy, as it was for earlier religious thinkers such as Joseph Butler in the eighteenth century. Recent English-speaking philosophers, however, have devoted relatively little attention to its moral complexity. They have tended to focus instead on the conceptual problems which self-deception poses for epistemology and philosophy of mind, especially the puzzling patterns of knowledge, consciousness, and willful belief sometimes involved in lying to oneself.

In this book, by contrast, self-deception is approached as a significant topic for both general ethical theory and applied ethics. I begin by analyzing self-deception as the evasion of acknowledging to oneself the truth (or one's unbiased view of the truth). Then I set forth a systematic framework identifying the main moral perspectives and traditions concerning self-deception that have emerged in western philosophy. In doing so, I clarify related concepts such as sincerity, authenticity, honesty, hypocrisy, and weakness of will.

While working on this book I received financial support in the form of a Fellowship for College Teachers from the National Endowment for the Humanities during 1981–1982 and an Arnold L. and Lois S. Graves Award for teachers in the humanities during 1984–1985. Chapman College gave me a sabbatical leave and reduced my teaching load to aid in completing the manuscript. Permission to draw upon my previously published articles was kindly granted by the editors of *Dialogue: Canadian Philosophical Review, Man and World, Mind, the Personalist* (now the *Pacific Philosophical Quarterly*), and the *Philosophy Research Archives*.

Several persons made helpful criticisms of parts of this book or of my earlier writings, from which the book developed. I wish to thank Kent Bach, Alan Drengson, Herbert Fingarette, Shannon Snow Martin, A. I. Melden, Joseph Runzo, Gerasimos Santas, David Smith, and Aaron Snyder. I am especially grateful to Robert Audi and John King-Farlow for reading the entire manuscript and offering numerous suggestions. Kate Torrey gave me ideal editorial guidance and encouragement.

My interest in self-deception as a philosophical topic was focused by Fred Hagen's spirited and inspired teaching at the University of Utah. It was sustained under the mentorship of A. I. Melden while I was a graduate student at the University of California, Irvine. Herbert Fingarette, through his books and personal correspondence, provided a constant stimulus.

Above all, I thank my mother, Ruth Lochhead Martin, and my wife, Shannon Snow Martin, for their support in every way and for their love.

1

Introduction

How little absolute sincerity is to be expected, even from persons otherwise honest, whenever their interest in any way bears on a matter, can be judged from the fact that we so often deceive ourselves where hope bribes us, or fear befools us, or suspicion torments us, or vanity flatters us, or a hypothesis infatuates and blinds us, or a small purpose close at hand interferes with one greater but more distant.
—Arthur Schopenhauer, *The World as Will and Representation*

We are accustomed to trust our commitment to truth and to truthfulness. Our errors are easily dismissed as inevitable, given the complexity of the world and the limits of our intelligence. Self-deception disturbs us because it calls into question the purity of this commitment. It reveals how at any moment we act on passions and interests capable of filtering, deflecting, and garnishing an impartial concern for truth. It confronts us with the possibility that we may be our own greatest obstacles in a search for self-understanding and insight into the world. And it leaves us perplexed at the irony of a creature whose rationality is rivaled by a capacity for distorted reasoning, deliberate ignorance, and self-directed lies.

Self-deception is even more perplexing when it contributes to immorality. Does it thereby increase guilt for willful inattention to misconduct and voluntary ignorance about vices, or does it diminish guilt by making us unaware of what we are doing? Does all self-deception involve some guilt, and is it among the most abhorrent evils, as some moralists and theologians have charged? Or is it only wrong sometimes, such as when it has bad consequences? Could it on occasion

1

be permissible or even desirable to deceive ourselves, just as we are sometimes justified in deceiving other people? Are self-deceivers perhaps more like innocent victims than like perpetrators of deceit and, as such, deserving of compassion and help? Or, paradoxically, are they best viewed with ambivalence: culpable as deceivers and simultaneously innocent as victims of deception?

Answers to these questions promise an enriched understanding of sincerity, honesty, and authenticity. These values have survived largely unscathed in a century in which moral skepticism and nihilism have had something of a heyday. Beginning with Freud, the clinical sciences elevated honesty with oneself to a paramount virtue, essential in overcoming neurosis and promoting mental health. Inspired by Nietzsche and Kierkegaard, existentialist philosophers like Jean-Paul Sartre treated authenticity as essentially the sole virtue and regarded self-deception as the supreme vice. Following Dostoyevsky, Tolstoy, and Ibsen, a string of twentieth-century writers made authenticity and self-deception central themes in their novels and plays: André Gide, Marcel Proust, T. S. Eliot, Eugene O'Neill, Jean-Paul Sartre, Albert Camus, Ralph Ellison, Katherine Anne Porter and John Barth, among others.

Precisely what is the relationship between avoiding self-deception and embracing the positive values of honesty, sincerity, intellectual integrity, and authenticity? Is avoiding self-deception the sole or primary element in being authentic and honest with oneself? How should these values, in turn, function within a comprehensive moral perspective? Can authenticity be justified as the primary value? Or is it a mere preparatory virtue that serves as a means to acquiring more substantive virtues?

In addressing ourselves to these questions, we will be departing from the emphasis of most recent philosophical debates concerning self-deception. Those debates have centered on the epistemological paradoxes suggested by the idea of lying to oneself—paradoxes concerning knowledge, consciousness, and willful belief. The central controversy has been over whether it is possible to lie to oneself in the sense of intentionally persuading oneself to believe what is simultaneously known to be false. How could this take place without a division of the self involving seeming impossibilities—believing and disbelieving the same thing, knowing and not knowing it, being conscious and not conscious of it, and willfully creating a belief by fiat? In his seminal book, *Self-Deception*, Herbert Fingarette broke new ground by shifting the emphasis to questions about personal identity. Yet even he devoted only a few pages to the moral status of self-deception.

The task of resolving the epistemological puzzles is important because of the light it sheds on the concepts of belief, knowledge, intention, consciousness, and self-identity. Moreover, the paradoxes cannot be ignored because they bear on understanding the moral status of some forms of self-deception. Nevertheless, a full-scale attempt to resolve them here would leave space for little more than adumbrating the moral issues.

As a compromise, in Chapter 2 I present a working analysis of self-deception and indicate how it relates to the epistemological paradoxes. This view of self-deception as evading self-acknowledgment provides the flexibility needed for grappling with the diversity of approaches to self-deception adopted by moral philosophers. In Chapter 2 I also discuss the apparent moral paradox that self-deceivers seem to be both guilty as deceivers and innocent as victims of deception.

In subsequent chapters I explore the four main traditions, which offer strikingly different moral perspectives. The *Inner Hypocrisy Tradition* is preoccupied with self-deception about immorality. It regards self-deceivers as culpable cheats who corrupt their own moral understanding and thereby harm others. The *Authenticity Tradition* makes more sweeping condemnations of self-deception as constituting cowardice and contemptible self-betrayal. The *Moral Ambiguity Tradition* views self-deceivers as behaving in morally ambiguous ways that preclude holding them fully responsible. For the most part, they are victims who lack self-awareness, suffer from mental illness, are compelled by unconscious forces, or are determined by social and genetic factors beyond their control. The *Vital Lie Tradition* offers a positive assessment of how self-deception can help sustain self-esteem, viable human relationships, and other significant goods.

I discuss major thinkers in each tradition, but I do not systematically survey the development of the traditions in literature, religious thought, social science, and philosophy. The present inquiry is philosophical rather than historical. It is concerned with clarifying moral concepts related to self-deception, evaluating the acts and states involved in it, inquiring into the justification of moral attitudes toward it, and developing a comprehensive framework for exploring its moral dimensions. Nevertheless, because this framework is provided by the four historical and interdisciplinary traditions, I will draw attention to a rich heritage of writing on self-deception in philosophy, literature, religious thought, and the social sciences.

Chapter 3 is devoted to the Inner Hypocrisy Tradition. In it I examine how the notion of self-deception functions within traditional ethics as an explanation of wrongdoing. By traditional ethics I mean any ethical theory that treats judgments about moral obligations as objectively justifiable by appeal to reasons making a valid claim on us. Ethicists such as Bishop Butler and Max Scheler criticized self-deception only when it corrupts conscience and warps moral understanding. They treated it as a kind of derivative wrong, censurable for its role in supporting immoral conduct. Kant, by contrast, condemned all self-deception as inherently immoral. I argue that much self-deception is indeed blameworthy for its harmful effects on others and for its hypocritical violation of standards of honesty, but Kant went too far in condemning all self-deception. I then explore the conceptual connections between self-deception and hypocrisy and between self-deception and moral weakness of will.

The striking shift in approach to the ethics of self-deception that occurs in existentialism, the main current within the Authenticity Tradition, is identified in Chapter 4. Existentialists regard the avoidance of self-deception as the substance of their paramount virtue, authenticity. Kierkegaard was the key transitional figure who initiated this shift in approach. Although he retained a conception of objective values, Kierkegaard was preoccupied with avoiding self-deception by authentically committing ourselves to those values. Much of the chapter deals with Sartre's influential account of self-deception. More than any other modern thinker, Sartre saw the perils of self-deception. Yet he was mistaken in regarding its avoidance as the primary moral value. The chapter concludes with a discussion of the two primary ingredients in most conceptions of authenticity—autonomy and acknowledgment of significant truth—and my recommendation for rethinking these ingredients.

The fact that self-deception often causes harm does not mean that self-deceivers are always responsible for that harm. Justified ascriptions of moral responsibility presuppose that people acted voluntarily or can be expected to have done so. These ascriptions presuppose that agents knew or should have known what they were doing and that they had control over or could reasonably be expected to have exercised control over their conduct. The Moral Ambiguity Tradition questions whether these presuppositions are satisfied by self-deceivers.

Two branches of the Moral Ambiguity Tradition are distinguished in Chapter 5. One branch derives from the psychoanalytic view of self-deceivers as suffering from the effects of unconscious forces. Influenced by psychoanalytic theory, R. G. Collingwood contended that an absence of conscious control renders the actions of self-deceivers morally opaque. More recently, Herbert Fingarette charged that self-deception is morally ambiguous because it undermines capacities for personal and moral agency. I argue that Collingwood and Fingarette have overgeneralized. Whereas many variables need to be considered in assessing moral responsibility for self-deception and its effects, much self-deception is not morally ambiguous. And even from Freud's perspective, it need not be tied to mental illness.

A second branch of the Moral Ambiguity Tradition proceeds from a deterministic worldview. According to it, each of us is completely determined by genetic and social forces beyond our control, and because of this we lack responsibility for our conduct. Mary Haight has expressed sympathy for this perspective. She contended that the concept of self-deception is paradoxical and confused; we employ it metaphorically because of uncertainty about whether we are free or determined. Without attempting to resolve the issue of free will versus determinism, I reject Haight's claim that the prospect of determinism automatically places in doubt the moral responsibility of self-deceivers.

Chapter 6 is devoted to the Vital Lie Tradition. This tradition regards self-deception as a valuable coping technique shielding us from unbearable realities and debilitating truths and contributing to personal growth, self-respect, love, and community. To unmask it without sensitivity to the vital needs it serves can be disastrous. And to treat respect for truth as the supreme value undermines equally important values, such as kindness and social cooperation. In responding to the legitimate claims of this tradition, however, I reassert the importance of rationality based on a respect for truth. I also indicate how non–self-deceiving forms of faith, hope, and imaginative expression can serve the vital needs emphasized in this tradition without abandoning respect for truth. The chapter concludes with a discussion of honesty with oneself, combined with a summary of some of the main themes of the entire book.

In the epilogue I expand the summary while adding a caution about ascribing self-deception to people on the basis of values whose precise implications are in doubt.

Throughout, my concern is not to apply general ethical theories about what makes actions right or wrong. Some readers may be surprised by this because moral philosophy has been dominated by the development, defense, and criticism of such theories (theories such as utilitarianism, duty-based ethics, human-rights ethics—each of which has several main versions). Since the 1960s, however, ethicists have explored a multitude of fresh approaches to moral questions. This development was spurred by the growth of applied ethics, which seeks to enrich practical moral reflection without adjudicating among competing general standards of right conduct. It has also been influenced by a resurgence of interest in virtue ethics, that is, the ethics of character traits, motives, and attitudes. Both of these movements have influenced me in writing this book.

2

Evading Self-Acknowledgment

It is easy to show that man is, in fact, guilty of many *inner* lies, but to explain the possibility of an inner lie seems more difficult.
—Immanuel Kant, *The Doctrine of Virtue*

Self-deception, as conceived here, is the purposeful or intentional evasion of fully acknowledging something to oneself. Contrary to Kant's assertion, it need not consist of an "inner lie," that is, lying to oneself by persuading oneself to believe something one knows is false. It need not even involve persuading oneself to hold a false belief. It *may* involve these things. Or it might consist of maneuvers not centered on belief formation. As with interpersonal deception, self-deception typically involves concealing a truth or one's view of the truth, but the concealment can take many forms.

In this chapter I develop a view of self-deception as the evasion of self-acknowledgment, explain its rationale, and sketch how it applies to several paradoxes discussed in recent philosophy. In the first section several patterns or strategies of evasion are distinguished and related to one another. In the next section I further clarify the notions of evasion and self-acknowledgment, and in the last section I deal with the paradoxes.

PATTERNS OF EVASION

There are many ways of sorting self-deception into characteristic patterns. Rougher and finer-grained distinctions are possible, and

6

the complexity of human behavior precludes an exhaustive categorization. Sartre distinguished various patterns in terms of his basic (phenomenological) distinctions concerning human consciousness. Freud identified patterns of unconscious self-deception paralleling the main forms of psychological defense he encountered in his clinical work. Ethicists have drawn a variety of distinctions to aid them in evaluating self-deceit. The following classification is intended to identify only a few everyday ways in which people evade acknowledging to themselves truths or their honest views of the truth, ways that will aid us in developing a working account of self-deception.

The marketplace provides fertile ground for self-deception, such as where white-collar crime is a temptation. Until recently, crime among white-collar workers was largely neglected by the law, and even today the penalties are relatively light. One of the earlier large-scale prosecutions of white-collar criminals occurred in 1960.[1] Some forty-five individuals from twenty-nine corporations were convicted of secretly fixing consumer prices for electricity in violation of the Sherman Anti-Trust Act. The guilty ranged from the vice-presidents of General Electric and Westinghouse Corporation to lower-level managers and their assistants. As a group they were described as having high moral character, and many of them were active in churches, charities, and civic organizations. Let us imagine how they might have evaded acknowledging to themselves that their actions were improper. What sorts of tactics might they confess to once they overcame their self-deception? In answering this question let us also bring to mind some of the reasons that might have led them to adopt these tactics.

Willful Ignorance. Jack, a low-level manager who played a minor role as a messenger, testified in court that he really had not known he was doing anything illegal. He admitted, however, that his previous ignorance was not altogether accidental. It resulted largely from his own actions or, rather, from his purposely omitted actions. He suspected that he might be involved in illegal activities and had a general knowledge that something might be amiss. Yet he did not want to make waves, which could hurt his upward mobility within the corporation. Acting on his suspicions, he refused to question his colleagues about what was going on. Whereas this refusal was purposeful (that is, not just serving a purpose, but actually done on purpose), it was never reflected upon sufficiently to be called deliberate. On one occasion the idea of checking with a lawyer entered his mind, but he let the idea drop immediately. In this and other ways, he avoided appropriate inquiries and discussions that he sensed might uncover information he preferred not to know.

Systematic Ignoring. Jill, like the rest of the conspirators to be discussed, knew what Jack did not. Instead of mere suspicions, she and the others had detailed and full knowledge that what was going on was illegal and had recurring feelings that it was immoral. But Jill systematically refused to think about the implications of her involvement in an illegal conspiracy. If the topic came up in conversations, she would *distract* her thoughts to more pleasant topics. When the idea of impropriety began to enter her thoughts, she quickly blocked it from becoming the focus of her attention. She also *disregarded* the legal and moral liabilities in the sense of not taking them into account and not giving them due weight when she reflected on her life. Her motive for the systematic ignoring was a genuine desire to be a cooperative "team player" serving the good of the corporation.

Emotional Detachment. Dick, unlike Jill, was sometimes willing to attend to the fact that he was engaged in illegal activities and to use this fact in his reasoning. Anxious about the prospect of lowered self-esteem if he acknowledged (to himself and others) that he was a criminal, he detached himself emotionally from what this involvement meant for his character. He blocked, hardened, and froze the emotions he would feel if he were to open up his mind to what he knew. In conversations with fellow conspirators about their roles in the price-fixing, he would display a coldness and an almost clinical detachment. His usual warmth and ease were replaced with tensed muscles, constricted breathing, and a hardened countenance. Occasionally he would reveal a contrasting, though equally uncharacteristic, bubbling glibness which enabled him to dismiss the seriousness of the topic. In retrospect he said he "intellectually believed" that what he was doing was wrong, but he avoided emotional recognition and heartfelt conviction about his wrongdoing.

Self-Pretense. Jane was like Dick in that she would sometimes become emotionally detached. But she engaged in a wider range of additional behaviors in pretending to herself that nothing seriously immoral was involved. Spurred in part by greed and in part by a vague fear of taking a stand against her colleagues, she struggled to believe (without complete success) that her actions were permissible. Consumers, she told herself, actually benefited from the price-fixing because it helped stabilize the market and protected it from the vacillations caused by cutthroat competition. She made every effort to talk, think, and act confidently as she carried out her part at secret meetings; she even reassured a colleague who expressed qualms about the activities. She did much the same with her own qualms, which occasionally brought with them a deflating awareness that her self-pretense was a charade. She often would try to restore her confidence by imagining how good things would be after she made her first million dollars. For the most part she managed to live in a kind of fantasy world, but a world of self-pretense rather than false belief.

Rationalization. Whereas Jane tried hard to convince herself that her actions were permissible, Tom actually succeeded. He admitted that his acts were "technically illegal," but he persuaded himself to believe they were not significantly wrong or unethical. Yes, a law was being broken, but it was a bad law and hurt business. So he rationalized matters to himself and others. Participants in the price-fixing were not criminals out to gain personal advantage; they were serving the interests of the corporation. Tom would not have said this about other white-collar criminals, and his evaluation of his involvement in the conspiracy was surprisingly at odds with his general sensitivity in moral and religious matters. His self-deception arose as an effort to silence an otherwise anguished conscience.

A few caveats are appropriate at this point. These five patterns of self-deception, to reiterate, are not intended to constitute an exhaustive list. Moreover, each pattern may have significant variations. For example, systematic ignoring might be (and often is) aided by using alcohol; emotional detachment might be fortified by the dulling effects of compulsive overeating. Again, in keeping themselves willfully ignorant, individuals may have varying degrees of consciousness of their purposes, all the way from an occasional dim awareness to recurrent moments of attentiveness, leaving us unsure whether the person really is self-deceived. Furthermore, the labels attached to the patterns are intended only to draw attention to the primary psychological strategy employed. There is no suggestion that these types of behavior—willing to be ignorant, systematic ignoring, emotional detachment, self-pretense, rationalization—always involve purposeful self-deception.

Finally, the examples of the conspirators are deliberately simplified. In actual situations self-deception tends to be multifaceted, with the patterns becoming interwoven and mutually reinforcing. This can be illustrated with Tolstoy's description, in *Anna Karenina*, of Karenin's self-deceiving reaction upon learning that his wife, Anna, is in love with Count Vronsky.[2]

Arriving late at a party, Karenin sees Anna seated alone with Count Vronsky and engaged in an intimate conversation. Karenin notices that acquaintances present in the room regard the situation as socially improper (as indeed it was within upper-class Tsarist Russia). Karenin decides to talk with Anna about the incident later that evening. But as he formulates what he will say, he begins to sense that Anna's conduct may reveal more than social indiscretion and that perhaps she has fallen in love with Vronsky. Although he has been married seven years to a woman much younger than himself, such a possibility has never occurred to him. Indeed, the very idea that Anna might have an emotional life separate from his own strikes him with horror. His feeble effort to understand her is short-lived. Telling himself that he has no right to enter into her private thoughts, he directs his attention to composing the homily he will deliver to her.

When Karenin confronts Anna, she blithely dismisses his comments about the importance of social decorum. From then on she puts up an "impenetrable stone wall of gay bewilderment" against his criticisms and innuendos about her frequent meetings with Vronsky. This is so conspicuously out of keeping with her characteristic openness that Karenin is left with no basis for doubting that she loves Vronsky. Though he has no absolute proof, he knows "deep inside him" that the couple are having an affair. But throughout the following year, he evades acknowledging to himself what he knows. He simply "refused to recognize" and confront it.

Karenin's evasion of self-acknowledgment is displayed in a cluster of mutually reinforcing patterns of behavior. He remains *willfully ignorant* of the details of Anna's affair. Acting on his suspicion (or tacit knowledge) that Anna and Vronsky are in love, he studiously keeps himself ignorant of Anna's specific whereabouts. He "did not see and did not want to understand" why Anna insists on moving to their summer home, closer to where Vronsky lives. Nor does he question Anna or their friends along lines made pertinent by what he already knows, and he "did not want to see" how his acquaintances shun Anna.

Karenin's willful ignorance is sustained by avoiding reflection about Anna's relationship with Vronsky. He *systematically ignores* this entire topic; indeed, for the most part he ignores Anna altogether. After allowing her to live in a separate house and deciding to visit her only once a week, he does not allow his thoughts "to stray further about anything that concerned her." Skillfully he maneuvers to prevent situations from developing that might force his attention to the affair. For example, "without acknowledging it to himself," he looks for opportunities to have other persons present when he meets with Anna in order to forestall intimate conversations which might lead in the direction of painful truths.

Perhaps the most striking aspect of Karenin's evasion of self-acknowledgment is his *emotional detachment*. Already his life is characterized by rigid conformity to conventions, obeisance to public opinion and formal religion, and a disposition to withhold many of his emotions from himself and others. All these tendencies become more pronounced and focused as he "locked and bolted that compartment of his heart which contained his feelings" for Anna and their son.

Karenin engages in various acts of *self-pretense* which help support his ignorance, ignoring, and detachment. When an acquaintance raises the topic of Vronsky and Anna, he aggressively insists that he believes everything is proper. Spontaneously and without reflection on what he is doing, he invents work for himself and then plays the role of the overworked official who is too busy to think about personal problems. While in Anna's presence at a social gathering, he manifests a "peculiar loquaciousness" as he adopts the role of the sparkling conversationalist. This artificially induced chatter aids him in concealing from himself his uneasiness and also helps suppress some of his thoughts about Anna.

All this behavior predisposes him to engage in *rationalization*—that is, biased and distorted explanations—when he forms beliefs. "He only saw the outward signs" of the relationship between Anna and Vronsky and believes what he wants to believe about it. Eagerly he accepts Anna's lies and explanations. By the time Anna decides to confront him with the truth, he is "ready to believe anything" rather than have his worst suspicions confirmed.

Later, after Anna forces him to recognize her affair with Vronsky, Karenin engages in a series of new rationalizations designed to reject any responsibility for wrecking his marriage. All along he has known that Anna is a depraved woman, he tells himself, and pity and compassion have led to his self-deception about her depravity. This illustrates something we shall have occasion to comment on again later: accusations of self-deception are themselves highly susceptible to self-deception, whether they are directed toward oneself or others.

EVASION AND ACKNOWLEDGMENT

Ordinary descriptions of self-deceivers employ a bewildering medley of ideas and images. Using concealment terms, we say they hide, conceal, and camouflage the truth from themselves. In visual imagery, we describe them as preventing themselves from seeing the facts, obscuring their own vision, blinding themselves, and intentionally overlooking what is before their eyes. Auditory imagery has them refusing to listen or hear and being deaf to the truth. Recognition terms have them avoiding apprehension, identification, or recognition of what they suspect. In the language of consciousness, we say they ignore or refuse to attend to a harsh reality or that they suppress and repress ideas and topics. With the imagery of confrontation, we characterize them as refusing to face up to a harsh reality. In terms of belief and knowledge, we describe them as keeping themselves ignorant and persuading themselves to hold false beliefs. We press into service a number of epithets which are pejorative or invite evaluative judgments: lying to oneself, dishonest role playing, conning and duping oneself, inner insincerity, hypocrisy before oneself, inauthenticity—and, indeed, self-deception and self-deceit. Finally, we often say that self-deceivers refuse to acknowledge, avow, admit, or confess something to themselves.

Recent philosophical theories of self-deception reflect this diversity of language. Nevertheless, there has been one widely preferred starting point: the assumption that in clear-cut cases, deceiving oneself entails persuading oneself to hold a false belief. The problem has been to explain when false beliefs constitute a state of self-deception and how self-deceivers generate and maintain these beliefs. Explanations have been developed in many directions: self-deceivers simultaneously know or believe at some lower level of consciousness that their self-deceiving belief is false;[3] they know this unconsciously;[4] they hold ''second-order'' false beliefs about their contradictory beliefs;[5] they cause themselves to believe what they know to be false and then act on their self-contradictory cognitive states in differing types of circumstances;[6] they ignore the contradiction in their beliefs;[7] they refuse to attend to the detailed contents of their self-deceiving belief;[8] they maintain the self-deceiving belief despite strong contrary evidence available to them;[9] they explain away, discount, and distort this evidence while reasoning;[10] their belief is motivated by a bias which they are free to discern;[11] they only half-believe;[12] there are conflicting criteria for saying they believe and do not believe something;[13] or they are in a semi-belief state, intermediate between belief and nonbelief.[14]

All these approaches have yielded valuable insights. Invariably, however, they emphasize a few cases while neglecting others, or they single out only some elements of self-deception. Perhaps that is inevitable. Not only does self-deception take innumerable forms, but there are also different uses of the expression *self-deception* in everyday language. For example, sometimes the expression refers to purposeful and intentional conduct and sometimes to the mental states that result from this conduct. Other times it is used to encompass inadvertently biased beliefs, unintentional wishful thinking, and nonpurposeful ignorance. At times it is used to refer specifically to misconceptions about oneself, excluding false beliefs about other people and the world. It may be used either with derogatory connotations or in contexts where no negative appraisal is implied. And even when self-deceivers do persuade themselves to hold false or unjustified beliefs, there are many variations in the manner in which the belief is held and the context in which it is generated. This complexity of everyday language, combined with the richness of human behavior, leaves plenty of room for mutually enriching philosophical conceptions.

It will be helpful here to adopt a working analysis of self-deception which meets several requirements. The analysis should not imply that self-deception is always bad because that is something to be explored rather than stipulated at the outset. Yet it should focus attention on the purposeful and intentional forms of self-deception involving actions open to moral appraisal. In doing so it must leave open the question of how voluntary the actions are. That will vary greatly and be a morally relevant variable we wish to examine without built-in conceptual biases. For the same reason we want to avoid restrictive presuppositions about the motives of self-deceivers, which, as we saw with the conspirators, can vary greatly: from ambition, greed, and fear to self-esteem, cooperativeness, and conscience. Finally, we want to include a wider variety of states of self-deception than those centering on false beliefs.[15] As the patterns of self-deception in the last section suggest, we are also interested in such things as willful ignorance, which can amount to a mere absence of true beliefs rather than the presence of false ones; systematic ignoring of something known, believed, or suspected, where ignoring may include both distraction of thoughts from a topic and disregarding evidence while reasoning; emotional detachment and attitudinal distortion; and self-pretense (acting as if one believes, and typically trying to believe without succeeding, or trying to play a role or have emotions and attitudes that are not genuine).

These requirements are met by a conception of self-deception that makes central the notion of acknowledging (admitting, confessing) to oneself. Deceiving oneself is the evasion of full self-acknowledgment of some truth or of what one would view as truth if one were to confront an issue squarely. The truths or apparent truths may concern oneself, others, one's immediate situation, or the world at large. The evasion may have any number of motives, although in general what is evaded will be perceived as unpleasant or onerous in some way.

Acts of deceiving oneself consist of the actions involved in forming and sustaining projects of evasion. A project of evasion can be carried out using an assortment of strategies and patterns of behavior, but the project and its unifying intention do not involve continuous mental activity. In this respect it is like the project of avoiding another person's company, which is accomplished without any one ongoing mental activity but with a variety of dodging tactics on different occasions: avoiding parties where the person is likely to show up, glancing away when the person enters the room, not initiating conversations or phone calls, not expressing one's emotions to him or her, or not responding to his or her needs.

Self-deception can also refer to the mental states that result from the project of evading self-acknowledgment. These states come in many forms: false beliefs, unwarranted beliefs (whether true or false), absence of true beliefs, inappropriate emotions, unfitting attitudes, dispositions to self-pretense or ignoring, and emotional detachment.

If self-deception is evasion of self-acknowledgment, what is self-acknowledgment? Let us answer this by comparing and contrasting self-acknowledgment with sincere acknowledgments made to other people.

Acknowledging to others is typically an act of openly conceding something that has been concealed or might be refused recognition. Thus, someone might acknowledge an embarrassing fear of public speaking or a shameful indulgence in drugs or overeating. In their explicit forms, such acknowledgments are speech acts, whether performed in words or in gestures, such as nodding the head in response to a question. Sometimes the acknowledgment is more tacit and gradual, encompassing a cluster of speech acts and other actions. ("It took me years to confess to you, bit by bit, the full horror of my war experiences.") Full and sincere acknowledgment to others entails knowing or believing what one is saying. But it goes beyond mere cognitive states by being a revelation or open expression of what is known.[16] It may include emotional expression, as contrasted with detached verbalization of a belief. Finally, acknowledging otherwise-private aspects of one's life can create more intimate relationships with others, although the intimacy has the potential to generate either interpersonal harmony or conflict.

Acknowledging to oneself need not be a speech act, although it can be performed with speech acts. Essentially it is a form of acceptance and psychological integration. Consider the fact that we all know very well we will someday die and yet often manage to postpone fully acknowledging that truth until our death becomes imminent. Then we may be like Mr. Casaubon in *Middlemarch:*

> Here was a man who now for the first time found himself looking into the eyes of death—who was passing through one of those rare moments of experience when we feel the truth of a commonplace. . . . When the commonplace "We must all die" transforms itself suddenly into the acute consciousness "I must die—and soon," then death grapples us, and his fingers are cruel.[17]

For Mr. Casaubon to fully acknowledge to himself his impending death requires integrating what he knows into his feelings, thoughts, and attitudes, as well as into his system of beliefs.

There are some rough analogies between acknowledgments to others and to oneself. Both involve bringing into the open something that has been or is a likely candidate for concealment. This time, however, it is an openness before oneself, in the forum of one's own consciousness. Both can be brief acts or activities that occur more gradually. In both cases sincere and full acknowledgment entails belief in what is acknowledged but also requires more than abstract intellectual assent. However, self-acknowledgment especially requires that the belief (or knowledge) become active by being brought into an intimate relation with other aspects of the personality. There must be a willingness to integrate it into one's conscious thoughts, reasoning, emotions, attitudes, values, and actions. In this respect it not only adds to but may alter the internal relationships among the elements of the personality, generating either harmony or conflict.

In sum, full acknowledgment to oneself of a given proposition has several aspects. An individual must: (a) understand it, (b) be willing to attend to it in explicit consciousness, (c) believe it, (d) have a disposition to use it in reasoning (where relevant), (e) undergo emotional and attitudinal responses to what it expresses, as appropriate given one's personality, and (f) have at least some disposition to express it in actions made appropriate by one's desires, beliefs, and basic commitments.

This enables us to see why evasions of self-acknowledgment come in a variety of patterns. Self-deceivers might (a) evade understanding by blurring their own grasp of what they know, (b) evade attention through systematic distraction, (c) evade belief via willful ignorance or rationalization, (d) evade cogent argument by disregarding evidence, discounting relevant facts, or refusing to let oneself see clearly what follows from what, (e) evade appropriate emotional responses and attitude adjustments by using emotional detachment, (f) evade appropriate action using self-pretense or any of the preceding strategies, and so on.

The term *evasion* is not intended to have negative connotations in this context. It implies avoiding something by using dexterity, stratagem, or cleverness, whether the avoidance is morally unjustified, permissible, or even desirable. This is consistent with ordinary usage where negative connotations become attached to the word only within special contexts. Charging a politician with evasion of issues usually imputes a fault. That is because politicians ought to confront issues directly and because we distrust their motives for failing to do so. By contrast, when a soldier is characterized as evading a direct confrontation with a more powerful enemy, no negative appraisal need be implied. And when a police officer is described as evading a sniper's trap, the implication is that evasion is admirable.

Evasion does imply purposefulness and hence serves to exclude unintentional forms of self-deception, which are not under discussion here. In particular, it rules out beliefs that are nonpurposefully influenced by desires, hopes, and wishes (much wishful thinking), hatred and fear (much prejudice), undue readiness to believe (much credulousness, gullibility, naïveté), undue reluctance to form reasoned beliefs (much obstinacy, bigotry, closed-mindedness), or any other unintended misinterpretation of evidence (much bias). We should be wary, however, that what superficially appears as nonpurposeful negligence may actually be a partially intentional failure to exercise reasonable care in evaluating evidence or in reflecting on issues. Evasion involves purposeful omissions as frequently as it involves positive acts.

It was remarked earlier that not all willful ignorance, systematic ignoring, emotional detachment, self-pretense, and rationalization constitute self-deception. For example, employees might have every chance to learn about computers easily in the evening from a delightful teacher and thereby receive a bonus from their company. Yet they could willfully remain ignorant about computers because they prefer television. Again, individuals might systematically ignore an ugly decoration on a neighbor's house in order to avoid the displeasure it gives them (without in any way refusing to acknowledge that it is there). Medical students may engage in emotional detachment while watching their first autopsies in order to cope with the traumatic experience.[18] Public speakers engage in non–self-deceiving pretense before themselves and others when they assume a posture of confidence in order to subdue their nervousness. And some rationalization is the unintentional result of biases and wishes whose influence might not be under our control.

How do we tell when these techniques are functioning as strategies of self-deception? The quick answer is that they must enter as integral parts of an evasion of self-acknowledgment. But how do we tell when that occurs? If this is a request for a precise set of necessary and jointly sufficient conditions for evading self-acknowledgment, then no answer is possible. As with most interesting concepts in ordinary language, the meaning of self-deception cannot be captured in a manner setting rigid boundaries for applying the expression. Yet we can identify some of the criteria used in applying it to central, or paradigmatic cases, leaving room for problematic, or borderline, cases in which some of these features are absent.

First, persons must take account of what they are said to be evading and use this as a basis for engaging in the evasion. In some cases, taking account of consists of tacitly knowing or unconsciously believing (without acknowledging to oneself) what one is deceived about. But more frequently a mere suspicion or intimation suffices. Thus, we sense that something unpleasant would be uncovered if we exercised our attention, reasoning, or information-gathering skills in a certain direction, and on that basis we proceed with avoidance tactics. Other people may tell from our circumstances, our general intelligence, our usual abilities of discernment, combined with our subtle behavioral give-aways that we must have at least sensed the truth and then turned away from it.[19]

Second, what is evaded must be of some personal concern. That is one reason the individual who avoids learning about computers because of a sheer lack of interest is not a self-deceiver. But personal concern does not imply any specific motive. Self-deception can be motivated by fear in response to a terrifying situation, laziness in taking the easy way out of a dilemma or avoiding an onerous task, callousness about obligations, vanity, pride, a desire to maintain self-esteem, a compassionate desire to downplay a friend's faults, loving concern to support hope in a troubled relationship, and so on.[20]

Third, the sheer number of reinforcing patterns helps us identify self-deceivers. Often we are fooled by isolated tactics such as mere emotional detachment. It is easier to spot self-deceivers like Karenin who display interlocking and reinforcing behaviors that impede self-acknowledgment.

Fourth, the extensiveness and duration of evasion tactics can be considered. The white-collar criminals engaged in long-term and systematic ignoring, emotional detachment, self-pretense, willful ignorance, or rationalization. This is unlike what is involved with the medical students who, witnessing their first autopsy, for a limited time steel their emotions and pretend not to be afraid. Their conduct is a special way of confronting a difficult task rather than evasiveness about death. To be sure, self-deception can be short-lived. A person can form an intention to evade self-acknowledgment and then quickly abandon it. In such cases it is difficult to identify the self-deception unless the person offers a retrospective public confession (and even then it may be preferable to speak of "trying" to deceive oneself).

Fifth, sometimes it is careful selectiveness, rather than extensiveness, that provides the clue that a person is engaged in self-deception. Ignoring, for example, can be systematic without being complete. Karenin is willing to talk with a casual acquaintance about Anna's relation to Vronsky. But he studiously refuses to talk about it with Anna herself because that might prompt a disarming intimacy that could force acknowledgment of the truth. Like all of us, self-deceivers are skillful in knowing when to ignore a topic in order to foreclose a possible revelation.

Finally, evasions of self-acknowledgment usually include or are accompanied by a self-covering evasion of the self-deceiving strategies and motives. Self-deceivers typically evade acknowledging to themselves their willful ignorance, systematic ignoring, emotional detachment, self-pretense, rationalization, or whatever other pattern of evasion in which they engage. In doing so they may use the same tactics at a second order level, with respect to the primary use of the tactics, but usually the primary use of the tactics suffices to cover their own tracks.

In connection with this last point, it is useful to draw a distinction between the primary and secondary targets and evasions. The primary target is the main thing the person is deceived about. For Karenin it is the love affair between Anna and Vronsky and Anna's emotional life. Accordingly, evading self-acknowledgment of the primary target may be called the primary evasion. Secondary targets are any related things persons deceive themselves about as a means of evading the primary target. In Karenin's case they include the motives for the primary evasion and the details about the affair (such as why Anna wants to change residences). Evading self-acknowledgment of these secondary targets is the secondary evasion.

Secondary evasion supports the primary evasion by concealing things whose acknowledgment would threaten the success of the primary evasion. For example, if I were to acknowledge to myself that I am engaged in systematically ignoring my aggressiveness (the primary target), I would thereby acknowledge the aggressiveness—just what I am avoiding. Hence the motives for the primary evasion carry over to the secondary evasion. But there can also be further motives for the secondary evasion which need to be concealed. In particular, it can be less than flattering to recognize that we have been deceiving ourselves and to admit to the reasons we have done so.[21] Although the motive for primary evasions varies too greatly to generalize about, it seems safe to view self-esteem as the most frequent supporting motive for secondary evasions (in addition to being one of the most frequent motives for primary evasions).

PARADOX

To deceive other people is to mislead them intentionally. Generally, one gets them to believe what one knows is false or at least to be ignorant of what one knows. (Other measures, however, may suffice, such as distracting them momentarily from something they know.) A number of philosophers have insisted that the genuine, literal, cases of self-deception involve something just like this except that the process occurs in one person. But is it possible to persuade oneself intentionally to believe what one simultaneously knows to be false? Acting on such an intention would require knowingly using one's grasp of the truth in the very attempt to make oneself ignorant or to make oneself believe the opposite falsehood. Would not this knowledge about the attempt subvert it from the outset? In any case, would it not be impossible to succeed, because it seems we cannot willfully manipulate our own beliefs nor simultaneously hold directly contradictory beliefs nor otherwise cognitively divide ourselves into a deceiver and a deceived victim?

These are epistemological paradoxes in that they center on knowledge and belief. The question is whether they are paradoxes in the philosophical sense: contradictions that could not describe possible situations. Or are they paradoxes in the literary sense: merely seemingly absurd statements that actually turn out to be coherent and to express genuine possibilities? Full answers to these questions would deflect us from our main inquiry into the moral issues surrounding self-deception. Yet they deserve brief consideration because of their twofold relevance to our inquiry. On the one hand, they constitute a challenge to the account of self-deception given in the previous sections, for they portray self-deception in the literal sense as centering on conflicting beliefs and willful belief formation rather than as evasion of acknowledging to ourselves what we suspect or know. Hence we must at least sketch how our account would apply to them. On the other hand, if there are such puzzling instances of self-deception, moral assessments should take them into account because what people believe is often relevant to how they should be evaluated.

Let us first consider the assumption that the literal sense of self-deception refers to something precisely like the deception of others, except occurring within one person. This assumption formed the backbone of Mary Haight's book, *A Study of Self-Deception*. She contended that deception occurs when one 'self' knows something, prevents another 'self' from knowing it, and usually gets the second self to believe the opposite of what the first self knows. Yet it is a contradiction, she continued, to claim that one self simultaneously knows and does not know the same thing. Moreover, interpersonal deceivers are readily able to bring to consciousness what they know, while their victims are precluded by ignorance from ready consciousness of the truth. It would be a contradiction to say that the same self is both readily able to become conscious, and not readily able to become conscious, of the same information at the same time.

Haight asserted that it *is* possible to conceive of two selves housed in one body. That is what is meant by a split personality. She also cited instances where one of the selves composing the split personality had privileged access to the other self, but not vice versa, enabling one self to deceive the other by manipulating its consciousness. Only in those instances was she willing to say that *deception* has a literal use as applied to the divided person. Yet that is not self-deception because the literal use of *self-deception* requires that one and the same self be both deceiver and deceived. Thus, she concluded, there is no self-deception at all in the literal sense.[22]

Now, it is misleading to claim that the literal, genuine, central, or full-blooded cases of self-deception are only those that parallel the epistemology of interpersonal deception. Consider an analogy to Haight's line of thinking.[23] Imagine someone arguing that self-taught or self-educated individuals are impossible in the literal sense of those words. Teaching requires knowing something and being readily able to become explicitly conscious of it, whereas learning something entails first being ignorant of it. In order to be self-taught, a person would have to know and not know the same information and be readily able and not readily able to call it to consciousness. Even if this occurred within a single person having a split personality, it would not, strictly speaking, be one self teaching itself. Hence, the idea of one person being teacher and student with respect to the same information is incoherent, and self-taught individuals could not exist.

This reasoning is not the result of paying strict adherence to the literal sense of the expression *self-taught*. Instead, it is the result of giving a mistaken interpretation to an intelligible expression by applying a potentially illuminating analogy in a too-rigid manner. In thinking about self-teaching, the model of teaching others is illuminating in limited respects because both activities involve purposeful endeavors directed toward acquisition of new knowledge and skills. But the interpersonal model does not by itself accurately give the literal or standard meaning of self-teaching. Similarly, Haight's allegedly literal construal of *self-deception* is a fiction created by applying the interpersonal model in a misleading way. Self-deception can best be viewed as a set of related phenomena which are analogous to interpersonal deception in some but not all ways.[24]

Our account of self-deception as evading self-acknowledgment captures the primary elements of purposeful behavior that roughly parallel those found in interpersonal deception. Interpersonal deceivers evade acknowledging to others something they know, believe, suspect, feel, and so on. Often they engage in pretense, withhold their emotions, prevent others from having explicit consciousness about something, keep others ignorant, or persuade them to hold false beliefs. There are analogies here with self-pretense, emotional detachment, systematic ignoring, willful ignorance, and rationalization. In fact, as we shall see in Chapter 5, Haight was sensitive to many of these patterns of self-deception which in her view were only metaphorically and misleadingly called self-deception.

We should determine the literal sense of *self-deception* by surveying the phenomena to which the expression is paradigmatically applied, not by being preoccupied with the interpersonal model embedded in our language.[25] I believe that such a survey not only justifies an account of self-deception as evasion of self-acknowledgment but also helps us make sense of some of the more puzzling varieties of self-deception. Let us examine a few of these varieties, bearing in mind that anything more than a brief discussion would require full-scale investigations of the concepts of belief, knowledge, intention, consciousness and unconsciousness—investigations beyond the scope of this study.

Believe and Disbelieve. Is it possible for a self-deceiver to hold beliefs that explicitly contradict each other? Are we contradicting ourselves when we describe others as believing propositions that directly (as opposed to in their implications) contradict each other?

We need to distinguish among the following descriptions. Assume that we are talking about the same person at the same time and let q stand for a proposition that is either true or false.

(1) Jane believes q and Jane believes not-q.
   —That is, Jane concurrently believes two propositions (q; not-q), one of which is the explicit negation of the other.
(2) Jane believes q and Jane disbelieves q.
   —That is, Jane believes that a proposition is true and concurrently believes that the same proposition is false.
(3) Jane believes q-and-not-q.
   —That is, Jane believes that an explicit contradiction is true.
(4) Jane believes q and it is not the case that Jane believes q.

If we asserted (4), we would be contradicting ourselves unless we added the qualification that different senses of *believe* were being used. Stated another way, as it stands (4) does not describe a possible situation. There is no formal contradiction, however, in asserting (1) through (3).[26] In fact, occasionally these statements do apply to self-deceivers.

Here is one possibility. Sometimes self-deceivers obscure their understanding of the concepts they use in forming beliefs. George Orwell had this in mind when he defined *doublethink* as the power to hold two contradictory beliefs in one's mind simultaneously and accept both of them. Orwell contended that in the real world of politics, as in his imaginary world of *1984*, language and concepts were being systematically abused in order to form contradictory ideas about freedom, government coercion, and war. He identified the use of a subtle mixture of conscious obfuscation and more-unconscious self-deception:

> To use logic against logic, to repudiate morality while laying claim to it, to believe that democracy was impossible and that the Party was the guardian of democracy, to forget, whatever it was necessary to forget, then to draw it back into memory again at the moment when it was

needed, and then promptly to forget it again, and above all, to apply the same process to the process itself.[27]

Doublethink does occur, and it can be used by self-deceivers to create states described by (1), (2), and, perhaps rarely,(3).

Is it possible, however, for persons to hold directly contradictory beliefs when they clearly understand the concepts they use? Restricting discussion to only (1) and (2), it is possible as long as we grant the possibility of unconscious beliefs.[28] One of the two contradictory beliefs can be held consciously in the sense that the self-deceiver is readily able and willing to attend to it. The other belief can remain unconscious in the sense that the person cannot readily attend to it except when under special influences such as drugs, psychotherapy, or stress. The self-deception is purposeful when the unconscious belief is the basis for evading self-acknowledgment of what is believed unconsciously. It is at least partially intentional when the person has some degree of knowledge of the evasion.

There are also many cases where one of the beliefs is not wholly unconscious or inaccessible to consciousness. Here self-deceivers evade acknowledging one of the beliefs to themselves, using the techniques described earlier: manipulating attention, disregarding evidence, giving special weight to evidence favoring what one wants to believe, emotional detachment, and so on.

Whether or not one of the beliefs is wholly unconscious, both beliefs can be expressed in actions, words (directly or via implications), feelings, and attitudes that taken as a whole are inconsistent. This is made possible by the enormous variety of contexts for human expression, combined with our limited tendency to keep all aspects of our lives interrelated. Not infrequently, each belief will have characteristic habitats in which it is expressed.[29] Thus, the classic Sunday-only Christian displays one set of beliefs (or half-beliefs) on Sunday, another on weekdays. Sometimes the conflicting beliefs might be displayed on the same occasion. Beneath a nervous arrogance and consciously held belief in one's superiority, for example, there might be a self-disguised belief in one's inadequacy. To the trained eye or the psychotherapist with a "third ear,"[30] this may be as obvious "as if a man feared that he was too small and walked on his toes to make himself seem taller."[31]

To be sure, there can also be a point in denying that such individuals really hold either belief or in ascribing to them only the belief that makes them look better or worse. To say that lip-service Christians do not believe at all in Jesus' teachings is to make actions speak not only louder than words, but decisively in ascribing beliefs. To say instead that they sincerely believe but are merely weak willed gives priority to speech and feelings of conviction in ascribing beliefs. Either way, we alter the normally loose criteria for belief in order to make a special point.[32]

Could a self-deceiver or anyone else bring to consciousness two directly contradictory beliefs at the same time, formulate them in words, be clear about their meaning, believe they are contradictory, be sane and not intoxicated, and still hold them? David Hume once reported a not-uncommon experience in doing philosophy: "There are two principles, which I cannot render consistent; nor is it in my power to renounce either of them."[33] The principles, however, were apparently only indirectly contradictory in that they seemed to entail a contradiction, so he could hope they might turn out to be reconcilable. Could he or a self-deceiver accurately make such a statement if the 'principles' or propositions were directly contradictory?

If it is possible, it would have to be extremely rare in persons having normal degrees of rationality. Certainly self-deceivers would be highly motivated to avoid explicit awareness of their inner conflicts. As one possibility, however, consider something Othello says while still deceived by Iago into believing that Desdemona is having an affair with Cassio and while still a victim of his own self-deceiving jealousies and self-doubts. Confronting Iago he exclaims:

> By the world,
> I think my wife be honest, and think she is not;
> I think that thou art just, and think thou art not:
> I'll have some proof.[34]

One interpretation is that, at the moment, Othello believes nothing that he says he believes; he is merely expressing conflicting inclinations to believe two sets of directly contradictory propositions. Yet perhaps his subsequently inconsistent behavior might lead us to say that he was caught in an even more desperate epistemological conflict, unable to entirely abandon his deeply entrenched beliefs in Desdemona's honesty (fidelity) or in Iago's being just (truthfulness). He also accepts evidence that he thinks justifies denying one of each of the sets of contradictory beliefs. Recognizing his conflicting beliefs (or at least partial beliefs), he demands further proof to enable him to abandon his self-contradictions.

Know and Disbelieve. Could a self-deceiver ever know q and concurrently believe not-q? Let us assume that knowledge consists in having a true and warranted belief. If, as we just suggested, it is possible to hold directly contradictory beliefs, we need an example in which a person is justified in believing the true belief in the pair. Perhaps the following two reports by a psychoanalyst provide such examples:

> Each time Clarence B., a man of thirty, turned off a light, he would be seized with the thought "My father is going to die." "I *know*

that this is a silly idea,'' he said. ''I *know* that it couldn't possibly happen. But I can't convince myself that it's silly, and I get very nervous about it.''

[After being informed of the death of her husband,] it suddenly seemed to her that her husband was *not* really dead. *Intellectually* she knew that he was, but somehow she felt that he was alive, but away on a business trip from which he would return. . . . In the late afternoon she would behave as if he were returning from work. At 5:30, the time at which he usually came home, she would begin looking out the window from time to time, watching for him to drive up to the house. Rationally she knew all of this was silly, and yet she found herself frequently cooking enough food to include his portion, or setting a place at table for him.[35]

Nothing forces us to say that these individuals believe what they know to be false. We can simply say they are obsessed with ideas and feelings that lead to actions that are irrational, given what they know. Still, the ordinary concept of belief seems sufficiently flexible to allow us to say they irrationally believe what they know to be false, and this belief explains the conflicting emotions and behavior. And while pathological forms of self-deception are involved in these two examples, there is no reason to deny that less disturbed self-deceivers could know the truth while believing the opposite.

Know and Not-know. Neither a self-deceiver nor anyone else could know a proposition to be true and also know it to be false in the same sense of *know,* in the same respects, at the same time. This is because knowledge requires by definition that what is known is true, and a proposition cannot be both true and false at the same time. Presumably, however, a person with a personality split into two or more distinct selves could simultaneously know and not know the same thing. We simply ascribe knowledge to one of the selves and deny it to another.

Short of split personality, however, there is room for self-deceivers to display a variety of cognitive divisions or what have been called ''schizoid states.''[36] Perhaps some of these states can be described by ascribing knowledge and its absence using two different senses of *know:* for example, consciously know versus unconsciously know, or intellectually know versus emotionally know. Drawing such distinctions may aid us in understanding some self-deceivers who discern in some respects what they do not grasp and respond to in other respects or who display clusters of speech, actions, emotions, and reasoning that cohere to form two conflicting patterns.

Intentional Ignoring. It seems especially puzzling that some self-deceivers can systematically ignore what is so easy for them to grasp. Interpersonal deceivers act on the basis of what they know in order to conceal it from their victims. But how could self-deceivers use their knowledge or suspicions of some truth as a basis for intentionally ignoring that truth (whether via distraction or disregarding)?

There are actually two problems here. First, in forming and trying to act on the intention to ignore, would using the knowledge of what is to be concealed not block the very effort of concealment? In the words of Jean-Paul Sartre, deceivers apparently "most know the truth very exactly *in order* to conceal it more carefully." Yet that seems impossible when only one person is involved.[37] Second, must not there be self-knowledge or self-consciousness of the intention to conceal the truth, and would not that knowledge or consciousness thwart the project of concealment? As Sartre poses the problem, "that which affects itself with bad faith [i.e., self-deception] must be conscious (of) its bad faith since the being of consciousness is consciousness of being [what it is]."[38]

If the first of these problems represented a genuine difficulty, then it would be a difficulty concerning all intentional ignoring, not just the self-deceiver's ignoring. But is it a genuine difficulty? Sartre seems to be misled by a certain picture of ignoring which he expresses at one point in the following way:

> I can in fact wish "not to see" a certain aspect of my being only if I am acquainted with the aspect which I do not wish to see. This means that in my being I must indicate this aspect in order to be able to turn myself away from it; better yet, I must think of it constantly in order to take care not to think of it.[39]

Surely in order to ignore or stop seeing something, it is not necessary to think about it constantly. Sartre's problem arises only if we conflate beliefs and attention. Intentional ignoring entails having and using suspicions, beliefs, or knowledge about what is ignored. It does not entail bestowing any kind of ongoing attention to it. We have the capacity to distract our attention from things we sense, to selectively focus it elsewhere, and to disregard troublesome facts. There is room for psychological accounts of how this occurs, but there is no conceptual obstacle to its possibility.

A similar confusion reappears to generate the second problem. Acting intentionally requires acting knowingly. But it does not require that this knowledge is constantly attended to. We engage in many intentional activities without deliberately attending to them all the while: shifting gears on a car, sipping a glass of water, impulsively making a snide remark. Self-deceiving forms of ignoring are most often spontaneous. The intentions involved are typically not deliberately thought about with focused consciousness nor constantly attended to with any degree of consciousness. Despite the claims of another writer, the self-deceiver is not at all like the person "who is given the self-defeating command, 'try not to think of pink elephants!' "[40]

Willful Belief. Much philosophical puzzlement about self-deception has centered on the idea of willful belief. Deceiving others typically proceeds from an intention to create or sustain in them a false belief. But can rationalization or other techniques be used in purposefully creating a false belief in oneself?

This problem arises primarily from the traditional model of beliefs as states that arise in us entirely without purpose or intention. In Hume's words, a belief consists in "something, that depends not on the will, but must arise from certain determinate causes and principles of which we are not masters."[41] This model captures an important truth: beliefs are not actions but are cognitive states that enter into explanations of actions. It also conveys the fact that beliefs normally cannot be chosen arbitrarily, at least not without employing esoteric techniques like hypnotism, drug injections, and brainwashing. Yet the model is one-sided and exaggerates the differences between actions and belief formation. On the one hand, most actions are not chosen arbitrarily but are themselves based on a consideration of reasons and evidence. On the other hand, certain key aspects of belief formation often are intentional. For example, we frequently make an intentional effort to acquire or avoid acquiring evidence on a given topic. And we can make an intentional effort to guard against the operation of our biases or purposefully allow them to operate.

Some intentions involved in forming beliefs are truth centered in that they involve efforts to acquire knowledge. Yet none of us is so completely dedicated to truth that we do not have competing intentions and motives as we form our beliefs. We seek the truth; we also seek to adopt beliefs that make us happy, support our self-esteem, provide a comfortable worldview, and align with our basic loves and commitments. Self-deception is often a special case of forming and holding beliefs on the basis of mixed concerns.

Self-deceivers need not be completely blind to the operation of such biasing influences, and they are not wholly oblivious to the truths they are fleeing. Although rationalized belief is not a deliberate choice, neither is it always entirely nonconscious and nonintentional. In forming or maintaining beliefs, self-deceivers can intentionally (even if spontaneously and without deliberation) disregard evidence that goes against what they want to believe. They can also refuse to guard against the operation of their biases and refuse to make inquiries that they suspect or know are appropriate. To the extent such tactics are used, rationalized beliefs are willful. In saying this we need not describe self-deceivers as "intending to believe what they want to believe," a phrase that misleadingly suggests that beliefs are actions. It is enough to describe them as intending to disregard evidence, to emphasize other evidence, to avoid inquiries, to avoid self-critical scrutiny of possible biases, and so on.

Doubled Selves. With interpersonal deception, one self deceives a second self. In self-deception does one self deceive itself, or are there two selves within one person—the deceiver and the deceived? Kant worded the problem this way: "A lie requires a second person whom one intends to deceive, and intentionally to deceive oneself seems to contain a contradiction."[42] In a few cryptic remarks, Kant tries to make sense of self-deception as a "lack of conscientiousness, i.e., of sincerity in our avowals before our *inner* judge, whom we conceive as another person when we think of sincerity in its utmost strictness."[43] More generally, anytime we make self-assessments, we think of ourselves as "a twofold personage, a doubled self": a flawed, finite, person ("phenomenal self") appearing before an "inner judge" who is the ideal moral self we aspire to be ("noumenal self").[44]

Self-deception, in fact, only sometimes involves duplicitous inner talk within the mental tribunal described by Kant. Yet it often does involve inner division: ambivalent emotions or attitudes, conflicting desires, self-contradictory beliefs or inclinations to believe, self-defeating actions that undermine one's own best interests or one's commitments, and so on. Plato postulated that psychic conflicts of these sorts reveal different parts of a person set against one another, and then he personified the parts by speaking of them metaphorically as distinct selves. That initiated a tradition that has created a folk psychology of dichotomies: Appetites versus Reason, Reason versus Will, Will versus Heart, Heart versus Lust, Passion versus Intellect, Lower Self versus Higher Self, and so on. Usually such distinctions obscure as much as they clarify, and certainly they are too simplistic to capture the more complex divisions that characterize self-deceivers.

Herbert Fingarette suggested that a self-deceiver—indeed, each of us—is a community of subselves which are organized clusters of desires–attitudes–emotions–beliefs–purposes, each of which can be expressed in semi-independence from other clusters. In self-deception a wider community of selves shuns a subself unacceptable to it. Fingarette and others who think in these terms[45] acknowledge that this image of multiple selves is a metaphor extending a social concept to the inner mind. Given this understanding, the image seems to me insightful in picturing how one person can play the two roles of deceiver and deceived, assuming that the subselves are not viewed as so autonomous and dissociated as those involved in multiple personalities. At the same time, nothing in our account of self-deception as evading self-acknowledgment forces us to embrace this picture. We can instead rest content with saying that there is only one 'self' involved in self-deception—namely, the person—who acts as deceiver while engaging in the evasive activities and is deceived insofar as the evasion serves to conceal a truth (or one's view of the truth).

Before proceeding to the last paradoxes, let us add a general caveat concerning the preceding epistemological paradoxes. Although I have suggested that some of the paradoxes can be resolved, I am aware that the brief discussions I have given will not convince those who deny the possibility of intrapersonal analogs to interpersonal deception. Lest it seem that those skeptics need not read further, it should be re-emphasized that my account of self-deception applies to much more than just the paradoxical and controversial forms of self-deception. There are avenues for evading self-acknowledgment other than willfully persuading oneself into believing what one knows deep down is false (or fails to represent one's real view): for example, willful ignorance, systematic ignoring, self-pretense, emotional detachment, and so on. Most skeptics who deny the possibility of what they call literal self-deception (as construed on the model of interpersonal deception) would allow that these other modes of evasion can be employed in refusing to acknowledge things to oneself; hence they are free to focus on them for the remainder of this study.

One possible exception is David Kipp, who vigorously denies the possibility of anything that can be called willful self-deception. According to him, so-called self-deceivers are really either sincerely ignorant or hypocritical conscious pretenders before others. Most of them, indeed, are pretenders who have a specific motive and aim: "They are trying to fend off, through deceptive pretense, what they regard as defeat, or unacceptable loss of face, in a not entirely unreal, socially staged power struggle, or status-seeking contest, whose goal is to appear, in the eyes of others, a maximally enviable existential success."[46]

On the surface this two-pronged fork—sincere ignorance versus conscious hypocrisy—embodies an overly simple view of human nature, if not an overly cynical one. Yet perhaps even Kipp must allow that pretenders may have different degrees of consciousness of their own pretense, aims, and motives. They range from individuals who are fully aware and deliberate about these matters to those who avoid acknowledging their purposes and pretense to themselves.[47] My conception of self-deceivers as evading self-acknowledgment applies to the latter range of cases.

Moral Paradoxes. At first glance self-deception appears shrouded in moral paradox. Regarded as deceivers, self-deceivers seem guilty for their deception and any harmful effects; regarded as deceived, they seem to be innocent victims. Viewed as liars, they appear insincere and dishonest; viewed as victims of a lie, they appear sincere and honestly mistaken. As deceivers, they seem responsible and blameworthy for cowardly hypocrisy; as deceived, they apparently deserve compassion and help in gaining full awareness of the guile perpetrated on them.

Fingarette made these paradoxes prominent on the opening page of *Self-Deception*:

> Whether in morally assessing ourselves or others, whether in the court of law or in everyday life, we are beset by confusion when once we grant that the person in question is in self-deception. For as deceiver one is insincere, guilty; whereas as genuinely deceived, one is the innocent victim. What, then, shall we make of the self-deceiver, the one who is both the doer and the sufferer? Our fundamental categories are placed squarely at odds with one another.[48]

Fingarette believes there is indeed something morally baffling about self-deception, but he believes these moral paradoxes fail to capture the real perplexity. He finds it true, though morally unhelpful, to portray self-deceivers as believing or sincerely affirming (qua deceived) what they know in their hearts is false (qua deceivers): "This 'epistemological' paradox generates moral paradox since ignorance and blindness exculpate, whereas knowledge, insight and foresight inculpate."[49] The solution he recommends, as we shall see in Chapter 5, is to redescribe self-deception using the language of action, volition, and personal identity, rather than using cognitive terms like "know" and "believe."

It is false, however, that describing self-deception with cognitive terms generates moral paradoxes. Instead, these paradoxes arise because of two assumptions. (1) Interpersonal deception is an appropriate general model for understanding the moral status of self-deception. (2) One simple moral appraisal of deceivers and their victims can be given—namely, the deceiver is always guilty, responsible, insincere, blameworthy, whereas the person deceived is always an innocent victim, exculpated, not insincere, deserving compassion. Both assumptions are false.

To begin with the second assumption, deceivers and liars are not always guilty or blameworthy. If a police officer discerns that the best way to save a hostage's life is knowingly and skillfully to deceive the kidnapper, knowledge is anything but inculpating. If a kidnapper forces a hostage to lie to the police or press, the hostage is usually not blameworthy if he or she complies under duress, especially when he or she acts to protect innocent lives. A parent using deception to prevent a three-year-old child from learning the details of a grisly murder is not guilty of insincerity or hypocrisy. And a lie often serves as a justified means of protecting against mischievous intrusiveness. Much interpersonal deception is morally permissible, and some of it is morally admirable or even obligatory.

Furthermore, victims of deceivers are neither always lacking in responsibility and guilt nor always deserving of compassion and sympathy. Perhaps they allow, encourage, or provoke the deception in the first place. The kidnappers in the preceding case represent one example, but there are many others. Citizens who apathetically allow their leaders to deceive them are partially responsible for the effects of the deception. Parents who excessively pressure their children to obtain high grades may be partly to blame when their children deceive them with forged report cards. And people who invade others' privacy sometimes provoke them into engaging in self-protective deception, thereby making themselves partially responsible for the deception and for being victims of it.

All of these examples also help explain why the first assumption is false. Interpersonal deception cannot provide a simple, general moral model for self-deception because the moral status of interpersonal deception varies too much from case to case. It cannot be generalized about in a simple manner that would yield a helpful standard. Of course we might selectively focus on cases of interpersonal deception that do involve a guilty deceiver and an innocent victim and then try to employ those instances as a model for self-deception. But why do that? Nothing in the concept of deception forces us to do so. If anything, we should expect the morality of self-deception to vary from case to case as much as the morality of interpersonal deception. Examination of some instances of self-deception may reveal that guilt and innocence are both involved, in different respects. Yet in other instances it may uncover only guilt or only innocence. Prior to our investigation there should be no paradox-provoking assumptions.

3
Inner Hypocrisy

It is no doubt an evil to be full of faults, but it is a still greater evil to be full of them and unwilling to recognize them, since this entails the further evil of deliberate self-delusion.

—Blaise Pascal, *Pensées*

The Inner Hypocrisy Tradition is preoccupied with self-deception insofar as it conceals immoral acts and character faults. It is therefore not surprising that it portrays self-deceivers as contemptible cheats who cause harm. The writers discussed in this chapter share the view that morality is objective in the sense of being based on defensible standards that make a claim on our commitments and that can be used in evaluating acts and attitudes. Like Pascal, these writers also distinguish between two wrongs involved in self-deception about immorality: the initial immoral act or fault which constitutes the main target or object of the deceit and the self-deceit itself. The self-deceit is a second-order wrong, bad in part because of its role in generating or supporting the primary immorality and in part because in this role it constitutes insincerity, untruthfulness, and hypocrisy.

The opening section contains a survey of writers in this tradition who rely heavily on the concept of self-deception in explaining wrongdoing. The next section discusses the main criticisms of self-deception made by these and other writers in the Inner Hypocrisy Tradition. The last two sections explore the relationship of self-deception to hypocrisy and to moral weakness.

31

EXPLAINING WRONGDOING

In many ways Socrates set the backdrop for the Inner Hypocrisy Tradition by wedding moral understanding to intellectual honesty and courage in confronting truth. He also placed self-reflection and inquiry into the objective moral values at the heart of significant life—the life worth living. Nevertheless, Socrates does not himself belong to the Inner Hypocrisy Tradition. In the Platonic dialogues he makes only rare and unelaborated allusions to self-deception, such as the following: "I cannot trust myself. And I think that I ought to stop and ask myself, What am I saying? For there is nothing worse than self-deception— when the deceiver is always at home and always with you."[1] It is almost certain that in such passages *self-deception* refers to nonwillful ignorance about oneself and unintentional wishful thinking. This is because the very possibility of willful self-deception is ruled out by the fundamental Socratic doctrine that knowledge is virtue, that to know moral truth is to act on it, and hence that people are never willfully immoral. Willful self-deception designed to foster wrongdoing is too much like knowingly doing wrong to have been recognized by Socrates.

Disagreeing sharply with Socrates, Aristotle insisted there is voluntary and intentional wrongdoing. He also emphasized that we are not automatically absolved of responsibility because we are ignorant of the harm we cause, for our ignorance may be the result of our own blameworthy carelessness or negligence:

> Indeed, we punish a man for his very ignorance, if he is thought responsible for his ignorance, as when penalties are doubled in the case of drunkenness . . . since he had the power of not getting drunk and his getting drunk was the cause of his ignorance. And we punish those who are ignorant of anything in the laws that they ought to know . . . since they have the power of taking care.[2]

Yet Aristotle had little to say about how motivated carelessness and purposeful negligence merge into self-deception so as to dim or destroy understanding of one's own immorality. It is Christian rather than Greek thinkers who were most preoccupied with willful clouding of moral consciousness.

To my knowledge, the first book-length study of self-deception was the Reverend Daniel Dyke's treatise, *The Mystery of Selfe-Deceiving*, published in 1630. Quoting Jeremiah 17:9, Dyke enunciates his central theme: " 'The heart is deceitful above all things, who can know it?' So mystical are these hearts of ours; so deep and abstruse are her mysteries of deceit."[3] By the mysteries of self-deceit, Dyke did not mean the paradoxes discussed in the last chapter. Instead he referred to the morally baffling ways in which self-deception fosters wrongdoing and the enormous difficulty in being honest with oneself about morality and religion.

Dyke was well aware of his heritage of earlier Christian thinkers who invoked the concept of self-deception to explain sin. He cited St. Thomas Aquinas, for example: "Ignorance is sometimes directly and intrinsically voluntary, as when one freely chooses to be ignorant so that he may sin more freely."[4] What was new in Dyke was the extent to which he tried to explain virtually all sin as the result of self-deception. Self-deceit was for him the primary explanation of why people turn away from God, fail to sustain genuine faith, misunderstand divine grace, refuse to repent, and dismiss their sins by blaming external forces or characterizing them with euphemism.

It would take us too far astray to pursue Dyke's development of these Christian themes. Nevertheless, the philosophers we shall discuss more fully are essentially following his lead in making self-deception the key to understanding much or most wrongdoing. Certainly this is true of Bishop Joseph Butler, who provided an insightful discussion of the self-flattering forms of self-deceit that generate "a very great part of the wickedness of the world."[5]

Writing a century after the Reverend Dyke, Bishop Butler devoted three of his major sermons to this topic.[6] His interest was in that form of "internal hypocrisy," or hypocrisy before one's own conscience, that enables people to remain largely blind to vices in themselves which they manage to see quite clearly in others. Although in passing he mentions self-deception in matters of prudence, he is preoccupied with how self-deceit allows moral conscience to be laid asleep, enabling an individual to proceed in a course of wrongdoing with little emotional disturbance.

Accordingly, when Butler stated the typical "occasions" of the phenomena he wished to explore, he cited only two main categories in which self-deceit serves as a cover for wrongdoing. One category is the violation of duties not specifiable by exact rules. Much of morality, as he noted, leaves considerable room for exercising personal judgment. Our specific duty should be determined on the basis of a sincere concern for justice and the good of others. With respect to the positive duties to promote others' good—to be kind, compassionate, charitable—there is always the question of precisely how much we are required to do. With respect to the negative duties not to harm others, it is impossible to draw a sharp line distinguishing acceptable from forbidden acts. There is no moral algorithm for determining what constitutes oppression of others, as opposed to the legitimate assertion of self-interest. Nor can we specify exactly the border between liberty and licentiousness. Self-deceivers take advantage of these areas of vagueness. They draw their own lines of demarcation according to what is convenient for them rather than on the basis of a genuine good will to be fair and loving.

The second category is the clear-cut and often gross violation of determinate rules. Here what is obvious to a sensitive and unbiased observer becomes clouded and distorted to the rationalizer. People palliate, extenuate, or even totally excuse their wrongdoing by appealing to alleged good intentions or extenuating circumstances.

Butler used two biblical stories as illustrations of this second category. The first was King David's adultery with Bathsheba and his subsequent order that her husband, Uriah, be sent to the front lines during a war. David is an otherwise morally admirable leader, and hence it is baffling how he could proceed without experiencing guilt (none is recorded in the Bible). His behavior is inexplicable without postulating that he deceived himself. Butler did not speculate about the precise form David's self-deception took, but we might imagine that David told himself it is not murder for a king to order a soldier to the front lines. And perhaps he rationalized the adultery under the pretext that kings deserve special privileges.

The second illustration is the story of the prophet Balaam who is requested by a Moabite king to issue a ceremonial curse on the Israelites before attacking them. Balaam receives what he interprets as a direct commandment from God not to issue the curse, but, tempted by the king's bribes, he ignores the intent of the commandment and seizes on a simplistic reading of it. The command only forbids making the curse given the Israelites' present spiritual state. It does not command concern for their future spiritual welfare. Balaam ingenuously contrives a plot to encourage them to engage in widespread adultery and idolatry in order to make them deserve God's curse, punishment, and destruction.

Butler saw little obscurity in how such self-deceit occurs. He described the tactics of willful ignorance, systematic ignoring, disregarding evidence, laxity in uncovering bias, and rationalization in numerous forms. Inner hypocrites, he suggested, are like persons who glimpse a disagreeable scene and then shut their eyes. They have an "implicit suspicion" of where their faults lie and act on that suspicion in turning attention away, thereby avoiding detailed and honest self-scrutiny. As he observed, "the eyes of the mind" can be closed as readily as those of the body, with a willfulness that is spontaneous and not itself attended to.

Nor is there any great mystery, in Butler's view, about the motives for inner hypocrisy about wrongdoing. They are varied: general complacency and self-trust about our character; specific passions that conflict with our value principles; and above all, a general selfishness and overfondness for ourselves in seeking our own good at the expense of others. While most of us have some concern for goodness, we allow these other motives to prompt actions inconsistent with that concern. Self-deception provides an easy way to engage in wrongdoing while making our sins "sit a little easy" on our minds.

Early in this century, Max Scheler developed these themes further. Like Butler, Scheler focused on self-deceivers who distort values they nevertheless appreciate. In his book *Ressentiment*, Scheler identified how mixed motives can lead to a perversion of genuine values. In doing so he progressed beyond Butler's preoccupation with individual actions to consider more systematic warping of moral sensitivity.

The state of *ressentiment* is smoldering, suppressed, wrath permeated with self-deception. It begins when a person experiences intense feelings of hatred in the form of envy, spite, or vindictiveness. Normal outward expression of the hatred is blocked because of fear and a felt lack of strength to display it before others. Gradually a process of repression occurs in which negative emotions and their specific objects are less readily available to consciousness. Focused hate is replaced with general negativism and malice that spill over into patterns of vicious criticism, cruelty, or betrayal. These indirect outlets do not remove the suppressed hate, however, which continues to smolder unattended to. By this stage, full-blown *ressentiment* has developed, bringing with it self-deceiving "value delusions."

Value delusions are unacknowledged attempts to discredit something under the guise of valuing something else. They take two forms: (1) self-deceiving judgments that another person, group, institution, religion, or commodity has failed to meet a certain standard of excellence, and (2) self-deception about standards of excellence themselves.

Scheler discussed the first form only briefly. Self-deception in evaluating particular things is as familiar as the fable of the fox who called the grapes sour because he could not obtain them. Similarly, when we greatly desire the love or respect of another person but fail to gain it, there is a natural tendency to attend to the person's faults.[7] As we do, the faults seem to multiply before our eyes. When *ressentiment* develops we do not simply change our initial view. All along we retain a sense of the genuine worth of the person, which initially attracted us to him or her.

In the second, more interesting form of value delusion, *ressentiment* extends to the standards of excellence themselves: the grapes are not sour, but their very sweetness is undesirable. Frustrated in their attempt to live by standards they correctly appreciate, self-deceivers construct an "illusory hierarchy of values" more comfortable to them. Positive values like good health and freedom are inverted, for example, into prizing suffering and obedience. Once again the value delusion is not a complete blindness induced by bias, for appreciation of the positive values is never entirely lost:

> The phenomenal peculiarity of the *ressentiment* delusion can be described as follows: the positive values are still felt as such, but they are overcast by the false values and can shine through only dimly. The *ressentiment* experience is always characterized by this "transparent" presence of the true and objective values behind the illusory ones—by that obscure awareness that one lives in a sham world which one is unable to penetrate.[8]

Scheler applied this analysis to a variety of personality types and social groups where *ressentiment* is especially likely to occur. He mentioned, for example, prudes whose long-suppressed sexuality generates obsession with uncovering and condemning sexual behavior in the name of purity, even though they still value sexual pleasure (without acknowledging as much to themselves). Another example is the apostate who devotes a lifetime to secret vengeance against previous commitments that were never completely cast off and replaced with new affirmations. Likewise, *ressentiment* motivates those romantics whose longing for the past conceals a contempt for the present.

Scheler's most provocative examples concerned ideologies and philosophical perspectives. He contended that the alleged humanitarian ideal of egalitarianism in all aspects of life is really an attempt by the weak and slavish to bring the strong down to their own level. Again, subjectivism in ethics, which reduces values to personal tastes, constitutes a sweeping attempt to debunk all objective norms because they are difficult to live up to. The subjectivist dodges criticism by dismissing it as sheer subjective bias.

The concept of *ressentiment* was earlier developed by Friedrich Nietzsche in *The Genealogy of Morals*, a work that greatly influenced Scheler. It is therefore especially interesting that Scheler rejected Nietzsche's best-known application of the concept. Nietzsche had argued that Christianity arose from a slavish mentality of envy for the Greek and Roman values which, combined with social repression, blocked participation in the society based on those values.[9] The ensuing frustration, anger, and desire for revenge were then transformed by means of a value delusion based on self-denial, suffering, humility, and love of enemies. Scheler argued, convincingly in my view, that Nietzsche misunderstood the positive nature of at least some Christian virtues. Christian asceticism, for example, is aimed at nurturing inner strength, not at degrading the positive worth of the body. Again, Christian love is an overflow of positive strength, not a hidden tactic of the slavish in dealing with the powerful.[10] And as long as they are not perverted, humility and some acceptance of suffering are required for maturation and honest self-insight.

Whatever one's views about the origin of Christian values, there is an important lesson to be gained from the dispute between Scheler and Nietzsche. Nothing is easier or more tempting than charging one's opponents with self-deception for subscribing to value perspectives different from one's own. Religious thinkers have often been eager to criticize one another and attack nonbelievers as willfully ignoring God's truth.[11] In turn, atheists like Nietzsche, Marx, Freud, and Sartre were all too eager to ascribe *ressentiment* and other forms of self-deception to theists (as well as to their critics). Overlooked in these disputes is the possibility of honest and non–self-deceiving differences concerning value perspectives, differences that should be met with tolerance rather than accusations of self-deceit.

Thus it is a short step from using "self-deception" as an explanatory concept to using it as an ideological weapon, whether in religion, morality, or politics. To call someone's value perspective self-deceptive is not merely to suggest that it arose or is held in a certain way. Most often it is also implied that the view is false, unsupported, or otherwise unwarranted, given the available evidence. Ascriptions of self-deception, therefore, usually require two sorts of justification. First, there must be evidence that purposeful or intentional evasion has occurred, as opposed to inadvertent bias, the effects of limited intellect, or good-faith differences in outlook. Second, there must be independent evidence for believing the view is false or unwarranted. Because decisive evidence-giving is often difficult where value differences are involved, unjustified ascriptions of self-deception represent a real danger for members of the Inner Hypocrisy Tradition who rely heavily on "self-deception" as an explanatory concept.

DERIVATIVE WRONG

Given the preceding qualification, writers in this tradition are insightful in emphasizing how frequently self-deception conceals wrongdoing and moral insensitivity. Several factors suit it well to this role. Evading self-acknowledgment of our faults enables us to avoid painful moral emotions: guilt and remorse for harming others; shame for betraying our own ideals; self-contempt for not meeting even our minimal commitments. We also bypass the sometimes onerous task of abiding by our values and manage to sin freely and pleasurably. We avoid the need to make amends and restitution for the harm we do. And above all, we maintain a flattering self-image while pursuing immoral ends, often in the name of virtue.

Were they writing today, these authors could press their points with examples of greater cruelty than they had witnessed. Consider Albert Speer, Hitler's powerful minister of armaments and war productions. Contrary to what we might like to think, Speer was not a complete monster lacking all moral sensitivity. He was a talented architect and bureaucrat, a loving family man, and considerate to his circle of peers. Yet he managed to remain blind to some of the most horrifying proceedings of the Third Reich. If we can believe his memoirs, he intentionally avoided any inquiries that would have made him aware of the holocaust: "I did not investigate—for I did not want to know what was happening" at Auschwitz and elsewhere.[12] In addition, he evaded acknowledging to himself his own cruelty in placing war prisoners in slave conditions within his armament factories, the crime for which he was convicted at Nuremberg. Speer reported that he was moved emotionally by the faces of prisoners as he inspected factories. But he kept his feelings at the level of pure sentimentality, divorced from morally responsive action.[13]

Examples like this make it easy to understand Butler's castigations concerning inner hypocrisy: "The temper is essentially in its own nature vicious and immoral. It is unfairness; it is dishonesty; it is falseness of heart: and is therefore so far from extenuating guilt, that it is itself the greatest of all guilt in proportion to the degree it prevails; for it is a corruption of the whole moral character in its principle.[14] The "principle" of character referred to here is conscience, the central element in Butler's ethical theory. According to his faith, God gave each of us a dependable conscience that should authoritatively guide us in identifying and acting on moral duty. Deceiving ourselves about our duties and character flaws amounts to "deceiving our consciences" and thereby undermining an otherwise reliable moral guide.

In Butler's view, the "temper" of deceiving ourselves about our immorality gives rise to a vast amount of further immorality. It leads us to disregard the moral instruction most likely to be of service in improving our character. It supports complacency about our character (even though complacency may have been part of its origin in the first place) and thereby indirectly causes much preventable wrongdoing. In a sufficiently selfish person, it provides scope for explaining away virtually any obligation. In a callous person it can support all degrees of wickedness.

Let us agree that when self-deception contributes to immorality it should be condemned, and condemned in proportion to the magnitude of the wrongdoing or character fault. It should also be criticized when it even threatens to lead to wrongdoing by warping moral understanding in the way Scheler described. Hence the Inner Hypocrisy Tradition offers this significant truth:

> *Derivative-Wrong Principle:* Self-deception often leads to, threatens to lead to, or supports immorality, and when it does it is wrong in proportion to the immorality involved.

This principle criticizes self-deception only when it is a derivative, second order, wrong because of its relation to other, primary, wrongs. The principle can be justified by any fundamental moral appeal (or ethical theory) about what makes acts primary wrongs: for example, harmful consequences (teleological theories such as utilitarianism), violation of duties (deontological theories), or infringement of rights (human rights theories).

Surely, however, not all self-deception is about immorality or fosters immorality in any obvious way. Thus, the Derivative-Wrong Principle provides no basis for a universal condemnation of self-deception about other topics. Nevertheless, a few writers in the Inner Hypocrisy Tradition have argued that self-deception always poses an indirect threat of wrongdoing. Immanuel Kant, for example, suggested in *The Doctrine of Virtue* that all self-deception encourages violations of duties to others. He was especially critical of those theists who lie to themselves about their self-interested motives for believing in God "in order hypocritically to win His favour if He should happen to exist" or in obeying commandments from a fear of punishment rather than a recognition of the validity of moral requirements.[15] But he even chastised the "frailty" of lovers who are self-deceived about their partners' flaws. Any lie to oneself, Kant sternly warned, "deserves the most serious blame, since it is from such a foul spot . . . that the evil of deceitfulness spreads into man's relations with other men, when once the principle of truthfulness has been violated."[16]

W. K. Clifford, a nineteenth-century spokesperson for the scientific community, also criticized all self-deceivers. In "The Ethics of Belief," he construed self-deception as a form of biased judgment and held that we are blameworthy whenever we allow our wishes to influence our assessments of evidence. Even if a biased belief does not directly influence conduct negatively, it still has the potential to influence other beliefs that could cause harm by entering into decisions. Directly or indirectly, all biased beliefs have the potential to cause harm. Hence it is "our duty to mankind" to guard against any belief that goes beyond the hard evidence available to us: "It is wrong always, everywhere, and for anyone, to believe anything upon insufficient evidence."[17]

Kant and Clifford offered what are called slippery-slope arguments: taking a first, otherwise innocent step in a potentially dangerous direction will initiate a slide down a disastrous slope. Not all slippery-slope arguments are fallacious. It all depends on available information about whether, in the specific context, the alleged series of events is likely to be initiated by the first step. The arguments of Kant and Clifford, however, are fallacious. For not every instance of self-deception appreciably threatens to cause wrongdoing.

To refer to Kant's examples, self-deception in love relationships need not encourage immorality and in some circumstances promises closer bonding and bliss. His examples of self-deception about motives for moral and religious commitments are plausible but represent special cases. We understand how self-deception of that sort can deflect and distort those commitments, precisely because the motives involved also function as motives for actions that could conflict with duty.

Clifford also provided a compelling example but for reasons other than he gives. He described a shipowner who from selfish economic motives deceives himself about the condition of his emigrant ship.[18] As a result he sends an unsafe ship to sea and its passengers to their deaths. Here the self-deception is culpable because of the motive (greed) and the specific features of the context. The man knows he is in a situation in which people's lives will be endangered by an error in judgment on his part, and he has a special moral obligation as shipowner to be fully aware of the ship's condition. Hence he is responsible for making a special effort to guard against any kind of bias, complacency, or purposeful self-deception. It is these circumstances that make his self-deception appalling, beyond the vague potential for harm embedded in all self-deception and all unwarranted beliefs.

Granted, there is always a logical possibility for any given instance of self-deception to generate wrongdoing. But that is a far cry from providing reasonable grounds for expecting it to do so or for criticizing all self-deception. The abstract possibility of unforeseeable bad consequences is present in all human endeavors and is no basis for criticizing them. It is unforeseeable that buying a car may lead ultimately to a fatal car crash, but that does not by itself make it immoral to buy a car. It is unforeseeable that having a child may indirectly lead to far more bad than good because of the child's actions as an adult, but that does not make it immoral to have a child. Morality focuses on reasonable expectations and takes account of unrealistic dangers only in unusual circumstances.

More-plausible slippery-slope arguments, however, can be developed concerning general tendencies or dispositions rather than individual acts or states of self-deception. Dostoyevsky has Father Zossima voice one such argument in *The Brothers Karamazov:*

> Above all, don't lie to yourself. The man who lies to himself and listens to his own lie comes to such a point that he cannot distinguish the truth within him, or around him, and so loses all respect for himself and for others. And having no respect he ceases to love. And in order to distract himself without love he gives way to passions and coarse pleasures and sinks to bestiality in his vices—all this from continual lying to other men and to himself.[19]

There is hyperbole here, but Zossima is voicing a genuine danger. Continual self-deception can undermine our general ability to discern truth. This may have two consequences. First, it makes us indirectly vulnerable to self-deception about immorality and thereby is subject to the Derivative-Wrong Principle. General habits of self-deception are bound to dull sensitivity to moral requirements or to interfere in living up to them. Second, most of us will eventually gain some sense of our habitual disregard for truth. This awareness may weaken confidence in our capacity for understanding and thereby lessen our sense of self-worth as rational beings. In lowering self-esteem, a nagging sense of living a lie can also undermine our relationships with others.

None of this has to occur, of course. Before it does we may gain full awareness of the self-deceiving tendency and abandon it or simply remain unaware of it. But the slippery-slope argument provides a reasonable caution against habitual self-deception. Thus, we can endorse a variation of the Derivative-Wrong Principle:

> *Modified Derivative-Wrong Principle:* Dispositions to engage in self-deception about any threatening topic typically contribute to immorality eventually, and in that respect they are immoral.

Kant also had a second argument for regarding all self-deception as immoral. According to it, self-deception is inherently wrong, whether or not it contributes to further immorality, for it constitutes blameworthy insincerity in expressing one's thoughts to oneself. Kant developed this argument by referring to the experience of guilt. To feel guilty is to feel as if one is condemned by another person, although the other person is experienced as oneself: "The man who accuses and judges himself in conscience must think of himself as a twofold personage, a doubled self."[20] Self-deceivers make insincere avowals before this moral alter ego which functions as a judge within us: "Insincerity is a mere lack of *conscientiousness, i.e.,* of sincerity in our avowals before our *inner* judge, whom we conceive as another person when we think of sincerity in its utmost strictness."[21] The inner judge is an ideal moral being with whom we identify and who we strive to become; it is what gives us a reason to reverence ourselves for our "splendid disposition for the good." But to the extent we lie to ourselves, we make ourselves contemptible by violating our dignity as persons.

Respecting the dignity of all persons, including ourselves, is central to Kant's deontological, or duty-based, ethics. Respect is manifested by adhering to specific duties that categorically prescribe or forbid certain types of actions. Some duties are "imperfect" in the sense that they enjoin an effort in a certain direction but not compliance on every occasion: for example, the duty to help others (benevolence). Others are "perfect" duties which require adherence on all occasions and do not admit of exceptions, such as the duty not to murder. Kant believed that the duty not to deceive—either other people or oneself—is a perfect duty: "By a lie a man makes himself contemptible—by an outer lie, in the eyes of others; by an inner lie, in his own eyes, which is worse still— and violates the dignity of humanity in his own person."[22]

Surely this is an exaggeration.[23] Not all interpersonal lies are immoral, insincere, or self-degrading, as we noted in the last chapter. And Kant provided no reason for thinking that all self-deception involves insincerity. His only argument was that all liars have "a purpose directly opposed to the natural purposiveness of the power of communicating one's thoughts."[24] Even if that were true, it would not establish his conclusion because it is not automatically immoral to alter a natural (biological or cultural) purpose. If it were, contraception and voluntary celibacy would be immoral. Yet, more important, there is no fixed, natural purpose for language. People have innumerable purposes in using language, and therefore language has many purposes. Wittgenstein drew attention to this multiplicity of "language games" other than truthful communication of thoughts: for example, joking, giving and receiving orders, playacting, and "lying [which] is a language-game that needs to be learned like any other one."[25]

In developing Kant's ideas, W. D. Falk suggested that avoiding self-deception has special significance within a Kantian ethics centered on self-respect. The basis for moral self-respect lies in viewing oneself as morally autonomous, and hence as having the ability to discern and live by moral principles. In turn, this requires truthful reflection and forbids self-deceiving evasion. The conscientious person is committed "to live without evading any issue—to seek out and weigh what cogent reasons would lead him to do, and to submit himself without self-deception or evasion to their determination . . . [and to accept] the principle of non-escapism as an over-all rule of life."[26] Only through this commitment can a person "preserve himself intact as a living and functioning self: mentally in possession of himself and what he is doing without having to hide from himself. The penalty for slighting this need is his undoing as a person."[27]

In part, Falk is criticizing habitual self-deception. Surely he is right that an entrenched habit of evading truth self-deceivingly, like a habit of drunkenness, undermines rationality and threatens to undo moral character. He is also stating—or overstating—a more positive thesis about the importance of dispositions to confront truth. In saying that we must "live without evading any issue," he creates the impression that each instance of self-deception is immoral and that even a restricted tendency toward self-deception in a matter having little to do with morality is immoral. These views are far too strong. Yet there is an important truth in what Falk is saying, which we might formulate as follows:

> *Autonomy-Supporting Principle:* In all matters relevant to morality, dispositions to truthfulness and non–self-deceiving truth seeking are essential in enabling us to discern moral requirements, act on them, and retain whatever unity of character is based on moral autonomy.

This principle embodies two caveats. First, it is restricted by subject matter: the self-deception concerned must be relevant to morality. Second, it is a statement about general dispositions, not individual acts and states of self-deception. It allows, for example, that a person could be effective as a morally autonomous agent while displaying occasional lapses into self-deception (because an episode does not destroy a disposition). And it allows that there might be examples—many of them—in which self-deception or even a limited tendency to self-deception is not about a subject relevant to morality. For example, there might be a tendency to deceive oneself about the beauty of one's family members (as compared with the beauty of strangers), which is morally permissible and which remains insulated without spreading to self-deception about other topics.

Taken together, the Derivative-Wrong Principle, the Modified Derivative-Wrong Principle, and the Autonomy-Supporting Principle specify the moral importance of avoiding self-deception about wrongdoing and character faults. They are all implied by a wider principle:

> *Due-Care Principle:* There is a duty to take appropriate care before we act to be sure we are not violating our moral obligations.

This is a second-order moral duty, derived from our primary moral responsibilities: having any moral obligations entails having obligations to take appropriate steps in meeting those obligations. Hence, self-deception that is either a general habit or specifically about our own immorality constitutes moral negligence.[28]

HYPOCRISY

The label "Inner Hyprocrisy Tradition" derives from Butler's expression, "internal hypocrisy." Are these terms appropriate? If they are, then self-deception about immorality can be wrong for a further reason than its contribution to other wrongdoing or character faults, for hypocrisy is a fault by itself, whether or not it adds to further immorality. But is self-deception about immorality appropriately viewed as a form of hypocrisy? Or does hypocrisy suggest a degree of self-awareness incompatible with self-deception? And if self-deceivers can be hypocrites, does their absence of full self-awareness make them less bad than fully aware hypocrites?

Butler used the adjective "internal" to refer to hypocrisy before oneself—self-directed hypocrisy—although he allowed that normally it also constituted hypocrisy before other people.[29] Let us begin by clarifying hypocrisy before others, or "outer-directed" hypocrisy.

It is tempting to think that hypocrisy before others is a species of deception, but that is not quite correct. A person can be a hypocrite even though no one is deceived. Senator Joseph McCarthy remained a self-righteous, pompous, intolerant hypocrite even after everyone saw through his hypocritical posturing, and other hypocrites are more easily seen through before they deceive anyone. Hypocrisy is a form of pretense, whether or not the pretense leads to actual deception. But the relevant sort of pretense requires that the hypocrite either intend to deceive or knowingly and voluntarily allow a misleading appearance to continue.

If not all hypocrisy is deception, neither is all deception hypocrisy. Using security lights to mislead burglars into thinking someone is at home does not make one a hypocrite. Not even all blameworthy deception is hypocritical. Terrorists who achieve immoral goals by sending deceptive messages to their victims need not be hypocrites. The definition given in the *Oxford English Dictionary* explains why this is so. Hypocrisy is "the assuming of a false appearance of virtue or goodness, with dissimulation of real character or inclinations." The hypocrite is "one who falsely professes to be virtuous or religiously inclined; one who pretends to have feelings or beliefs of a higher order than his real ones; hence generally, a dissembler, pretender." If we omit the erroneous suggestion that all pretenders are hypocrites, these definitions accurately report that hypocrisy involves pretending to be better than one is,[30] unlike terrorists who may not try to con anyone about their character traits.

The definitions fail, however, to capture the strongly derogatory connotations of "hypocrisy" and "hypocrite." Originally, being a hypocrite meant acting a part on the stage. But according to contemporary usage, actors are not hypocrites, even when a roguish actor plays the role of a virtuous character. To call someone a hypocrite, without joking or qualification, is to criticize him or her. Thus, hypocrites are (a) pretenders, (b) who intend or willingly allow themselves to appear better than they are (whether better according to valid moral standards, unwarranted conventional moral standards, or other norms), and (c) who are at fault for doing so.

Ascertaining fault and blameworthiness for pretense is a case-by-case procedure. Any number of reasons may stop us from blaming individuals for appearing better than they are. For example, insofar as we indulge or even enjoy the braggadocio of children (and some adults), we do not view it as hypocrisy. We may admire, not blame, spies disguised as ministers or undercover police officers disguised as social workers so long as their ruses are necessary for achieving praiseworthy goals. And we withhold the pejorative epithet "hypocrite" from individuals who are confronted with situations in which the only way to endure social tyranny is to pretend to meet conventional standards of virtue, as with Jews in Nazi Germany, black slaves in the United States, or women in oppressive patriarchal societies.[31]

What reasons do we use in singling out and blaming as hypocrites only certain pretenders who appear better than they are? Here again there are many different reasons, but they fall into two main categories. First, we speak of hypocrisy when immoral consequences are involved, such as stealing, betraying, or unfairly winning a promotion. Second, we criticize it for what it is in itself: for its bad intentions, its unfairness, or its violation of relationships with others. Sometimes we despise it as a subtle form of coercion.[32] For example, hypocrites often seek to manipulate us into esteeming them more highly than we would esteem them if we were not deceived. In this way they try to manipulate and exploit our attitudes in a blameworthy manner, whether or not they actually bring about harmful consequences. Frequently hypocrites violate our trust in them not to deceive us.[33] Most often we are offended by hypocrites for trying to gain the benefit of social esteem in unfair ways. Our respect and the respect of others is a good to be won by meeting appropriate standards, and in pretending to meet the standards the hypocrite is a cheat (whether or not harmful consequences result).

If hypocrites pretend to be better than they are in blameworthy ways, it is clear that not all self-deceivers are hypocrites. For one thing, not all of them are culpable and blameworthy, as we have seen. Moreover, some self-deceivers appear to themselves and others to be much worse than they really are. People who display drastically low estimates of themselves, suffering from inferiority complexes, may do so because of self-deception about their own positive attributes and self-worth.[34]

Our definition of hypocrisy also clarifies why many self-deceivers *are* hypocrites, especially the self-deceivers discussed by Dyke, Butler, and Scheler, for they engage in immorality while pretending not to be engaged in it. Of course, where we find mitigating circumstances we will not apply the negative epithet "hypocrite." But in the degree they are blameworthy for the self-deceptive pretense, they are hypocritical. They are *inner* hypocrites—hypocrites with respect to themselves—in the sense that they culpably pretend before themselves to be better than they are. They are also outer-directed hypocrites insofar as they cause, and are blameworthy for causing, a morally inflated image of themselves before others. Moreover, some self-deceivers are outer-directed hypocrites even though their self-deception is not about immorality. An example is a writer who is so charmed by himself that he self-deceivingly thinks his minor novel deserves world recognition as a literary masterpiece and as a result behaves pompously.

Nevertheless, there does seem to be a (misleading) temptation to regard self-deception and hypocrisy as mutually exclusive. The temptation seems to arise from our preoccupation with hypocrites who are fully aware of their pretense, including classic characters in literature. Mention of hypocrisy brings to mind the villainous Iago, who sadistically betrays Othello while pretending to be his loyal servant. Or we think of Uriah Heep in *David Copperfield:* the slimy, contemptuous cynic who pretends to be humble in order to camouflage his exploitation of people around him. Perhaps we recall Molière's conniving Tartuffe, who is fully aware of how his pretense of religious devotion enables him to earn a comfortable living.

All these hypocrites are self-aware in that they acknowledge to themselves their pretense, intentions, motives, and strategies. Of course, they are most unlikely to make a heartfelt confession to themselves that they are hypocrites. "Hypocrite" implies a condemnation, and honestly criticizing themselves is the last thing they want to do. They are just as callous, malicious, or amoral as they are self-aware. Yet precisely because of their complete self-awareness they are poor models for understanding most hypocrisy. The majority of hypocrites are much less self-conscious and less willing to acknowledge their false appearances.[35] They have some vanity and, it is hoped, some moral concern that would make them uncomfortable to admit to themselves their wrongdoing.[36]

Judge Pyncheon in Hawthorne's *House of the Seven Gables* provides a vivid illustration of a self-deceiving hypocrite. Pyncheon pretends before others and himself to be a model of virtue. In the eyes of virtually everyone, he is a faithful guardian of society's interests: zealous in politics, president of the Bible society, treasurer of a widows' and orphans' fund, supporter of the temperance cause, and widely renowned for adhering to high principles of conduct. Yet his financial success is founded on greed, cruelty, and betrayal rivaling that of Iago. As a youth he had once searched his uncle's room and was caught by the uncle, causing the old man to have a fatal seizure. Pyncheon ransacked the room to make it look as if a burglar were responsible for the death. Later he allowed his innocent cousin to go to jail as the convicted murderer. He also destroys a final will that gives the uncle's inheritance to the cousin, while preserving an earlier will giving the inheritance to himself.

During his later life of philanthropy and public service, Pyncheon used self-deception to shuffle this sequence of events "aside, among the forgotten and forgiven frailties of his youth, and seldom thought of it again."[37] He also deceived himself about his chicanery in depriving others of their land, burying such acts under "a sculptured and ornamented pile of ostentatious deeds." His apparent altruism draws only public praise, making it easy to blind himself to his thoroughgoing egotism: "A hard, cold man . . . seldom or never looking inward, and resolutely taking his idea of himself from what purports to be his image as reflected in the mirror of public opinion, can scarcely arrive at true self-knowledge."[38]

In addition to illustrating how self-deception can be hypocritical, Pyncheon also helps us understand the comparative moral status of self-deceiving and non–self-deceiving forms of hypocrisy. If we concentrate on self-aware and villainous hypocrites (like Iago, Uriah Heep, and Tartuffe), there appears to be a connection between awareness of one's pretense and moral callousness. This connection in turn suggests that self-aware hypocrites are more callous and detestable than self-deceivers. Pyncheon refutes these generalizations. He is as detestable as the self-aware hypocrites mentioned previously and is additionally contemptible for using self-deceit to unfairly reap the benefits of a flattering self-image.

Whereas Pyncheon illustrates how self-deceivers can be as cruel as many self-aware hypocrites, another Hawthorne character illustrates how self-aware hypocrites can have a higher degree of moral sensitivity than many self-deceivers. The Reverend Dimmesdale in *The Scarlet Letter* may be self-deceived in thinking he is best serving God by continuing as a minister rather than marrying Hester Prynne. But he is not self-deceived about his hypocrisy in doing so. He fully believes that his adultery with Hester makes him as guilty as the parishioners whom he calls to confession and a far greater hypocrite than most of them because of his hypocritical appearance of being more virtuous. In our view today, his worst sin consists in betraying Hester and their daughter, Pearl. Yet, like Hester, we feel some compassion for him because of his tormenting awareness of his guilt and hypocrisy. His self-punishment, self-contempt, and self-flagellation are at least partially the result of his acute moral sensitivity. As Hawthorne wrote, Dimmesdale is a "remorseful hypocrite" who suffers "without the momentary relief of being self-deceived."[39]

Dimmesdale shows that self-aware hypocrites may be unusually morally sensitive, both in general and specifically with respect to their hypocrisy (even though their sensitivity may be shown more in their suffering than in their conduct). Judge Pyncheon shows that self-deceiving hypocrites may be diabolical. If Dimmesdale had deceived himself into believing he was innocent of wrongdoing, then he would have shown less moral sensitivity than he did while suffering as a self-aware hypocrite. If Pyncheon had not been a self-deceiver, then his corruption would at least have been less convoluted and not compounded by unearned self-esteem. In general, self-aware hypocrites need not be less morally sensitive than self-deceivers. And the relative degree of their blameworthiness depends on the circumstances and the motives involved.

MORAL WEAKNESS

Self-deception about our immorality often supports or helps generate actions that go against our own better moral judgment. When these actions are intentional and uncoerced, they are referred to as acts of moral weakness—that is, weakness of will in moral matters. Hence it is not surprising to find the concept of self-deception frequently invoked to help explain why moral weakness occurs.[40] At the same time, self-deception about wrongdoing has been viewed by some philosophers as itself a form of weakness of will because it constitutes a failure to implement moral understanding in particular situations. Yet if self-deception is an instance of weakness of will, it would seem inappropriate to appeal to it in explaining weakness of will. Moral weakness apparently cannot be explained by appealing to moral weakness; something cannot explain itself.

To confuse matters further, the concept of moral weakness is itself used to explain wrongdoing in a way that is seemingly incompatible with self-deception. "Moral weakness" seems to suggest a lack of strength of will. And to act against one's better judgment because of a lack of strength is different from blurring one's judgment to begin with by engaging in self-deception.

I want to show that the following three statements are compatible and plausible. (1) Some moral weakness (though not all) can be explained in part by appealing to the presence of self-deception. (2) Self-deception and moral weakness are sometimes alternative and contrasting explanations of wrongdoing. (3) Self-deception about wrongdoing is often a form of moral weakness.

As we proceed, we will need to pay heed to an ambiguity in the expression "better moral judgment," especially in dealing with the first statement. This expression can refer to any of the following: (a) the general capacity (or ability) to form the correct moral view, (b) a specific judgment about what ought to be done made sometime earlier than the occasion of the moral weakness, or (c) a specific judgment about what ought to be done which is made at the time of acting.

(1a) The first of the three statements is that some moral weakness (though not all) can be explained in terms of self-deception. Consider the sense in which "moral judgment" refers to (a) the general capacity to form the correct moral view. Acting against our moral judgment in this sense is failing to exercise our moral competence in ways that can be expected. We have the general ability, for example, to discern that we owe a debt of gratitude to a friend for helping us, but we fail to exercise that ability. The explanation is that we tried to avoid an onerous burden by deceiving ourselves into thinking that the friend did not really help us significantly or was only trying to manipulate us into owing something in return.

Bishop Butler applied the concept of self-deception in this manner to understand specific acts of wrongdoing like those of David and Balaam. Scheler applied it in understanding *ressentiment* and distorted moral perspectives that in a more wholesale fashion undermine the ability to arrive at correct moral judgments.

(1b) Consider next the situation in which "moral judgment' refers to a moral appraisal made some time prior to the occasion of the moral weakness. Here we know or at least suspect the correct course of action, but we see no need to act right away. Time remains to blur our initial insight or to rationalize it away. Perhaps we deliberately procrastinate repaying a small loan from a colleague. Before long we convince ourselves that the loan is too small to bother with. Because the initial insight represents our better moral judgment and because self-deception facilitates acting against it, the self-deception helps explain why and how the moral weakness occurs.

(1c) Suppose that "moral judgment" refers to the specific judgment made at the time of acting against it. Here our better moral judgment is at least partially operative during the time we engage in wrongdoing. But we refuse to acknowledge it to ourselves, whether by ignoring, self-pretending, emotional detachment, on-the-spot rationalization, or whatever. For example, we know we should make a special effort to control our tempers during a debate on a controversial topic, but instead we work ourselves into a veritable emotional frenzy. Afterwards we admit to ourselves that we knew all along we were out of line but at the time ignored our better judgment (without earlier acknowledging to ourselves that we were doing so).

(2) The second statement was that self-deception and moral weakness are sometimes alternative and contrasting explanations of wrongdoing. This is the case when the morally weak individual is fully clear and undeceived about the correct course of action but fails to make a sufficient effort to act accordingly. For example, soldiers know they should obey orders but fail to muster the courage and self-control to do so. Or students are aware that cheating on exams is wrong and yet give in to a desire to pass the course even at the cost of cheating.

Socrates denied that such things could occur as described. To have moral knowledge, he insisted, is to be virtuous, and hence knowing what is right entails doing it (unless prevented by external obstacles beyond one's control). More-recent skeptics about moral weakness have reasserted the Socratic view in terms of commitment rather than knowledge. They contend that sincere commitment entails acting on the commitment unless external obstacles intervene. Such views carry to an extreme the commonsense insistence that actions speak louder than words in determining what a person knows, believes, or is committed to. In doing so, they depart from the flexibility of ordinary language that permits us to say that we can know what is right and yet fail to do it for a variety of reasons: we were too tired, afraid, or apathetic on a particular occasion to be responsive to what we knew or to what we were in general committed to; we failed to try hard enough to do what was right; we lacked the requisite habits which facilitate strength of character on particular occasions; and so on. Socratic skepticism about such phenomena can only be sustained by linguistic fiat in stipulating nonstandard senses of knowledge and commitment or on the basis of a normative theory that sets unusually high standards for what counts as commitment and moral insight.

Now frequently, "moral weakness" refers specifically to a lack of strength or to a loss of self-control and hence has a much narrower sense than merely acting against one's better moral judgment. It means acting against one's better judgment because of forms of weakness other than self-deception. Here, of course, moral weakness and self-deception become contrasting ways of explaining failures to follow one's better moral judgment.

(3) The third statement is that self-deception about wrongdoing is itself often a form of moral weakness. This is true whether "moral weakness" refers to all acts against one's better judgment or only to those involving a loss of self-control. A great deal of wrongdoing results from a lack of effort to maintain a clear moral vision, to form appropriate habits of rational belief and acknowledgment, and to exercise those habits on appropriate occasions.

There are, in fact, several senses in which self-deceivers might act against their better judgment. First, "better judgment" might refer to the judgment that they ought not to deceive themselves about moral matters. Not all self-deceivers make this judgment. But those who do are acting against this better judgment if they then deceive themselves about their immorality.[41] Second, "better judgment" might refer to the general ability to form and act on sound moral judgments. Most self-deceivers have this ability and hence act contrary to their moral judgment when they deceive themselves in moral matters.[42] Third, "moral judgment" can refer to self-deceivers' unacknowledged knowledge about how they ought to act (whether the knowledge is present at the time of acting or at an earlier time). Many self-deceivers can be viewed as morally weak for refusing to admit to themselves what they know.[43]

But where self-deception about wrongdoing is itself a form of moral weakness, how can self-deception function as an explanation of moral weakness? As we noted at the outset, an instance of moral weakness cannot be used to explain itself. Yet self-deception involves additional elements that go beyond the specific acts of moral weakness it is used to explain: namely, the psychological tactics comprising the evasion of self-acknowledgment. In self-deception about wrongdoing there are two actions (or sets of actions), either of which might be an instance of acting against one's better moral judgment: (1) the use of the self-deceiving tactics, and (2) the wrongdoing about which one is self-deceived. Recall King David, who violates his Judaic belief that adultery is wrong and, according to Butler, uses self-deception in making a special exception for himself. We distinguish between (1) his self-deceiving rationalization (or other forms of evading self-acknowledgment) and (2) the adultery itself. Both are instances of moral weakness, but that does not prevent the former from entering into an explanation of the latter.

The Inner Hypocrisy Tradition shows us that self-deception, whether episodic or habitual, is a derivative wrong when it supports immoral conduct, vices, bad character, or distorted moral perspectives.

This tradition does not establish that self-deception about other topics is always immoral. Blameworthy self-deception also constitutes an inherent fault by being a form of hypocrisy before oneself and others. Hypocrisy can be wrong for a variety of reasons, and self-awareness need not make it morally worse than when self-deception is present. The concept of self-deception can be used to help explain how many instances of moral weakness occur, even though it can itself be a form of moral weakness. Responsible moral conduct requires acknowledging to oneself (a) warranted moral principles, (b) the applicability of those principles in appropriate situations, (c) the facts relevant to acting on those principles in particular situations, and (d) our own moral concern. Self-deception can enter to lessen or block full self-acknowledgment in any of these areas.

4

Authenticity

> How much truth does a spirit *endure*, how much truth does it *dare*?
> More and more that became for me the real measure of value. Error
> . . . is not blindness, error is *cowardice*.
> —Friedrich Nietzsche, *Ecce Homo*

The Authenticity Tradition emphasizes a single ideal, authenticity, which is defined in terms of avoiding self-deception. This emphasis leads to intensified criticism of virtually all self-deception—not just self-deception about wrongdoing—as cowardly and dishonest. Whereas the Inner Hypocrisy Tradition regards self-deception as a derivative wrong, the Authenticity Tradition criticizes it as the primary or only wrong. Correspondingly, it transforms the avoidance of self-deception from a limited and secondary duty into the paramount virtue. There is also another, ironical, transformation. In contrast with the Inner Hypocrisy Tradition's attack on self-deception insofar as it undermines commitments to objectively justifiable moral values, the Authenticity Tradition deemphasizes or attacks the very possibility of such values.

It is not difficult to see in outline how these transformations occur. Existentialists, who represent the main current in the Authenticity Tradition, are preoccupied with the process of decision making, rather than with evaluating resulting actions by reference to objectively defensible values. Their concern is not so much with *what* choices are made as with *how* they are made. Decisions, they insist, must be made in a fully honest way, based on a courageous willingness to acknowledge the significant features of the human condition, of one's immediate situation, and of one's personal responses. While they differ over what these

53

features are, they always select features intimately connected (in their views) with all aspects of meaningful life—for example, freedom, personal responsibility, death, individuality, or personal fulfillment. This leads them to trace virtually all evasions of self-acknowledgment to fundamental evasions of significant truths about these features. The result is that virtually all self-deception is to be condemned, and condemned with the same intensity used to focus on one value—authenticity.

Sartre will receive special attention in this chapter. Not only is his discussion of self-deception the most systematic and influential among the existentialists, it is also the most technical and obscure. It will be worthwhile to unravel its main threads in light of my conception of evading self-acknowledgment. Before doing so, however, I offer a sketch of the views of Søren Kierkegaard, who is in some respects a member of both the Inner Hypocrisy and the Authenticity Traditions. As such, he is the key transition figure because he shifted attention to the process of decision making while retaining a belief in objective moral values. After the discussions of Kierkegaard and Sartre, I discuss briefly a few other writers in order to support the thesis that authenticity has two dimensions—autonomy and acknowledgment of significant truth—each of which receives different interpretations by different writers in this tradition. I also recommend an alternative interpretation that would lessen the likelihood of polemical abuse of the concept of authenticity.

CHOOSING ONESELF

References to self-deception permeate Kierkegaard's voluminous writings, but we will do well to focus on the second volume of *Either/Or* and *The Sickness unto Death*. Both works deal with the development of ethically concerned individuals who shape their personalities around autonomous moral commitments. In Kierkegaard's view, this development is guided by the "Eternal Power" of God. Yet his best moral insights, especially in *Either/Or*, are largely distinct from his religious perspective.

Judge Wilhelm, the fictional spokesperson for the ethical point of view in *Either/Or*, makes the following remark: "If you will understand me aright, I should like to say that in making a choice it is not so much a question of choosing the right as of the energy, the earnestness, the pathos with which one chooses. Thereby the personality announces its inner infinity, and thereby, in turn, the personality is consolidated."[1] One way *not* to understand the judge aright is to think he is denying there is an objective rightness that should guide and constrain choices.

As the judge later explains, genuine passion in choosing enables a person to identify and correct (objectively) wrong choices by purifying the personality and redirecting it toward dutiful conduct. Moral duty remains a universal demand on all of us, as Kant said, and is not something we invent.[2]

Nevertheless, extensive reflection about specific duties is of relatively little importance. What counts is the passion and energy with which choices are made. Passion is not mere enthusiasm—that would be a second way to misunderstand the judge's remark. Instead, it is single-minded commitment to live by principles of duty and therein to affirm oneself as an ethical agent.[3] Moral self-affirmation brings with it an assurance of one's "inner infinity"—one's unlimited worth. It also fosters unification of the entire personality by relating even the most mundane aspects of life to moral duties. Herein lies our highest duty and our greatest good: "to order, cultivate, temper, enkindle, repress, in short, to bring about a proportionality in the soul, a harmony, which is the fruit of the personal virtues."[4]

To underscore his shift of emphasis from knowledge about specific duties to passionate moral commitment, Kierkegaard replaced the Socratic dictum "know thyself" with an injunction to "choose oneself."[5] Choosing oneself as an ethical agent begins by affirming one's freedom to choose between good and evil. In this sense alone Kierkegaard says we are the authors of the good and bad created through our commitments: "The good [I can achieve] *is* for the fact that I will it, and apart from my willing it, it has no existence. This is the expression for freedom. It is so also with evil, it *is* only when I will it."[6] That is, we do not invent moral duty, but our commitments to act in morally concerned ways generate the good in meeting our duties and the bad in failing to do so.

Choosing oneself presupposes an initial awareness of oneself as being a morally imperfect self lacking singleminded moral concern. This awareness is *despair*. The ethical self can emerge only after we accept our despair in humble recognition of our faults.[7] The crucial next step consists in acknowledging our freedom, together with our personal responsibility and guilt for unjustified expressions of that freedom, and thereby being moved to repentance.[8] Thus, choosing oneself as a moral self involves fully acknowledging our freedom, despair, responsibility, guilt, and need to repent. This acknowledgment, like the choice to be a moral agent, is not a momentary resolve made once and for all. It is a gradual shaping of attitude and commitment that needs to be reaffirmed in all subsequent choices. All aspects of our lives must be interpreted in light of duty, for only this enables ethical agency to unify the personality. Other overriding passions, such as desires for fame or wealth, fragment us in many directions rather than provide continuity and consistency to our lives. Only moral commitment generates sufficient unifying power and discipline by imparting a sense that it matters unconditionally whether we choose the good or the bad.[9]

All of Kierkegaard's specific applications of the concept of self-deception in *Either/Or* relate to the fundamental choice of oneself as an ethical agent. For example, he charged hedonists with immersing themselves in pleasure seeking because of fear of the discipline required in unifying their personalities around moral commitments.[10] Intellectuals, by contrast, use abstract thinking as a potent anesthetic to remain emotionally distanced from themselves.[11] Many of us refuse to deal responsibly with features of our lives we did not voluntarily initiate, even though self-acceptance requires accepting responsibility for all aspects of our lives. A contrasting deceit is to adopt the attitude that we can make ourselves anything we want to, forgetting entirely the facts about our lives that cannot be altered.[12]

In *The Sickness unto Death* Kierkegaard elaborated on these themes more systematically than in the somewhat desultory *Either/Or*. Sickness unto death is despair, now understood as the failure to choose oneself as an individual, or self, in relation with God. God's commandments provide the objective basis for moral duty, rather than any limited human perspective on duty (such as Judge Wilhelm's largely Kantian outlook). The forms of despair are catalogued from two main perspectives, which we can summarize using Kierkegaard's own numbers and letters.[13] Because despair is sin and sin is the product of self-deception, these forms of despair are also general forms of self-deception.

(A) The first perspective from which to view despair and self-deception is in regard to the fundamental aspects of the person that need to be unified in creating an ethical self.

(a) The self is a synthesis of the infinite and the finite. That is, it emerges only as the potentially unlimited areas of personal growth (the infinite) are related consciously to the firm limits to what we can become (the finite). Correspondingly, there are two types of self-deception. (1) We might deceive ourselves with inflated notions about our unlimited potential. In this case our sense of ourselves becomes so ethereal and abstract that it is as if the self becomes volatile. An extreme example is the God-inebriated mystic who loses attachment to this world and the responsibilities it entails. Another example is the intellectual who in searching for unlimited quantities of general knowledge loses detailed, practical self-understanding. (2) In contrast, we might conceive of ourselves as so finite that we lack any potential for growth, creative accomplishment, and genuine distinctiveness. This is the self-deceiving despair of the person who flees individuality, who "does not dare to believe in himself, finds it too venturesome a thing to be himself, far easier and safer to be like the others, to become an imitation, a number, a cipher in the crowd."[14]

(b) The self is also a synthesis of possibility and necessity: it is aware of both its genuine options and the respects in which it is determined. Here again there are two corresponding forms of self-deception and despair. (1) We might conceive of ourselves as a pure possibility. For example, we might continuously attend to our bright prospects without undertaking the hard effort required to overcome obstacles and as a result squander life with Pollyanna-like fantasies. Alternatively, our fantasies may be somberly preoccupied with the horror of life, leading us to an anxiety-ridden melancholy existence. (2) In contrast, we might view ourselves as wholly determined. This denial of our freedom as moral agents suffocates the self, which can thrive only with faith in the prospect of moral self-transformation based on personal initiative.

(B) The second perspective from which to classify despair and self-deception is the degree to which we are conscious of our despair. Essentially, this is the extent of our awareness of our failures to be morally concerned and autonomous agents.

(a) Being completely unaware of our moral imperfection would extinguish the moral self and even a sense of the possibility of becoming a moral agent. Such a state is better called dread. Dread usually arises when immersion in immediate gratifications stifles unification of the personality around moral commitments or when excessive intellectual abstraction generates emotional detachment from significant aspects of the personality.

(b) Most of us, however, are at least somewhat aware of ourselves as moral agents. (1) We are simply too weak to summon the discipline necessary to achieve a fully unified self. Our weakness is manifested in (i) a preoccupation with worldly concerns and an unwillingness to struggle to overcome faults or (ii) a sense of hopelessness about being able to accept our moral individuality. (2) Only rarely do we choose not to enter into a relationship with (what we believe to be) God, in full, defiant consciousness.

The preceding outline of Kierkegaard's interest in self-deception provides only a skeleton, which is given flesh by his many detailed analyses. But enough has been said to reveal his preoccupation with how the moral and spiritual self undermines itself by refusing to acknowledge, with varying degrees of awareness, its own particular potentials, limitations, realistic options, and actual characteristics. All such details, he urged, must be acknowledged and related to other aspects of the personality within the unifying framework of moral and ultimately religious concern. This ongoing process of unification generates an enlivening sense of individuality and worth as a unique being. Individuality and moral selfhood alike are undermined to the extent that self-deception conceals the personality and the environment in which it expresses itself. As a result, Kierkegaard tends to regard all deception— not just self-deception about moral values—as self-betrayal.

After presenting his classification in *The Sickness unto Death*, Kierkegaard posed a problem generated by two of his beliefs about wrongdoing. The problem deserves mentioning in order to better grasp his relation to the Inner Hypocrisy Tradition. On the one hand, Kierkegaard shared the Christian belief that sin is conscious wrongdoing. On the other hand, he believed that most sin is facilitated by a self-deceptive blurring of consciousness. The problem is how to reconcile these two beliefs.

Kierkegaard began by attacking the Socratic view that wrongdoing is always the result of ignorance or unawareness. This is not only inconsistent with the Christian doctrine that sin is conscious wrongdoing, but it neglects the psychological fact that moral ignorance can be willfully self-induced. For, as he wrote in a famous passage, there is a "little tiny transition from having understood to doing":

> In case then a man the very same second he has known what is right does not do it—well then, first of all, the knowledge stops boiling. And next comes the question how the will likes this thing that is known. If it does not like it, it does not follow that the will goes ahead and does the opposite of that which the intelligence understood, such strong contrasts occur doubtless rather seldom; but the will lets some time pass, there is an interim, that means, "We'll see about that tomorrow." All this while the intelligence becomes more and more obscured, and the lower nature triumphs more and more. . . . And then when the intelligence has become duly darkened, the intelligence and the will can understand one another better; at last they agree entirely, for now the intelligence has gone over to the side of the will and acknowledges that the thing is quite right as it would have it.[15]

This dialogue between personified will and intelligence identifies a familiar phenomenon. Self-deception often proceeds hand in hand with procrastination. Insofar as the obscuring tactics involved in the delaying are willful, the resulting wrongdoing is a product of our will rather than solely a result of ignoring, as Socrates had thought. Yet this does not by itself refute Socrates' view that at the moment of wrongdoing the person is ignorant of the moral truth. How then are we to understand the Christian doctrine that sin is conscious? We cannot: "No man by himself and of himself can explain what sin is, precisely because he is in sin."[16] We must simply embrace the Christian dogma on the basis of faith.

Later Kierkegaard made a half-hearted effort to soften his appeal to blind faith. Most of us, he suggested, are too far removed from God to have much sense of ourselves as conscious sinners: "How on earth can one expect to find an essential consciousness of sin (and after all that is what Christianity wants) in a life which is so retarded by triviality, by a chattering imitation of 'the others,' that one hardly can call it sin, that it is too spiritless to be so called?"[17] But this is a mere shuffle because he immediately added that the lack of consciousness, or the spiritlessness, is our own fault. Therefore, according to his faith, it is the result of conscious wrongdoing, and hence no solution has been found.

In his eagerness to appeal to faith, Kierkegaard failed to do justice to his own psychological insight. At least in its early stages, the self-deceiving procrastination he described frequently carries with it a degree of partial knowingness and consciousness which lead us in the first place to call it willful. This purposeful blurring of moral consciousness suffices to capture the main element in the Christian view of sin, as Bishop Butler saw. And it also expresses common sense.

Kierkegaard's interest in using the notion of self-deception to explain wrongdoing, together with his belief in objective values, made him a member of the Inner Hypocrisy Tradition. At the same time, he sounded a genuinely new note in shifting attention to the process by which individuals shape their own individuality as ethical selves by unifying their personalities around moral and religious commitments. Virtually all self-deception is bad because it constitutes a refusal to be conscious of some aspect of the individual (including his or her situation), which must be reflectively related to other aspects in order for a completely unified and distinctive personality to emerge. In this respect he was a member of—indeed, ushered in—the Authenticity Tradition.

As we shall next see, later existentialists like Sartre pursued many of Kierkegaard's themes, especially concerning freedom. Yet in turning to Sartre, the focus will be on the striking differences in how the themes were developed as a conception of objectively defensible values drops out. For Kierkegaard, moral responsibility in exercising freedom entailed conforming our lives to the requirements of duty and God's commandments. The authentic self is the morally better self and, ultimately, the spiritually higher self. It is autonomous not only in the sense of shaping itself on the basis of self-reflection but also in Kant's sense of rationally responding to the requirements of duty. For Sartre, these ideas were completely alien.

FREEDOM

Although Sartre intended *Being and Nothingness* as a purely descriptive study of consciousness, in it he provided the basis for his existentialist ethics. Its central ethical thesis is that "freedom is the unique foundation of values and that nothing, absolutely nothing, justifies me in adopting this or that particular value, this or that particular scale of values."[18] Conduct, commodities, and people are valuable only because we happen to commit ourselves to affirm them as having worth. They do not make justifiable claims on us that obligate us to make these commitments. To think otherwise is a primary form of self-deception or, as Sartre called it, "bad faith." Most of us engage in this form of bad faith because it is anguishing to acknowledge our freedom to create values (or our freedom from having a rational foundation for our values).

Freedom, together with our tendency to evade its acknowledgment, defines what it is to be human: "Human reality may be defined as a being such that in its being its freedom is at stake because human reality perpetually tries to refuse to recognize its freedom."[19] Yet there are several other types of freedom that Sartre had in mind.

First, we are free from complete causal determination of our consciousness. There are, of course, limits or constraints on how we may act, but these constraints do not force us to think or act in any one way. They merely comprise the hard facts—the "facticity"—that specify the situation to which we respond with complete freedom. Second, we are free to select from among a constant multiplicity of specific options that confront us at any moment. Especially important is our ability to control our immediate consciousness, to focus and ignore at will. Third, we are free to choose our "original project" to approach the world in certain general ways, such as rationally versus irrationally, benevolently versus selfishly, with self-esteem or with a basic sense of inferiority. Specific options are largely a result of these more fundamental choices. Even my options at this moment to go on typing, to rest, or to get a drink arise because of a self-conscious or "reflective" decision to write a book and, in turn, that decision is traceable to a less deliberate, "prereflective," original project to seek an understanding of the world. Fourth, we are free within limits to pursue our goals and to modify the world so as to increase our options. Whereas this last sense of freedom was largely dismissed as irrelevant in *Being and Nothingness*,[20] it played a major role in subsequent writings.

Fifth, we are free to interpret the world and our lives, to give them significance (both value and intelligibility in terms of values). This significance is expressed in detail through our emotions and attitudes, which, in Sartre's view, we also choose. We can even be said to choose to be born, for we can affirm our birth in pride and joy, or degrade it through shame and despair.[21] Sixth, we are free to acknowledge or evade acknowledging facts about the world and ourselves, including facts about how we have chosen to interpret and commit ourselves. Most important, we are free to acknowledge or evade acknowledging to ourselves the facts about the preceding kinds of freedom, of which each of us has some degree of awareness.

Authenticity is the constant willingness to acknowledge to ourselves all these freedoms and also all the specific ways in which we exercise them, especially in interpreting the world through belief, emotion, and attitude, as well as in commitment and conduct. As he succinctly defined it elsewhere, "authenticity, it is almost needless to say, consists in having a true and lucid consciousness of the situation, in assuming the responsibilities and risks that it involves, in accepting it in pride or humiliation, sometimes in horror and hate."[22] This definition dispels any appearance that Sartre was interested only in a narrow kind of self-deception. He was interested in all forms of evading self-acknowledgment; it is only that he sees freedom related to every aspect of consciousness about the world. In his view, each moment of consciousness is an act of interpreting what we are conscious of—what we perceive, conceive, imagine, feel, respond to, and so on.[23] Hence each interpretive act is an exercise of our freedom, always against the background of our freely chosen values. Because being conscious is synonymous with exercising interpretive freedom, authenticity has to do with avoiding self-deception about all topics to which consciousness is exposed.

Consciousness carries with it some sense of its freedom. Most often this is something less than knowledge, which for Sartre required making a thing an object of explicit reflection (thereby "positing" it in relation to ourselves, or becoming aware of ourselves in relation to it). In fact, we constantly try to avoid reflection on freedom by deceiving ourselves. Nonetheless, inherent in consciousness is a tacit awareness of freedom, which he labeled "nonpositional" or "nonthetic" awareness.[24] There is also an implicit awareness of other aspects of how we exercise freedom, including our values and our original projects in the world.[25] This unfocused awareness does not automatically enable us to articulate what we are aware of, but it suffices as a basis for evading its acknowledgment.

Fully acknowledging freedom involves coming to know it by recognizing it reflectively, but it also involves emotional and attitudinal responses (paralleling my analysis in Chapter 2). Sartre believed that anguish is an inevitable emotional response to awareness of all types of freedom; in fact, he simply defined it as the reflective apprehension of freedom.[26] He also stipulated that acknowledgment entails a specific attitudinal response: the willingness to assume responsibility for the particular ways in which we exercise freedom. This does not mean, as it did for Kierkegaard, being morally concerned to act on objectively defensible values. Instead, it means being disposed to recognize ourselves as authors of our lives, as the complete source of the significance we attach to our lives.[27]

Inauthenticity is essentially the evasion of self-acknowledgment of our responsibility for our interpretations of the world. Sartre's explanation of how this self-deceiving evasion takes place has four parts. First, he set forth several patterns of self-deception, as did Kierkegaard, though using his own fundamental distinctions for understanding consciousness. For example, there is the distinction between our freedom to interpret the world ("transcendence") and our simultaneous confrontation with facts about our situation ("facticity"), which includes such things as our immediate environment, our past, and our bodies. One pattern of self-deception consists in conflating these two aspects of our lives.

Sartre's famous example is of a woman who flees sexual realities by construing sexual desire as a purely Platonic choice or freedom ("transcendence"), while enjoying it as an unacknowledged biological given ("facticity").[28] She consents to date a man who, as she knows, intends to seduce her. While on the date she evades acknowledging to herself the man's intentions by stripping away the sexual overtones in his words and conduct, disregarding their wider meaning as an overture to an intended tryst. In this way she denies his disturbing and freely chosen intention (transcendence) and "glues it down with all the facticity of the present"—that is, she keeps her attention focused solely on immediate events and on the man's present politeness. At the same time, without admitting it to herself, she enjoys the sexual desire directed toward her and also enjoys her own arousal. By the time he takes her hand, she has entirely distracted herself with a sentimental conversation. For the moment, she regards herself as a pure mental freedom (transcendence), divorced from the given reality of her body (facticity). In these ways she achieves her goal of evading, or at least postponing, an anguishing decision.

A second basic duality is that we exist both "for ourselves" and "for others." That is, we are free to form our own view of ourselves (and always have some form of self-awareness), yet simultaneously are aware of and interested in being viewed by others. When it suits our purposes we use self-deception to disregard our own interpretations and embrace those of others or vice versa.[29] If we find our view of ourselves painful, we readily embrace an admirer's more flattering view of us. If we are confronted with criticisms from others, we rest comfortably with our own higher self-appraisals. More important, we avoid anguished reflection on our freedom by viewing ourselves through the eyes of an undifferentiated set of people—"the Other."[30] One way to accomplish this is to distract ourselves from our genuine options by considering all but one of them as "purely *conceivable* eventualities" that another person in our situation might pursue. This makes one course of action stand out with a sense of inevitability, thereby destroying our anguish about being responsible for choosing it.

Classifying self-deception into patterns is only a preliminary part of Sartre's explanation of "bad faith."[31] The second part is to characterize self-deception as founded by an "original project" to avoid using rational standards for evidence whenever it serves its purposes.[32] In bad faith, we resolve to ignore evidence contrary to what we want to believe, to be satisfied with minimal evidence for our favored beliefs, and to allow ourselves to adhere to dubious propositions. This attitude toward truth and evidence is embraced spontaneously, without conscious deliberation, and with an ease comparable to falling asleep. Furthermore, just as once asleep we can only dream about going to sleep (as we dream about anything else), the original project of self-deception includes a self-covering dimension in which evidence about our self-deceptive strategies is disregarded or distorted.

In the next part of his explanation, attention is drawn to the nature of the beliefs (or "faith") that make bad faith possible.[33] Holding a belief, as opposed to having knowledge, means lacking conclusive evidence establishing the belief as true. As a result all beliefs are "troubled": we are tacitly conscious (nonpositionally) that the belief could turn out to be false. In response, the rational or scientific mind attempts to strengthen beliefs by searching for further evidence. But the person in bad faith is content that the self-deceiving belief, like all beliefs, is unsupported by conclusive evidence.

Lastly, bad faith is facilitated by various psychological tactics. For example, we distract attention, either while reflecting on ourselves or in prereflective consciousness of the world.[34] Another tactic is to rationalize away our freedom and responsibility by viewing ourselves as determined, either in general or on specific occasions: "Psychological determinism, before being a theoretical conception, is first an attitude of excuse, or if you prefer, the basis of all attitudes of excuse."[35] In this connection we also frequently engage in equivocal reasoning to support our rationalizations.[36]

Having outlined Sartre's conception and explanation of self-deception, we are in a position to turn to his moral critique of it. If all values are the product of free commitments and are never justifiable independently of them, what basis remains for morally criticizing self-deceivers? And if being responsible merely means recognizing oneself as freely authoring one's actions and interpretations, how could self-deceivers be *morally* irresponsible or blameworthy?

Sartre answered these questions in "Existentialism Is a Humanism." He began by reaffirming that there is no objective basis for criticizing people who do not deceive themselves, and in doing so made one of many somewhat careless remarks in that essay: "Whenever a man chooses his purpose and his commitment in all clearness and in all sincerity [i.e., authentically], whatever that purpose may be, it is impossible for him to prefer another."[37] Of course it *is* possible that he could have preferred another—his freedom assures that it is possible. What Sartre meant is that it is impossible for authentic individuals (given his definition of them) to recognize good reasons for restricting their choices in light of compelling moral obligations. Yet self-deceivers can be blamed, and blamed harshly. His argument for this had four main steps.[38]

> [1] "Freedom, in respect of concrete circumstances, can have no other
> end and aim but itself; and when once a man has seen that values
> depend upon himself, in that state of forsakenness he can will only
> one thing, and that is freedom as the foundation of all values."

From this first premise on, the argument clearly proceeds from the perspective of authentic persons who recognize free commitments as the origin of values. It was designed only to show that authentic individuals are in a position to criticize self-deceivers. There was no attempt to defend authenticity itself, consistent with the view that no value, not even authenticity, is justified by objective reasons that obligate us to commit ourselves to them.

A key idea in the argument is expressed in this premise as to "will freedom" and elsewhere as to "will liberty," "make liberty one's aim," "the will to freedom," and "the quest for freedom." If we are already free, in what sense can we "will" freedom? Sartre's answer was that we can commit ourselves to value it. This is done by fully acknowledging and cherishing its role in making possible all choices of values. To will freedom as the foundation of values is tantamount to affirming authenticity as the guiding norm in how we form all other commitments. This affirmation is not an abstract intellectual act but rather the tacit implication of all specific choices made authentically. This explains why the authentic person "can will only one thing": to be authentic is to choose in awareness of freedom and, in turn, that is tacitly to express one's commitment to choose in this way.

[2] "And in thus willing freedom, we discover that it depends entirely upon the freedom of others and that the freedom of others depends upon our own."

In what sense is the freedom of individuals interdependent? Sartre hastened to add that "obviously, freedom as the definition of man does not depend upon others." Whether or not others recognize it, we are free in most of the senses noted earlier: free from causal determination of consciousness, constantly confronted by options, creators of our own values and interpretations, and so on. But which options we have at any given time, and how far we can attain the goals we value, turns entirely on the willingness of others to allow us to act, and to give or withhold their help. In these ways freedom is interpersonal and interdependent.

[3] Thus, "as soon as there is a commitment, I am obliged to will the liberty of others at the same time as my own. I cannot make liberty my aim unless I make that of others equally my aim."

That is, authentic persons are obligated to will the liberty of others, to will it in the sense of affirming its value. Why? Presumably because commitment to any goal requires commitment to the necessary means for securing that goal (by definition of "commitment"). Because exercising my freedom depends on other people's acknowledging and respecting my freedom, and because they would presumably be inclined to do so only on the basis of reciprocity of recognition, I am tacitly committed as an authentic person to value their freedom. Insofar as I fail to do so, I encourage them to suppress my own endeavors in pursuing authentic commitments. They may kill me or interfere in any number of less drastic ways. They may also fail to give me the positive aid I need.[39] Whereas not everyone must be authentic in order for me to be so, a world permeated with delusion about and suppression of freedom would undermine my attempts to exercise authenticity.

It follows, Sartre thought, that authentic persons are justified in morally criticizing self-deceivers:

[4] Therefore, "in the name of that will to freedom which is implied in freedom itself, I can form judgments upon those who seek to hide from themselves the wholly voluntary nature of their existence and its complete freedom. Those who hide from this total freedom, in a guise of solemnity or with deterministic excuses, I shall call cowards. Others, who try to show that their existence is necessary, when it is merely an accident of the appearance of the human race on earth—I shall call scum. But neither cowards nor scum can be identified except on the plane of strict authenticity."

Understood in this way, the argument is provocative—but is it sound? Notice, to begin with, that even if it were sound, it would establish very little. All it defends is the flaccid hypothetical that if a person makes the choice to be authentic, then that person is warranted in criticizing others who do not make that choice. One wants to retort, "So what?"

Consider an analogy. Two groups who disagree about euthanasia for terminally ill people in severe pain criticize each other. One group calls the other murderers, and the second group responds by calling the first group callous. We request arguments justifying these criticisms. But instead of appeals to moral values, we are given arguments showing that if one thinks euthanasia is murder, then one is warranted in criticizing its supporters as murderers, and that if one thinks it is inhumane to allow needless suffering, then it is callous to allow it. It is understandable why the members of each group make their criticisms. If they did not, we might even question how committed they are to their beliefs. But their sincere commitment can only help explain why they make their criticisms; it cannot justify them. By analogy, Sartre's argument does not justify moral criticisms of self-deceivers. At most, it merely helps explain why a genuine commitment to authenticity might lead one to criticize self-deceivers.

In spite of this, Sartre's argument does raise considerations that, if true, would constitute a justification of criticizing self-deceivers for those who retain a conception of objective moral values beyond authenticity. To the extent that self-deception underlies hurting others or suppressing their liberty, it warrants criticism. This much was established by the Inner Hypocrisy Tradition. It seems to me that here, as in other places, Sartre was tacitly defending authenticity by presupposing other humane values. He was admirably inconsistent with his own official tenet that "*nothing*, absolutely nothing, justifies me in adopting this or that particular value." *Of course* there are justifying reasons, and Sartre's defense of authenticity would have no interest unless he tacitly alluded to them.

When Sartre engaged in practical moral commentary he clearly assumed a conception of human decency. Especially revealing is his book *Anti-Semite and Jew*, which was written about the same time as "Existentialism Is a Humanism." In the book he analyzed bigotry against Jews (and, implicitly, racial prejudice in general) as a product of self-deception. Anti-Semites adopt fear as their basic attitude toward truth about themselves and others and dread the agonizing process of rational inquiry. They are "impervious to reason and to experience" and passionately cling to simplistic explanations of the world.[40] Yet the main objection to anti-Semites is not their threat to authenticity *per se* but, instead, the ways in which their self-deception renders them insensitive to humane values: "A man who finds it entirely natural to denounce other men cannot have our conception of humanity."[41] The self-deception of the anti-Semite is immoral because it spawns cruelty, suppression of liberty, and irrationality. The "reason" and rationality from which anti-Semites flee includes moral reasonableness, which must be understood in terms of more than either authenticity or the rights of authentic people to criticize self-deceivers.

There are two further difficulties with Sartre's argument. It is far too much to suggest that gross inhumanity (such as suppression of liberty) is either always or primarily the result of self-deception about freedom. In spite of his aperçus on this topic, Sartre leaves us with overly simple explanations. Many determinists who are paradigms of inauthenticity in his terms have no tendency to suppress the liberty of others. And if authenticity is to be allowed to flourish in the way he desires, there must be other values beyond authenticity acknowledged within a community. Justice is one of them. Another is tolerance of ideological and philosophical differences (such as those concerning the nature and extent of freedom). This kind of tolerance begins with the affirmation that even those who reject our most cherished convictions and values need not be self-deceiving cowards or scum.

This brings us to the next point. Sartre's argument is not valid: his concluding criticisms do not follow from the premises (even assuming the premises are true). Moral criticism, blame, and condemnation are actions that themselves stand in need of moral justification, and the harm caused by some self-deceivers does not warrant blaming all self-deceivers. We can hope that authentic and humane people will find it appropriate to forgive some and accept other inauthenticity. Sartre's own examples remind us of how potent stereotypes have confronted women and minorities with special obstacles in achieving authenticity and should temper moral criticisms.

Finally, we noticed that Kierkegaard's elaboration on authenticity involved appeals both to autonomy and to certain views that he found especially important about human beings. Similarly, we can distinguish two aspects of the concept of authenticity used by Sartre and in doing so question whether the emphasis he placed on them was too extreme.

On the one hand, authenticity involves autonomy in the sense of shaping one's life on the basis of one's own honest reflections. The failure to do this was what Sartre found most objectionable in people who live primarily through the eyes of other people or who, like the woman on the date, postpone decisions in order to allow events to restrict their options. Yet, however much we may share this value, there is no reason to single it out as having any greater importance than communal values such as kindness, tolerance, and justice. Sartre's existentialist ethic is in this sense excessively individualistic, as many of his critics have said.

On the other hand, Sartre confidently asserted as significant truths certain theses that, he alleged, any rational person must accept and, indeed, that we are all somewhat aware of. The trouble is that some of these theses could not be more highly controversial, especially his extreme insistence that consciousness is free from causal determination[42] and that no values are rationally defensible. In the last section of this chapter I will return to the implications of building into one's concept of authenticity such controversial theses. I will also offer an alternative conception of authenticity that removes the temptation to condemn as inauthentic those people whose autonomous reflections lead them to disagree with one's cherished beliefs.

SINCERITY

Sartre made several startling assertions about sincerity or what he sometimes and with irony called "good faith." It is impossible, he told us, ever to be sincere. Moreover, we all sense this, and as a result we are self-deceptive and inauthentic when we adopt sincerity as an ideal. In fact, self-deception is possible only because we sense our inability to be sincere.

These remarks were not made flippantly or in passing. Nearly half of the chapter in *Being and Nothingness* entitled "Bad Faith" is devoted to defending them. In order to explain and appraise them, let us first compare and contrast a few of the ordinary uses of *sincerity* and *authenticity* and identify some familiar ideals of sincerity.

In standard usage, the term *sincerity* rules out unwarranted dissimulation, intentional deception, hypocrisy, duplicity, bad-faith commitments, and doublemindedness. Frequently it retains the positive connotation of purity derived from its Latin root *sincerus*, which means unadulterated. Talk about sincerity usually presupposes some positive standard for good motives, intentions, or attitudes against which insincerity is condemned.[43] Promises, for example, are insincere when they are made without the appropriate intention to keep them and normally only when this is felt to be blameworthy. Again, deceivers and self-deceivers lack sincerity to the extent that their aims are corrupted by undesirable motives. Furthermore, usually only desirable types of motives are called sincere or insincere depending on the absence or presence of conflicting motives: *sincere love* sounds natural, whereas *sincere envy* does not. Obviously in this context, Sartre did not intend to use the word *sincere* with these ordinary, honorific connotations.

By contrast, the various uses of *authentic* are captured by the idea of genuineness rather than purity. The authentic is the bona fide (insurance policy), real (Chinese tapestry), official (commemorative stamp), or authoritative (executive order), as opposed to the fake, imitative, unofficial, or unauthorized. Just as an authentic cowboy is the real McCoy, so there can be authentic con artists but only apparently sincere ones. An authentic compliment is one that succeeds in praising someone, in contrast to a sincere compliment, which need only be intended to express feelings of admiration. Here *authentic* attaches to the content of the compliment, whereas *sincere* attaches to the mental state of the person making the compliment.

In spite of such differences, there are many contexts in which genuineness and purity coalesce, making *authentic* and *sincere* apply to the same things in closely related senses. For example, sincere compassion is sympathy uncontaminated by such feelings as contempt or superiority. Authentic compassion is heartfelt sympathy flowing from within, as one's own personal response, rather than an imitation of what others are feeling or what others expect us to feel. Usually the two are found together and amount to much the same. Sincere beliefs are those held with conviction on the basis of an honest effort to get at the truth rather than by complacently accepting a popular outlook or by allowing biases to operate. This notion merges with the idea of authentic beliefs which express one's own view—the view generated by personal reflection. Again, saying that in her *Ariel* poems Sylvia Plath achieved authenticity as an artist means that she attained her unique poetic voice. One might also say that she achieved full sincerity as a poet in expressing her singular talents.

What do we intend when we apply these terms to the composite character of a person, when we say *tout court*, "She is authentic" and "He is sincere"? I believe that usually the terms are used in significantly contrasting, although overlapping, ways. Sincere people manifest a cluster of dispositions to purity in speech, conduct, and inner states, according to some model of purity such as those we shall mention next. Authentic individuals, however, are people whose speech, conduct, and inner states represent a full and genuine expression of their own abilities rather than a mere imitation uncritically modeled on others or on some social convention. Because Sartre viewed consciousness of freedom as the earmark of genuineness and the distinctive human ability, he equated authenticity with acting in full awareness of freedom, even though tacitly he also built in an emphasis on autonomy. This enabled him to attack sincerity as inauthentic when it involves restricted autonomy or an absence of full acknowledgment of freedom.

Let us now list several models of purity, or different conceptions of sincerity, as an allegedly praiseworthy ideal. Not all these ideals stand up under critical scrutiny, and most do not make exceptionless moral demands. In reviewing each one, we will take note of sincerity with other people and then sincerity with oneself.

Sincerity as singlemindedness. This ideal demands dedication to one's goals and strict consistency of inner resolve and attitude. The corresponding ideal of sincerity with oneself is essentially the same requirement of inner unity. The sincere person maintains beliefs, emotions, sentiments, and commitments that are wholehearted and untainted by conflicting mental states, and he or she acts consistently with these.

Sincerity as moral purity. This ideal is singlemindedness specifically with respect to fulfilling moral responsibilities. According to Lionel Trilling, this is the characteristically British conception of sincerity: "The English ask of the sincere man that he communicate without deceiving or misleading. Beyond this what is required is only a single-minded commitment to whatever dutiful enterprise he may have in hand."[44] In this sense, sincerity with oneself is achieved by unifying inner states and overt behavior on a foundation of moral concern. This was essentially Kierkegaard's interest (together with interpreting moral concern within a Christian framework). For him, inner sincerity demanded unrelenting earnestness in disciplining every aspect of one's life according to a commitment to the good.

Sincerity as avoiding unjustified deceit. Here the minimal ideal of being sincere with others is to avoid unwarranted deception and hypocrisy. Insincerity is unjustified deception. The corresponding ideal of sincerity with oneself demands avoiding culpable forms of self-deception.

Sincerity as openness. This ideal subsumes the avoidance of deception under a more positive goal of being open about oneself. According to it, secretive and extremely private individuals are not fully sincere, even though they may not intentionally mislead others. Sincere people are self-revealing, at least to the extent of letting others understand their basic commitments, motivations, and character. Moreover, their motive for being open is to be honest with others in appropriate ways on suitable occasions rather than having ulterior motives such as a desire to control or self-aggrandizement. In this conception, sincerity or candor with oneself entails avoiding self-deception as well as seeking self-understanding for its own sake.

Each of the preceding ideals of sincerity could also function as an ideal of authenticity or genuineness. None of them is what Sartre had in mind when he critiqued sincerity. Instead, Sartre was thinking of the following ideal, one that is not idiosyncratic with him but has frequently been conventionally accepted.

Sincerity as mere congruence. This ideal perverts the ideal of openness by only demanding concord between specific inner states and outward behavior—regardless of the motive for seeking this congruence. For example, Rousseau and some other romantics viewed sincere artists as those who accurately revealed and expressed what they felt. In practice, this often inspired narcissism and exhibitionist displays of the sordid aspects of life neglected by conventional artists.[45] It transformed truth-telling into a weapon of aggression, cruelty, and self-seeking (as Molière showed us in *The Misanthrope*). Sometimes it also encouraged living naturally in the sense of being unfettered by elaborate self-reflection. As Chamfort urged, "One must not watch oneself living" lest, like Hamlet, one becomes "sicklied o'er with the pale cast of thought."[46] The corresponding ideal of sincerity with oneself is congruence between specific attributes and one's immediate consciousness of them. It allows that the motives for the congruence may have little to do with striving for significant truths or an honest understanding of one's present attributes.

Sartre's critique of this ideal was insightful, albeit couched in hyperbole and paradox designed "to shock the mind and discountenance it by enigma."[47] He attacked the sordid motives that may prompt self-deceivers into embracing the ideal of sincerity as mere congruence.

Sartre stipulated that by *sincerity* and *candor,* he understood the ideal that "a man be *for himself* only what he *is.*"[48] "What he is" refers to the specific attributes of the person, though not the general trait of being free. Such attributes have *being-in-themselves* and are identical with themselves: just as a rock is a rock, so being six feet tall or the recipient of an award is that and nothing more. This assertion of self-identity cannot be made about consciousness because it always exists *for-itself* through either reflection or more tacit self-consciousness. A free consciousness assures that we are always more than our present attributes, for to be conscious of them is to transcend them, rather than be reducible to them, by freely giving them a meaning or by initiating actions to modify them. But the ideal of sincerity demands a reduction: it enjoins that we attempt to restrict ourselves to being just what we are now by focusing consciousness solely on our present and past and expressing it to others.

The demand for sincerity as mere congruence is thus an impossible one to satisfy. As long as we are conscious, we are never reducible to our present and past attributes or determined to be only them. Furthermore, inasmuch as each of us has a tacit consciousness of our freedom ("a vague prejudicative comprehension"[49] of it), each of us has a sense that we can never attain the goal of sincerity by reducing ourselves to any set of current attributes. But we evade acknowledging this awareness of our freedom, all the while relying on it to engage in self-deceiving equivocations whose effect is to degrade us and others by miring us in the past and immediate present.

In bad faith we evade evidence in order to deny our actual attributes or to ascribe inappropriate attributes to ourselves and others. In good faith or sincerity, by contrast, we accept evidence and accurately ascribe specific attributes to ourselves, to others, and to our situation. Yet the aim of bad and good faith is essentially the same: to escape the anguishing responsibility for our actions. Both can also involve the same psychological tactics of ignoring, rationalization, and equivocation.

Yet the basic strategy of good faith is more subtle and paradoxical: "The sincere man constitutes himself as a thing in order to escape the condition of a thing by the same act of sincerity."[50] Eager to confess, we initially view ourselves as identical to a causally determined evil thing. That enables us immediately to disavow our evil by viewing it as unrelated to the new self which emerges purged through our sincere confession: "The evil is disarmed since it is nothing, save on the plane of determinism, and since in confessing it, I posit my freedom in respect to it; my future is virgin; everything is allowed me."[51] Authentic confession, by contrast, requires a constant willingness to recognize ourselves as having authored an evil that cannot disappear by being expressed verbally.

Demanding sincerity of others is often motivated by similarly irresponsible aims. Indeed, it is part and parcel of the ongoing struggle to win mastery over others. To insist that the person who deceives himself about his homosexuality openly acknowledge it (to himself and others) may well be an attempt to degrade the person. The champion of sincerity views the homosexual as a thing whose homosexuality is a determined destiny rather than a free sexual response. The confession is demanded in order to dismiss the homosexual: "Who cannot see how offensive to the Other and how reassuring for me is a statement such as, 'He's just a paederast,' which removes a disturbing freedom from a trait."[52] The freedom is disturbing, in part because it raises our anxiety about ourselves being free and in part because its recognition would reveal our kinship as free beings. That would negate the aim of the champion of sincerity to elevate himself or herself at the expense of reducing others to one of their characteristics (their sexual orientation).

The same strategy is employed in restricting others to their particular social roles. We employ it when we want waiters in a restaurant to remain wholly absorbed in the task of serving our needs. We also use it in treating grocery clerks as mere functionaries on our behalf: "A grocer who dreams is offensive to the buyer, because such a grocer is not wholly a grocer."[53]

In short, the appeal to sincerity, understood as mere congruence between consciousness-admission and present-past attributes, frequently has the ulterior aim of limiting others or ourselves to a finite set of roles and characteristics. That amounts to a denial of our ability to transcend what we are and have been, and it is often spawned by the motive to degrade. While Sartre presented these theses without cautious qualifiers ("frequently," "often"), his discussion remains cogent and insightful.

AUTONOMY AND SIGNIFICANT TRUTH

Authenticity, I suggested, functioned for Kierkegaard and Sartre as a two-sided concept. One side is autonomy: exercising and acting on one's own powers of reflection rather than passively submitting to others' views or to social conventions. In this sense, authentic persons creatively shape their own lives, bestowing meaning on their activities through attitudes, emotions, beliefs, and commitments that are more than imitations of society. But that is not enough. The second aspect of the concept is the acknowledgment of significant truths, including truths about the appropriate goals in exercising autonomy. Because it is (in their view) anguishing to exercise autonomy and acknowledge these truths, we are continually tempted to deceive ourselves. And because the purported significant truths pertain to all aspects of human consciousness, virtually all self-deception constitutes a betrayal of authentic selfhood.

Kierkegaard and Sartre differed over what the relevant significant truths are, especially those concerning appropriate goals in exercising autonomy. For Kierkegaard, autonomy has the goal of achieving full individuality and personal uniqueness based on moral commitments and a relationship with God. Kierkegaard's view of significant truths includes not only freedom of consciousness to shape oneself autonomously but also the objectivity of moral duties based on a Christian interpretation of God's commandments. Sartre, in sharp contrast, rejected belief in objective values and in God's existence, charging that these beliefs are themselves products of self-deception. Moreover, he attached no special importance to individuality in Kierkegaard's sense of maximal personal uniqueness. The only universal goal of freedom he recognized was the full appreciation of freedom itself. The authentic individual affirms freedom as the defining mark of human beings, especially the freedom to create all values unguided by objective reasons or divine commandments.

Hence, the similarities in the concepts of authenticity used by Kierkegaard and Sartre are largely formal. The real substance in these concepts, which provides a basis for criticizing self-deceivers, lies in the conceptions of philosophical truths that they largely assume as true. In light of this, the appeals they make to authenticity, as opposed to more specific moral values, provide a dubious basis for moral objections to self-deception. Either they tacitly presuppose specific moral values, as with Sartre's defense of his criticisms of inauthenticity, and thereby return us to the appeals made in the Inner Hypocrisy Tradition, or they rely on philosophical or theological theses that are too controversial to support their harsh criticisms of self-deceivers.

We have considered, however, only two thinkers who appeal to authenticity. In order to widen our discussion we need to consider other examples of how appeals to authenticity rely on controversial conceptions of both autonomy and significant truths. Authenticity is much discussed in connection with the topics of death and self-realization. With respect to each of these topics, let us consider two thinkers who develop contrasting conceptions of authenticity.

In his *Confession,* Tolstoy recorded that after fifteen years of productive work he experienced a profound "arrest of life." Suddenly and without explanation all his endeavors struck him as meaningless and morally unintelligible. Indeed, his existence seemed an absurd and cruel joke. This experience was enduring and intense, bringing with it recurring temptations to commit suicide. The question that first presented itself to him was: "Why should I live, why wish for anything, or do anything?"[54] As he became preoccupied with the brevity of life in comparison with eternity, the question was transformed: "Why should I live, that is to say, what real, permanent result will come out of my illusory transitory life—what meaning has my finite existence in this infinite world?"[55]

The resolution of his crisis came in the form of a Kierkegaardian leap of faith in God and eternal life. His confrontation with death evoked in him a rapport with the childlike faith of Russian peasants, compassion for the people around him, and a deep love for humanity. Yet these moral responses had meaning for him only in light of his religious conversion.

Subsequently, in some of Tolstoy's finest works of fiction, the religious view moved into the background and the moral connectedness with all mankind became salient. *The Death of Ivan Ilych* is especially poignant in this respect. Ivan Ilych had spent his life immersed in the easy contentments of home and work, all the while suppressing annoying impulses toward personal autonomy and moral growth. During that time death seemed to him an abstract human occurrence rather than an item of personal concern. On his deathbed he comes to view this life as a sham, as something dishonest and inauthentic, as "a terrible and huge deception which had hidden both life and death."[56] "It occurred to him that his scarcely perceptible attempts to struggle against what was considered good by the most highly placed people, those scarcely noticeable impulses which he had immediately suppressed, might have been the real thing, and all the rest false."[57] There is no time now to change his outward life, but in his final moments he is moved to compassion for his family and servants, who waited on him during his illness. These final moments of authenticity enable him to accept death without despair.

Martin Heidegger agreed with Tolstoy that authenticity can emerge only when one confronts death. Indeed, he was more preoccupied with death than any other modern philosopher. Yet he offered a contrasting set of significant truths about what the confrontation with death has to offer. Whereas Tolstoy was a theist who emphasized emotional solidarity with other human beings, Heidegger was an atheist who also believed that death establishes the ultimate separateness of each of us. Full acknowledgment of death enables us to achieve authenticity by revealing our differences from *das Man*, that is, from the impersonal social masses with all their weight of authority and custom.

According to Heidegger, death is the most intimate and assured reality each of us must confront. It is our *"ownmost* possibility," which sets an absolute boundary to our lives.[58] At the same time it is the window that reveals all else in proper perspective. Unconfronted, death is dreadful. It generates vague fears and anxieties that drive us away from authenticity and toward immersion in conventionality and everyday pleasures. Inauthenticity consists in being preoccupied with social conventions and with the immediate present, for this disperses our consciousness of ourselves as beings who are distinct from mass society. If, however, we confront death and anticipate it continuously, we are liberated from preoccupation with petty concerns and social conformity.[59] In fully acknowledging death we are pressured to unify our lives, to relate our past experiences to our aspirations for the future, and to accept the ultimate transitoriness and insignificance of our lives.

Authenticity is also appealed to frequently by applied psychologists who are concerned with self-realization, self-fulfillment, or self-actualization. Here an authentic individual is typically understood as pursuing the higher self within the range of possible selves. This higher self is generally healthy (physically and mentally), unified, self-aware, and willing to exercise a full range of talents and skills. Inauthentic persons, by contrast, are fragmented, self-ignorant, frustrated, and self-alienated (alienated from both their higher selves and much of what they are at present). Specific conceptions of authenticity vary according to the brand of psychology invoked in unfolding accompanying conceptions of autonomy and self-insight.[60]

The psychoanalyst Karen Horney represents an example from the neo-Freudian literature. In *Neurosis and Human Growth: The Struggle Toward Self-Realization*, Horney located the authentic or real self in the active core of the personality containing the person's special talents and creative possibilities. Authentic persons are integrated in that they consciously interrelate the various dimensions of their lives, much in the way described by Kierkegaard (who influenced Horney). Neurotics, by contrast, are alienated from their real selves, which they betray through obsession with an idealized, unrealistic self-image. They are driven between the extremes of excessive pride, insofar as they actively seek to become this inflated self, and self-contempt, as they inevitably fail to do so. All the while they engage in purposeful self-deception: "The neurotic who, without knowing it, does lead a double life must similarly, *unconsciously*, blur the truth of what he is, wants, feels, and believes. And all his self-deception follows from this basic one."[61] Neurotics can be freed from their inner warfare only by gaining self-knowledge of the unconscious and compulsive inner forces uncovered by Freud.

Most writers in the Authenticity Tradition place a heavy emphasis on freeing oneself from obeisance to social expectations. This makes it interesting to consider the contrasting view of authenticity found in the modern ethicists who most emphasized self-realization. I have in mind Hegelians such as F. H. Bradley and Josiah Royce,[62] who share some similarities with the Authenticity Tradition even though they are not members of it.

For F. H. Bradley, the authentic individual is a thoroughly social-bound creature whose highest development is attained through commitments to social groups. Bradley's authentic individual might have said, for example: "I fulfill myself by participating in communities, both actual communities and the ideal community of rational beings. Rather than setting myself apart from others, I must eagerly embrace the ties that bind me within my specific social context and comprise 'my station and its duties' [the title of Bradley's most famous essay]." Although Bradley allowed for independent thinking in discerning these ties, he directly opposed the idea that one's true self is shaped independently of others. For him, that would have been the ultimate self-deceit.

Josiah Royce shared Bradley's view of the genuine self as the higher self defined through participation within a community. Influenced by the American tradition of individualism, however, he was more concerned with the autonomous determination of one's unique social vocation. That is, each of us is also free in Kant's sense of being morally autonomous. Our duty and moral identity are decided by personal moral interpretation of the claims emerging from our past and our society. The true self emerges through commitments to particular social causes and to the principle that the self-realization of all people is attained through interlocking loyalties (a principle he calls "loyalty to loyalty"). In addition to this, Royce believed that, ultimately, individual wills express a divine will, and hence he rejected Sartre's causal indeterminism and atheism.

These Hegelians recommended conceptions of the authentic self that are polar opposites to those of the existentialists. Historically this is no surprise, because existentialism began with Kierkegaard's sweeping attack on Hegel. What is of interest here is that Bradley and Royce shared with the existentialists a conception of the genuine self as autonomous and as acknowledging significant truths. That is, for them the authentic self still creates itself through rational effort on the basis of achieving insight into important truths, and they objected to passive (unthinking) social relationships. But their conceptions of the relevant significant truths about the true self and the goals of autonomy are very different. The preoccupation with independence from social conventions and with personal uniqueness gave way to an emphasis on participation within a community. For them, the genuine self must be understood as part of something much larger—a view shared, of course, by many religious traditions. Moreover, their conceptions of freedom are very different. In place of Sartre's causal indeterminism and essentially anarchistic view of moral autonomy, they saw freedom as liberation from the bondage of disruptive and alienating emotions such as anxiety, hatred, and (in contrast with Heidegger) dread of death.[63]

Enough has been said to show that conceptions of authenticity differ according to views about its two main ingredients. *Authenticity* is a value-laden term whose substance turns on the kinds of autonomous self-creation a thinker esteems and also on the specific truths judged most important for living a meaningful life. Before self-deceivers can be criticized for betraying their genuine (true, real) selves and evading significant truths, those value judgments must be brought to the surface and defended. What is problematic about the fervor of the existentialists' criticisms of self-deceivers is that both their favored view of autonomy—a highly individualistic one that neglects the claims of community—and their favored list of alleged significant truths are highly controversial and assume more than they defend. Nothing is more uncertain and perennially open to dispute than the nature and significance of human freedom, responsibility, death, and religious belief.

This conclusion does not undermine the appropriateness of linking the concepts of authenticity and self-deception. But greater tolerance is called for lest we condemn as inauthentic those people who do not share our particular views of human nature.

This conclusion also suggests the possibility of untethering the concept of authenticity from any controversial theses about values, consciousness, autonomy, or religion.[64] We might retain the notion of autonomous self-creation through sustained personal effort, commitment, and active reflection without insisting on any particular degree of independence from conventional society or communities. Then, in place of insisting that the authentic person must acknowledge particular theses, the emphasis would shift to exercising the character traits that define rationality: traits such as intellectual honesty, intellectual courage, openness to new experience, freedom from crippling biases and obsessions, and passionate truth-seeking. Authentic persons, on this revised conception, would be committed seekers after truth rather than discoverers of any particular truths. And they would be persons who shape their self-identities on the basis of that concern for truth.

In addition, we could build into our conception of authenticity certain areas in which it is important for intellectual honesty to be exercised. Here our conception of meaningful life would influence us (thereby allowing some differences among our conceptions of authenticity). Thus, perhaps most of us can agree with the existentialists that authentic persons must honestly and courageously confront fundamental aspects of human reality such as death, freedom, and the foundation of human values. But this view of authenticity requires honesty about certain topics, not acceptance of any particular philosophical theses about those topics.

On this new conception, authenticity could retain considerable substance and importance as a human excellence, with less likelihood of its being a conceptual weapon in disagreements over particular philosophical, religious, and moral perspectives (although I think it will always be abused to some extent in this way). According to this conception, self-deceivers would often fail to display this excellence, either by failing to exercise autonomous reflection, failing to integrate the results of that reflection into the rest of their lives, or failing to confront certain unpleasant aspects of life. But their failures would not always warrant the kinds of severe moral criticisms made by Sartre, for authenticity would be only one human excellence and would need to be weighed with other fundamental values such as compassion, love, justice, and appreciation of beauty. Equally important, the extent to which authenticity is a specifically moral requirement would remain an open question. Perhaps it would best be viewed as a distinct ideal of excellence that overlaps, in places, with the requirements of morality.

5

Moral Ambiguity

As long as there have been men and they have lived, they have all felt this tragic ambiguity of their condition, but as long as there have been philosophers and they have thought, most of them have tried to mask it.

—Simone de Beauvoir, *The Ethics of Ambiguity*

The Moral Ambiguity Tradition regards self-deceivers as morally perplexing in ways that thwart assessments of their responsibility for their actions. It views them, in whole or in part, as victims of forces beyond their independent control or at least calls into question whether their conduct is voluntary. One branch of the tradition is concerned with how self-deception causes, constitutes, or manifests mental illness and unhealthy adjustments to reality. Freud is the primary shaper of this branch. He applied the distinction between conscious and unconscious purposes to explain how self-deception can lead to involuntary compulsions, delusions, and other pathological behavior. R. G. Collingwood and Herbert Fingarette developed related philosophical perspectives, arguing that the presence of unconscious influences makes blameworthiness for self-deception ambiguous, opaque, or paradoxical.

A different branch of the Moral Ambiguity Tradition is based on a deterministic world view. It begins with the premise that self-deception, as well as all other human behavior, is caused not by personal agency but by such factors as psychological compulsions, genetic programming, environmental constraints, and social pressures. Determinists have contended that ascriptions of moral responsibility to self-deceivers are especially problematic because self-deceivers illustrate so vividly how ignorance and unconscious causes guide human endeavors. Recently this perspective was sympathetically presented by M. R. Haight.

In my view, we are very often unambiguously responsible, in whole or in part, for deceiving ourselves and for any resulting harm. In the first section, I assess the central claims of Collingwood and Fingarette. In the second section, I show that, contrary to what is sometimes assumed, Freud's theory of unconscious purposes and mental illness does not imply any one simple moral outlook on all self-deceivers. In the third section, I consider Haight's discussion of determinism and self-deception. And in the final section, I draw together some conclusions about moral responsibility for self-deception, conclusions based in part on genuine insights from the Moral Ambiguity Tradition into factors mitigating blameworthiness.

MORAL OPACITY

Collingwood's analysis of self-deception—what he called "corrupt" or "false" consciousness—is presented in his treatise on aesthetics, *The Principles of Art*. This seems surprising until the analysis is viewed in relation to his idealistic theory of art. Idealism regards the "real" work of art as the mental act of "expressing" feelings by clarifying and fully experiencing them in consciousness. Art objects, whether paintings, sculpture, symphonies, movies, or poems, are only outward signs of the "inner" works of art which are conscious acts. They also function as occasions for members of an audience to become artists by clarifying and expressing their own feelings. *Feelings* are any sensations and sense impressions about the world or oneself. *Consciousness* is a linguistic (or symbolic) activity that transforms feelings into emotions and ideas and simultaneously creates an understanding of them. It constitutes an explicit awareness of both the type of emotion (joy, guilt) and the emotion's specific object (an achievement, a failure).

Corrupt consciousness is the misperformance or the purposeful nonperformance of acts of expression within consciousness. Self-deceivers attend fleetingly and indistinctly to some alarming feeling or impression. Fearful of being unable to "dominate" or control it, they turn attention away and avoid developing it into an idea or emotion: "It is as if we should bring a wild animal indoors, hoping to domesticate it, and then, when it bites, lose our nerve and let go."[1] Self-deceivers do not really know the truth they flee because (for Collingwood, as for Sartre) knowledge entails having full consciousness. But neither are they naively mistaken in their beliefs, for they corrupt their own consciousness at a level prior to the intellect's formation of beliefs by assessing propositions for truth or falsity.

To express feelings in consciousness is also to affirm ownership of them, whereas to corrupt consciousness is to disown them: "A true consciousness is the confession to ourselves of our feelings; a false consciousness would be disowning them, i.e., thinking about one of them 'That feeling is not mine.'"[2] But this thinking occurs without explicit attention at the "threshold" of consciousness where feelings are granted or denied expression.[3] Disowning feelings leads to a loss of control over them because they continue to exert an unsupervised influence for which we do not assume responsibility.[4]

Corrupt consciousness is something very bad, according to Collingwood. Not only is it the greatest evil that can affect consciousness, but it can lead to any degree of suffering or wrongdoing:

> The falsehoods which an untruthful consciousness imposes on the intellect are falsehoods which intellect can never correct for itself. In so far as consciousness is corrupted, the very wells of truth are poisoned. Intellect can build nothing firm. Moral ideals are castles in the air. Political and economic systems are mere cobwebs. Even common sanity and bodily health are no longer secure.[5]

Yet corrupt consciousness is not classifiable as either an involuntary mishap or voluntary wrongdoing—the two familiar types of evils. It is not a mishap like a disease that is inflicted by an outside force, for it is the result of one's own activity. Neither, however, is it the product of a "choice" or a "decision" to do something. Collingwood reserved these terms for activities initiated with full consciousness, whereas disowning occurs at the line between the conscious and the unconscious. Therefore, he concluded,

> the symptoms and consequences of a corrupt consciousness . . . are a kind of sheer or undifferentiated evil, evil in itself, as yet undifferentiated into evil suffered or misfortune and evil done or wickedness. The question whether a man in whom they exist suffers through his misfortune or through his fault is a question that does not arise. He is in a worse state than either of these alternatives imply. . . . So far as that corruption masters him, he is a lost soul, concerning whom hell is no fable.[6]

There is much to be valued in Collingwood's analysis of corrupt consciousness as the evasion of self-confession. His models of consciousness and disavowal illuminate aspects of my own account in Chapter 2. Unfortunately, however, his analysis becomes obfuscating right at the point relevant to ethics, and his moral conclusions are little more than mystification.

Misled by his own analysis, he was unable to see how to classify self-deceivers by using familiar moral terms. So he invented a new category especially for them. Yet the category is unfathomable. In conjuring a special moral limbo or hell, it leaves us with nothing to say about moral accountability for entering into self-deception and for causing any resultant harm to oneself or to others. All that can be said is that we are confronted with a unique form of "undifferentiated evil" to which ordinary moral distinctions do not apply.

What led Collingwood into this dead end? His mistake was to restrict the concepts of action, choice, decision, wrongdoing, and fault to what occurs in full and attentive consciousness. Given this restriction, together with the fact that self-deceivers lack full and attentive consciousness about both what they evade and their evasive activities, it would follow that self-deception is morally opaque.

In order to escape this dead end, we need only insist that the choices and omitted actions for which we are accountable are not always the product of explicit consciousness. Perhaps the majority of what we ordinarily count as choices and actions are markedly less mindful than Collingwood allowed. This is true of physical acts, like making a bed or shifting the gears of a car we have driven for years. It is also true of the panoply of brief acts of attending and ignoring that form the warp and woof of our everyday consciousness. We are accountable when we negligently fail to give due attention to the everyday activities involved in meeting our obligations. The same is even more true with respect to spontaneous ignoring, whether or not the ignoring is initiated at the borderline between consciousness and unconsciousness. There is no reason to deny that at least many acts of ignoring and disowning involved in corrupt consciousness are chosen, chosen in a sense that makes them subject to appraisal using ordinary moral concepts.

Collingwood's way of understanding and evaluating self-deception shares striking similarities with Fingarette's approach in *Self-Deception*. Prominent in both accounts are the ideas of psychological disowning, fear of being unable to psychologically integrate what is disowned, refusal to focus explicit consciousness (where explicit consciousness is understood on a linguistic model), rejection of personal responsibility and control, and the resultant moral ambiguity. Yet whereas Collingwood adumbrated most of Fingarette's main themes, Fingarette developed them in fresh directions and with greater subtlety. This, together with the impact of Fingarette's book on contemporary discussions (including mine), warrants a lengthier discussion of his account.

According to Fingarette, self-deceivers can be described as persuading themselves to believe what they know ("deep down" or "in their hearts") is false.[7] Though true, however, this description is paradoxical and philosophically unhelpful. Hence, he proposed to redescribe them using the language of action, volition, and personal identity rather than relying heavily on cognitive terms such as *believe* and *know*. Self-deceivers, he suggested, pursue engagements that they disavow—that is, they refuse to avow as part of their identity or self-image. An *engagement* can be an activity, purpose, emotion, perception, belief, experience, or any other aspect of how we discover, interpret, or take account of the world and ourselves. To *avow* an engagement is to commit oneself to treating it as an aspect of oneself. In undertaking such identity-forming commitments, people authoritatively create their own sense of who they are. Self-deceivers, however, pursue an engagement that is inconsistent with their avowed values while simultaneously refusing to avow it.

Avowing an engagement has two primary dimensions, each of which self-deceivers avoid. First, it entails a willingness to focus explicit attention on the engagement on appropriate occasions. Fingarette referred to explicit attention as ''spelling-out'' because it is a linguistic act or something very much like one. But not only do self-deceivers systematically refuse to spell out an engagement, they also, in a ''self-covering'' manner, refuse to spell out the fact that they are refusing to spell out their engagements. Not infrequently, they engage in rationalization by inventing cover stories for themselves and others and engage in self-pretense.

Second, avowing an engagement involves integrating it into the set of other avowed engagements that together constitute our identity from our own point of view. The engagement must be brought under the influence of our avowed values, tastes, standards of rationality, and other guiding principles. If the engagement conflicts with these principles, as it does in self-deception, avowal would bring painful emotions such as anguish, guilt, or shame. It would also confront us with the need to reshape a new identity in the midst of inner turmoil. Self-deception enables us to pursue a disavowed engagement without having to suffer inner conflict and emotional turmoil.

There is a two-sided generic motive for all disavowal: a desire to maintain inner unity among the engagements presently avowed and a fear of undergoing inner conflict in reshaping our current identity. This motive reveals a ''concern for integrity'' (or ''inner dignity'') but also ''spiritual cowardice.''[8]

At this point it will be helpful to relate Fingarette's account of disavowal to my account of evading self-acknowledgment, especially as Fingarette was the primary influence on what I said in Chapter 2. Self-acknowledgment and its evasion, like identity avowal and disavowal, concern psychological integration rather than mere belief formation.

Both self-acknowledgment and identity avowal involve a willingness to attend to what is acknowledged, to make emotional and attitudinal adjustments to it, and to relate it to one's values and standards of rationality. Evading self-acknowledgment, like identity disavowal, involves purposefully avoiding these things. Moreover, both typically include evasions of acknowledging to oneself that one is evading self-acknowledgment.

Nevertheless, there are significant differences between the two accounts that are essential for understanding the different moral conclusions they imply or leave open.

One minor point of disagreement, or at least of different emphasis, is that my account of evading self-acknowledgment does not set out to describe self-deception without heavy reliance on cognitive concepts such as belief and knowledge.[9] Self-acknowledgment often involves having or forming beliefs, as well as making adjustments in emotion and attitude, altered patterns of attention and desire, and so on. Far from downplaying cognitive terms, I relied on them from the outset in distinguishing the patterns of self-deception, such as willful ignorance (choosing not to know) versus systematically ignoring something known or forming a rationalized belief versus engaging in self-pretense. Willingness to use cognitive terms in thinking about self-deception is important because moral evaluations of self-deceivers often turn on precisely what they believe or know and what they ought to have known. For example, evaluating the conspirators in the price-fixing scheme described in Chapter 2 requires understanding what they knew and should have known about the legality and probable consequences of their actions. Similarly, evaluating their motives and intentions requires understanding what they believed they were doing.

Fingarette inadvertently misled when he claimed to make the "essential discriminations" concerning self-deception without reliance on cognitive terms, even though he admitted that he did not propose to eliminate them from his analysis.[10] He invoked them tacitly at every critical juncture in developing his theory.[11] For instance, he stipulated that the refusal to spell out an engagement involves "sizing up" and "assessing" the engagement and its context and "taking account of" reasons against spelling it out.[12] These terms operate as partial synonyms for "form beliefs," "acquire relevant knowledge," and "make inferences from beliefs to other beliefs." Again, to spell out an engagement involves becoming conscious of what one believes about it (as contrasted with just entertaining it in one's thoughts). And the cover stories and rationalizations that self-deceivers fabricate are presumably believed, partially believed, or the objects of attempts to believe.

The most important difference between the two accounts is that only Fingarette defined self-deception in terms of defending one's present identity, and only he built into his conception of disavowal a generic motive: the desire to preserve current inner unity and identity, plus the fear of undergoing psychic turmoil. In contrast, viewing self-deception as the evasion of self-acknowledgment presupposes no particular motives and does not restrict it to an identity-preserving maneuver. This difference is crucial because motives and purposes are directly relevant to making moral appraisals. Fingarette has packed into his account a basis for seeing something good (prima facie) about all self-deception—namely, an apparently admirable concern for integrity—and also something bad (prima facie), a cowardly flight from reshaping personal identity in light of the truth.

In my view, self-deception does not have any one generic motive or aim (although I allow that a concern for self-esteem is usually a motive for not admitting to ourselves that we are engaged in self-deception). Certainly there are motives for self-deception that have little to do with fear of dealing with inner turmoil. Perhaps all of us, for example, have been motivated by sheer laziness in using self-deception to support a lackadaisical attitude about the need to study for an exam for which we are in fact ill prepared.[13] In fact, self-deception can be prompted by any number of more specific reasons for avoiding an unpleasant or onerous task: a desire to find an easy way out of a difficulty, a need to relax, a wish to make oneself fail, a hope of indirectly hurting others on whom one's actions impinge, and so on.[14] Nothing as momentous as protecting one's present self-identity need be involved. Self-deception can even be motivated by admirable and courageous desires,[15] as we shall see in the next chapter, and still be compatible with the person's basic values and guiding principles.

Of course, Fingarette might insist that in all these cases the individuals really are protecting their self-identities because they are obviously concerned not to have to recognize themselves as the person pursuing the engagement. Such a response would effectively reduce Fingarette's view to the thesis that self-deceivers have a personal stake in not wanting to acknowledge some engagement, where *personal stake* encompasses all desires, needs, fears, hopes, wishes, and commitments. His view would then be true, but it would lack the kind of substantive empirical insight into precisely what the self-deceiver's concerns are—an insight I think clearly is present in Fingarette's account, although exaggerated. Self-deceivers often are motivated by a specific concern for not having to rethink and emotionally confront the kind of persons they are; but they are not always so motivated, and they are so motivated in all different degrees and with all different mixtures with other motives.

Now let us turn to Fingarette's conclusions about the moral status of self-deception. Fingarette contended that disavowal involves an inability to become explicitly conscious of the engagement, which becomes isolated from the influence of avowed principles of rationality and values. This undermines moral agency so as to render self-deception morally ambiguous: "The move into self-deception is, as we know intuitively, a morally ambiguous move."[16]

Fingarette did not explicitly define what he meant by "moral ambiguity," thereby creating a problem of interpretation. It could mean having double moral meanings, that is, being immoral in some respects and permissible or excusable in other respects. This interpretation is tempting because, as we saw in Chapter 2, Fingarette took seriously the air of moral paradox surrounding self-deception: "For as deceiver one is insincere, guilty; whereas as genuinely deceived, one is the innocent victim."[17] He also said that self-deceivers are "insincere" because they spell out their engagements in purposefully mistaken ways and simultaneously "sincere" (in another respect) because they spell them out to themselves and others in the same way.[18] And he asserted that self-deceivers can be criticized for cowardice in not confronting their disavowed engagements and also partially forgiven because of "authentic inner dignity as the motive" for their self-betrayal.[19]

Even though I once put forth this interpretation,[20] I now think it is mistaken. For one thing, Fingarette did not intend the words "sincere" and "insincere" to carry connotations of moral praise and condemnation (contrary, I believe, to ordinary usage). For him, sincere spelling out is simply the absence of purposeful errors in spelling out, whether or not it is praiseworthy, and insincere spelling out is purposeful error, whether or not it is immoral. This explains why he discussed sincerity in Chapter 3 of *Self-Deception* where he developed a model of explicit consciousness as spelling-out, not in Chapter 7 where he presented his views on the moral status of self-deception.

Nor did Fingarette intend that the notions of courage, cowardice, dignity, and concern for integrity carry specifically moral connotations. This is shown by his liberal use of the words "spiritual" and "spirit," as in "spiritual courage," "spiritual cowardice," and "concern for integrity of spirit." The term "spirit," borrowed from Kierkegaard, is used as a synonym for the personal self—the self created by acts of avowal.[21] Spiritual values are those that concern shaping personal identity congruently or incongruently with one's engagements, and those values need not be viewed as moral ones. Admittedly this distinction between spiritual and moral might have been made more prominent in the text.

After all, Kierkegaard intimately linked "spirit" with moral values, and Fingarette even makes a point of emphasizing that "typically" the integrity that the self-deceiver is protecting is rooted in moral concern.[22] Nevertheless, the text allows that no specifically moral judgments of blame or innocence were being made.

Indeed, I now understand Fingarette's central point to be that straightforward judgments of blame or responsibility cannot be made about self-deceivers. This is because the normal presuppositions for applying moral terms have been at least partially removed. In particular, as he wrote in a later essay, "because of the inner split created by disavowal, personal agency is compromised, and so the voluntariness of conduct is compromised, the relevant conduct being no longer either straightforwardly voluntary or straightforwardly involuntary."[23] The compromise of agency, as I understand it, is present during the transition into self-deception as well as afterwards while the person is in a state of self-deception (because both constitute phases of the disavowal said to undermine agency). The upshot is that self-deception is morally ambiguous in the sense that it is morally obscure and opaque: "We are not in a position to ascribe moral properties, or to make paradigm moral judgments, in regard to the condition of self-deception."[24] Self-deception is a type of premoral condition in which the absence of full voluntariness makes moral responsibility uncertain.

To develop this further, voluntary agency is subverted because of the loss of direct control over the disavowed engagement. Direct control presupposes being able and willing to supervise the engagement in explicit consciousness. Only in that way can the engagement be discontinued or modified in light of avowed values and standards of rationality. Disavowal, by contrast, entails surrendering authority to spell out the engagement and express it as one's own, pursuing it in an irrational and compulsive manner, and losing the ability to deliberate about it while formulating other plans of action. It also entails a tacit abandonment of moral responsibility for it. Taken together, these features constitute "a genuine subversion of personal agency and, for this reason in turn, a subversion of moral capacity" which, when focused on, should incline us "not to hold the self-deceiver responsible but to view him as a 'victim' " to be pitied as helpless and suffering from "mental pathology."[25]

These statements are set forth as truths applicable to all self-deception. We are not told that only some self-deceivers are (in one regard) helpless and to that extent not morally blameworthy, or that a morally neutral approach or compassionate approach is suitable only within special contexts such as therapeutic relationships. Instead, the suggestion is made that a morally nonjudgmental perspective is appropriate for certain aspects of all self-deception, even though a "spiritually" judgmental perspective is appropriate with respect to its other aspects.

Fingarette's assessment of self-deception emerges as remarkably close to that of Collingwood. And his elusive terms like "spiritual courage" and "integrity of spirit" remain as unclearly related to ordinary moral concepts, as was Collingwood's notion of "undifferentiated evil." Nevertheless, the primary basis for Fingarette's conclusions is importantly different. Collingwood found self-deception morally opaque because he wrongly assumed that moral accountability presupposes being fully conscious about our actions. In contrast, Fingarette located its opacity in the inability of self-deceivers to become fully conscious of and to avow their engagements.[26] Taken by itself, this is a more plausible moral thesis. But it is false to claim that all self-deceivers are unable to attend to their unacknowledged engagements. Fingarette's claim is an overgeneralization based on the special examples of severe neurosis in which persons dramatically lose control.

To be sure, Fingarette's moral conclusions remain insightful with respect to some neurotic self-deceivers. For example, they square with his example of a man suffering from conversion hysteria.[27] Once unusually vigorous, the man becomes totally incapacitated following an operation on his back to relieve persistent pains. To all appearances he is eager to return to work, and no known physiological cause explains his incapacitation. Under the influence of truth serum, he reveals that he is in fact punishing his family for forcing him to have an operation against his wishes. Upon returning to normal consciousness, he is again oblivious to this repressed motivation for his physical ailments, and there is no reason to suspect him of deliberate lying or pretense. Presumably he is genuinely incapable without special professional help of spelling out and avowing his vengeful engagement.

Many other self-deceivers, however, are far more able, but simply unwilling, to confront what they refuse to acknowledge. The self-deceiving evasions of acting on moral requirements explored by the Inner Hypocrisy Tradition, for example, may have little to do with neurotic compulsions and incapacitating mental illness. Moreover, the ability to spell out and avow a previously disavowed engagement, which is so important in assessing responsibility and blame, varies too much from person to person to provide a basis for any moral generalization about self-deception.

Not surprisingly, Fingarette became caught in inconsistencies in this connection. In some passages he seemed to imply that self-deceivers are clearly (without ambiguity) not blameworthy. For example: "It happens—witness the self-deceiver—that an individual will be provoked into a kind of engagement which, in part or whole, the person cannot *avow* as *his* engagement, for to avow it would apparently lead to such intensely disruptive, distressing consequences as to be unmanageably destructive to the person."[28] Surely most self-deception is not provoked by a perceived trauma of this magnitude. But where it is thus provoked, blameworthiness is absent or greatly diminished.

In other passages he seemed to suggest that in general self-deceivers do meet the criteria for being held responsible. At one point he stipulated that a special interpretation is to be given to his claim that self-deceivers are "unable" to spell out their engagements: "This inability to spell-out is not a lack of skill or strength; it is the adherence to a policy (tacitly) adopted. 'He cannot admit it, cannot let himself become conscious of it,' here means 'He *will* not'; but the 'will not' refers to a general policy commitment and not an *ad hoc* decision not to spell it out."[29] This seems untrue of many self-deceivers, such as the man suffering from conversion hysteria, and also undermines the claim that self-deception is morally ambiguous. Whenever self-deceivers have the strength and skill to acknowledge their disavowed engagements, they are not helpless victims of compulsive unconscious forces.

Fingarette may have one further argument in support of a morally nonjudgmental approach. In an earlier book, he argued that before persons can be held morally responsible they must show a willingness to accept responsibility.[30] For this reason, sociopaths are never appropriately held responsible because they entirely lack the kind of moral concern that would lead them to assume any moral responsibility. This view was reaffirmed at the end of *Self-Deception*, perhaps implying that self-deceivers should not be held responsible because of their tacit refusal to accept responsibility.[31]

That conclusion does not follow, however. As Fingarette also emphasized, individuals' general moral concern can make them responsible for specific engagements for which they fail to assume responsibility. Tobacco executives, to use his illustration, might refuse to accept any responsibility for the effects of their vigorous advertising designed to attract young people to cigarettes. But they may be held responsible because of their general moral commitment not to harm others, a commitment manifested in other areas of their lives.[32] Consistent with this, at least many generally responsible self-deceivers might be blameworthy for the avoidable harm they cause, even though they have refused (through disavowal) to assume responsibility for it.

In sum, Fingarette made a daring attempt to reconcile the morally judgmental perspectives of Sartre and Kierkegaard with a nonjudgmental, therapeutic perspective. Agreeing with the existentialists, he regarded self-deception as the cowardly act of refusing to integrate an engagement into the avowed aspects of one's life. Disagreeing with them, he reconstrued the cowardice as a "spiritual" fault with respect to which specifically moral condemnations are not applicable. Much of the final emphasis of the book, especially in the stress placed on weakened capacities for moral agency, sided with a morally nonjudgmental approach linked to psychoanalytic theory. The result is a view applying straightforwardly only to the self-deception involving severe neurosis.

Once we eschew the drive to say something general about the moral status of all self-deception, Fingarette remains deeply insightful in revealing the possible roles of cowardice, compulsiveness, loss of direct control, and a desire to protect self-identity and inner unity. There are still the practical difficulties, of course, in determining the extent to which a given person is able, but simply unwilling, to summon the courage, insight, and concern to overcome the self-deception and the degree to which the self-deception and its effects may have grown beyond the person's independent control. Fingarette's vision of ubiquitous moral ambiguity should be transformed into a quickened sense of these important areas of vagueness and difficulty in evaluating individual self-deceivers.

MENTAL ILLNESS AND UNCONSCIOUS DEFENSE

Freud usually portrayed unconscious psychological defense against threatening impulses and situations as a purposeful evasion of truth. This makes it plausible to interpret psychological defense as a major type of self-deception. The processes, or "mechanisms," of defense represent different unconscious strategies used by the ego (which is our integrating and coping side) in evading acknowledgment of impulses from the id (biological instincts such as sex and aggression and unacknowledged ideas derived from them) and from the superego (socially instilled values), as well as dangers from the perceived external reality.

Fingarette went further in construing Freud's therapeutic perspective as suggesting a nonjudgmental approach to self-deceivers. This has some basis, not only because the therapeutic context makes it fitting at times to suspend otherwise-appropriate criticisms, but also because the victim of unconscious processes seems to be removed from blame on two traditional grounds: ignorance and involuntariness. Ignorance is present because defense mechanisms operate automatically outside of consciousness, and involuntariness is present because the mechanisms exert a compulsive force. Some post-Freudian clichés would even portray all of us as suffering from neurosis or other mental illness because we are pushed about by inner forces beyond our rational supervision.

I want to show that matters are not this simple. It is true that as a therapist Freud was preoccupied with unhealthy forms of self-deception and that he regarded the concept of unconsciousness as the key to understanding mental health and sickness: "The division of the psychical into what is conscious and what is unconscious is the fundamental premise of psycho-analysis; and it alone makes it possible for psycho-analysis to understand the pathological processes in mental life."[33] Yet Freud's account of the relationships among mental illness, unconscious defense, and moral responsibility for self-deception does not entail any one moral attitude toward all self-deceivers. In showing this, I begin with the relation between mental health and self-deception, then consider the relation between unconsciousness and self-deception, and finally relate these topics to moral responsibility.

Freud conceived mental illness in two distinct ways, corresponding to two of his guiding interests. One interest was theoretical: to define mental illness and compare it with mental health. In this connection he emphasized the similarities between the psychological functioning of neurotic and "normal" people, for he was concerned to establish that the same forms of purposeful, unconscious censorship present in neurosis often operate beneath everyday phenomena such as dreaming, forgetting, and slips of the tongue. This led him to characterize all unconsciously motivated phenomena as pathological.

Witness, for example, his popular book, *Psychopathology of Everyday Life*. As the title suggests, there Freud treated everyday misperformances (slips of the tongue and pen, misremembering, blunders) as pathological behaviors displayed by otherwise healthy people. In other works, Freud described the dreams of generally healthy people as a turning away from reality akin to psychosis, indeed, as being a brief psychosis, though less severe.[34] Or he spoke of dreams as neurotic symptoms, remarking that "a healthy person, too, is virtually a neurotic; but dreams appear to be the only symptoms which he is capable of forming."[35]

These remarks should be understood as part of an attempt to relate his revolutionary ideas to a wide audience at a time when psychoanalysis was under virulent attack. Nevertheless, it remains unfortunate that Freud suggested that the mere presence of unconscious defense provides a criterion for mental pathology. Not only does it conflict with his remarks on other occasions stressing the health-supporting role of much psychological defense, but it gives rise to the view that self-deception involves mental illness whenever unconscious defense operates. That is false and is based on a conceptual confusion. Just because unconscious defense is pathogenic when found in neurotics does not mean it is pathological when found in nonneurotics. Digestion and respiration are not pathological processes even though they function in unhealthy ways in sick people. Defense processes are pathological only when they operate to produce certain kinds of effects: namely, unhealthy ones.

Freud's second criterion for mental illness attempts to characterize what unhealthy effects are. This new criterion, which is more prominent in his writing, derived from his interests as a therapist devoted to healing neurosis. In order to help identify successful therapy, he defined *health* as the ability to work efficiently, the capacity to experience pleasures, and generally successful functioning within society.[36] Whereas each of these tests admits of degrees, the criterion does mark a rough distinction between sick and nonsick forms of self-deception, a distinction analogous to the difference between interpersonal deception used by healthy people and the compulsive deception of the pathological liar. Using this criterion, not all or even most self-deception involving unconscious defense constitutes mental illness. It depends on the extent to which the self-deception impairs social functioning, the ability to work, or the capacity for pleasure.

If, according to Freud's main criterion for health, not all self-deception embodies mental illness, we can now consider a more fundamental question: would Freud analyze all self-deception in terms of unconscious defense? Using my conception of self-deception, I think it is clear that he would not. In order to explain this, I will draw on Freud's threefold distinction among consciousness, preconsciousness, and unconsciousness.

We are *conscious* of something, in Freud's usage, when we attend to it, whether our attention is explicit and focused or more diffuse and peripheral. Accordingly, ideas, motives, beliefs, purposes, emotions and other "mental contents" are said to be conscious in the degree they are attended to. *Preconscious* mental contents are those of which we are not presently conscious but which we can attend to should we so desire. Sometimes Freud talked as if they are immediately accessible to attention, but usually he allowed that moderate (though not extraordinary) mental effort may sometimes be needed.

Unconscious mental contents are those to which we normally cannot attend except under special circumstances, such as while undergoing psychotherapy, hypnosis, or extreme stress. While there are many degrees of consciousness—from focused and vivid to indefinite and faint—the unconscious is "unnoticeable" except with a "very great effort" of attention.[37] *Dynamically unconscious* mental contents are those kept unconscious by the ego's mechanisms of defense—hypothesized processes that operate entirely outside consciousness and cannot be attended to.

Freud emphasized that unconscious defense is not the only way to resist sexual and aggressive drives or other alarming pressures. The ego has available other types of defense which are not inaccessible to consciousness. In fact, many classical unconscious defense mechanisms have preconscious and conscious analogues. Sublimation, for example, is the channeling of sexual and aggressive impulses into socially useful or acceptable directions. It can occur consciously after reflection and deliberation, or preconsciously (that is, accessible to attention though not actually attended to), or unconsciously. Another illustration is reaction formation, the process of keeping unconscious one of two ambivalent attitudes through an overemphasis on the other, conscious attitude. A conscious desire for extreme neatness, for example, may help control an unconscious desire to play with filth; excessive submissiveness may help subdue unconscious aggression. Analogous tactics can come into play at the preconscious and conscious levels. Thus, an individual may be aware that in taking four showers each day, a disturbed conscience is being symbolically cleansed, and some sycophants may be aware that in passively submitting to authority, they are controlling their anarchistic desires.[38]

One further example is especially important. Repression is the unconscious process whereby ideas (and other mental contents) are rendered incapable of being attended to with only moderate effort. Suppression, or what Freud also called condemnation, is its conscious and preconscious analogue: knowingly ignoring something. Sometimes suppression is an act of deliberately deciding to keep attention away from something. Yet it can also be a more spontaneous effort not to attend to a topic, an effort that itself is not attended to even though the person is able to do so if he or she were to make an appropriate effort. The latter form of suppression was emphasized by Bishop Butler and Sartre in their accounts of self-deception.

Any of the preconscious and conscious analogues to unconscious defense mechanisms may enter into self-deception. The defense activities, their motives, and purposes need not be buried deep within the unconscious. A less than extraordinary effort would enable us to attend to them and acknowledge them. Within Freud's own terms, then, we can draw rough distinctions among conscious, preconscious, and unconscious refusals to acknowledge something to oneself. In fact, because a given instance of self-deception might involve elements of all three, we can distinguish three possible dimensions of self-deception. It is conscious to the extent that it involves conscious suppression and other conscious analogues to the defense mechanisms. Typically these defense maneuvers are spontaneous, nondeliberative, and even themselves ignored. It is preconscious to the extent that the strategies of evasion could be attended to and acknowledged without great difficulty. It is unconscious to the extent that it involves evasive strategies which could be attended to only with extraordinary difficulty or special help. This holds true even if one rejects Freud's controversial hypothesis of dynamically unconscious defense mechanisms as the explanation for why the strategies are kept unconscious in this last sense.

We have reached two main conclusions about the implications of Freud's work. First, using Freud's primary criterion for distinguishing mental health and sickness, self-deception does not always constitute mental illness, even when it involves unconscious defense. Second, not all self-deception involves unconscious defense. Both of these conclusions are significant in assessing the responsibility of self-deceivers.

The first conclusion is important because mental illness is usually understood as weakening normal functioning so as to provide grounds for somewhat lessened responsibility. To be sure, we may be fully responsible for inducing our own sickness, whether physical or mental. Moreover, mental illness does not always diminish capacities for responsible conduct and rarely undermines all moral agency. Nevertheless, labeling someone mentally ill raises a presumption that the person has diminished resources for acting responsibly.[39] Because Freud was not committed to viewing all self-deceivers as mentally ill, he was not committed to the presumption that self-deception automatically lessens responsibility. In fact, his view allowed that the relevant psychological capacities of most self-deceivers are not impaired so as to diminish responsibility.

The second conclusion—that self-deception need not be unconscious—allows that not all self-deceivers are victims of uncontrollable forces. Insofar as the self-deception is conducted preconsciously or with conscious activity, individuals may be quite able and simply unwilling to acknowledge the truth. To that extent, they are responsible for the self-deception and its foreseeable effects.

It is interesting to note that one of Fingarette's descriptions (cited in the last section) nicely fits preconscious self-deception: a self-deceiver who is able to spell out an engagement refuses in a systematic way to spell it out. In cases fitting this description, the mere absence of explicit consciousness does not by itself lessen responsibility. However, this description would not be appropriate for unconscious self-deception that involves an inability under normal circumstances to spell out and acknowledge an engagement. Genuine inability to spell out constitutes one ground for diminished responsibility (although there might be some responsibility for getting into the state of being unable to spell out). For this reason Fingarette is misleading when he tries to make "disavowal" interchangeable with "unconscious defense."[40]

The degree of diminished capacity and responsibility, of course, varies, depending on just how difficult it is for a given individual to achieve awareness of the evasion. Even a diagnosis of neurosis does not cancel all accountability or all blameworthiness.[41] We must ask what kinds of compulsions are present, how strong they are, how difficult it would be to abandon the unconscious defenses, and what kinds of help are available. Moreover, just because an activity has its origin in unconscious desires does not mean we are unable to gain control over it. For example, a disposition to be rude to people having authority over oneself may result from childhood conflicts with parents, conflicts one has long since forgotten, but one may be quite capable of restraining that rude behavior.

My conclusions about the implications of Freud's views are consistent with his occasional remarks on the topic of responsibility. In one often-quoted passage, he wrote:

> Obviously one must hold oneself responsible for the evil impulses of one's dreams. In what other way can one deal with them? Unless the content of the dream (rightly understood) is inspired by alien spirits, it is a part of my own being. If I seek to classify the impulses that are present in me according to social standards into good and bad, I must assume responsibility for both sorts; and if, in defence, I say that what is unknown, unconscious and repressed in me is not my "ego," then I shall not be basing my position upon psychoanalysis.[42]

Even though this passage concerns unconscious impulses expressed in dreams, it would seem to apply to other unconscious desires as well. Here, Freud is not denying that the unconsciousness of a desire can be a mitigating factor in assessing blameworthiness. He is only emphasizing that in evaluating our own character, we must avow our unconscious impulses and be accountable for how they are expressed. The degree to which blame is appropriate in a given situation is another issue left open in the passage. Blame should be assessed in light of how difficult it is to become conscious of what we are deceived about, how able we are to control the unconscious impulses, and the kinds of help we may be expected to take advantage of in overcoming self-deception.

Freud was quite willing, and at times eager, to reprove what he regarded as dishonest or imprudent self-deception. The most notable illustration is his sweeping attack on religious beliefs in *The Future of an Illusion*. By *illusion*, he meant any belief substantially caused by wishes or desires, including purposeful self-deceptions. He charged that religious beliefs adopted for comfort and consolation, rather than strictly on the basis of a concern for truth, are harmful, irresponsible, and dishonest.[43]

Our discussion so far has centered on neurosis, which was the principal form of psychopathology explored by Freud. But we should at least pose the question of whether psychotic disorders like schizophrenia ever involve self-deception. Some philosophers have suggested that the answer is no because we do not ordinarily refer to psychotics as self-deceivers; we speak of them instead as suffering from delusions. Yet a simple appeal to what is ordinarily said is not decisive in this connection. The answer should turn in part on an account of what self-deception is and in part on the empirical data about psychosis discovered by scientists.

My conception of self-deception as evading self-acknowledgment is compatible with, although it does not entail, viewing some psychoses as partially the result of self-deception or as accompanied by self-deception. Many psychoses, of course, are traceable to brain damage, heredity, or other organic causes independent of any personal control. But perhaps others involve a radical evasion of acknowledging reality, as has been claimed by some distinguished psychiatrists,[44] anthropologists,[45] and social psychologists.[46]

Agreeing with these social scientists that some severe psychological disorders involve self-deception does not, however, settle the question of moral responsibilty for the self-deception and its effects. No doubt an answer would have to stress the extent to which psychosis leads to severly restricted capacities for responsible agency, hence drastically lessened accountability. In extreme cases the ability to act responsibly may be completely nullified. Yet at the same time, easy generalizations about responsibility and mental illness can blind us to a crucial fact: persons vary quite considerably in their capacities for living as moral agents.

DETERMINISM

Up to this point I have presupposed a contrast between being able to control one's actions and being determined by unconscious impulses not under one's control. The practical point of psychoanalysis, after all, is to enable people to take charge of their lives in areas previously controlled by unconscious motives and intentions. Nevertheless, Freud harbored a conviction that ultimately all human behavior is determined by physiological and environmental causes. Other scientists and philosophers have directly appealed to unconscious forces in defending determinism.[47] And in *A Study of Self-Deception*, M. R. Haight contended

that uncertainties about determinism, together with related considerations, renders all self-deception morally ambiguous so as to place
self-deceivers' responsibility in doubt.

The issues about determinism are subtle and enduring, and in
sketching my views here, I will not resolve them. My limited aim is to
consider Haight's arguments in order to explain why from my perspective her moral skepticism concerning self-deception is too extreme.

Recall from Chapter 2 that Haight believed that the expression *self-
deception* is self-contradictory. In her view, literal self-deception requires
that a "self" knows a proposition and is readily able to bring that
knowledge to consciousness and simultaneously does not know it and is
unable to affirm it consciously. I rejected that view, and here I set it
aside. Haight did, however, allow that *self-deception* refers metaphorically to a cluster of phenomena that are encompassed by my
conception of evading self-acknowledgment.

Self-deceivers, she suggested, usually hold a false belief which is
contrary to the implications of the evidence in their possession or
available to them. They avoid admitting the truth to themselves by
disregarding the evidence and engaging in self-pretense. Whereas they
may know the unpleasant implications of the evidence, they keep it
"buried"—that is, keep it unavailable to consciousness. Haight left open
how this is accomplished, whether via Freudian defense mechanisms,
neurological mechanisms, or by other means. "Buried knowledge"
contrasts with "free knowledge," which is readily recollected and used
in conscious reflection. At most, self-deceivers might allow their buried
knowledge to come to consciousness temporarily on occasions when
there is little realistic chance of acting on it. Or they might express it
obliquely in dreams, obsessive daydreams, jokes, or metaphors. Insofar
as they remain self-deceived, they will not admit to themselves that they
are employing such tactics. The ultimate goal of self-deception is to
avoid some particular undesired course of action or to engage in conduct
incompatible with one's values.[48]

Why do we use the expression *self-deception* to refer metaphorically
to such behavior? The first part of Haight's answer was that we sense
the inherent contradiction in the expression and use it precisely because
of its "*suggestion* of paradox: its ambivalence matches what we feel
about self-deceivers. We use it for a family of cases with this (typically)
in common: it is impossible either to settle or ignore the question 'Can A
help what he is doing?' "[49] The question cannot be settled because, on
the one hand, self-deceivers do not have full control over their actions
because they lack "free knowledge" of what they are deceived about.
On the other hand, they are not totally ignorant and lacking in control

because they do grasp enough evidence to warrant abandoning their false beliefs.

This first part of Haight's answer can be dealt with rather quickly. Essentially it restates Fingarette's claim that the ability and readiness to become explicitly conscious of what one is doing is a necessary condition for being responsible. As Haight put it at one point: "Knowledge—free knowledge—is at any rate *necessary* for virtue. . . . Free knowledge is necessary too for free choice, and free choice—whatever that may be— for responsibility."[50] This might be true if responsibility merely meant accepting or assuming responsibility. Accepting responsibility presupposes attentiveness to what one is doing and a willingness to keep available to consciousness all knowledge relevant to one's obligations. But as the context makes clear, Haight meant responsibility in the sense of being morally accountable and subject to moral blame and praise. Surely we are not relieved of moral accountability when through carelessness or negligence we fail to be alert while driving because of drinking alcohol or staying up all night. Similarly, we are accountable and often blameworthy when we refuse to acknowledge to ourselves morally relevant knowledge that we could reasonably be expected to acknowledge. Ignorance and buried knowledge resulting from self-deceiving evasions do not automatically cancel accountability.

The second part of Haight's explanation of why we use the expression *self-deception* derives from a more general thesis about all responsibility, not just responsibility for self-deception. Haight contended that instead of clear standards for ascribing responsibility, "we have a muddle."[51] Only in rare and extreme cases can we agree when individuals are acting freely and when they are unable to help themselves because of some form of coercion or compulsion: "Almost everything that is morally interesting or important seems to lie between what uncertain paradigms we may accept for freedom and compulsion."[52]

With respect to the bulk of actions where responsibility is debatable, "it is as though a stereotyped Judge and a stereotyped Social Worker confront each other every time."[53] The social worker adopts a "soft line": people are not blameworthy because they are not really free. The judge adopts a "hard line": people are fully free and accountable. In contrast with the judge and social worker, most of us are generally uncertain whether to adopt a hard or soft line on most occasions but especially those involving self-deception. Hence we fudge. We readily invoke the label *self-deceiver* to express our uncertainty and moral ambivalence. This enables us to sidestep a decision about responsibility because self-deception suggests ignorance and lack of control (the social worker's view) and simultaneously suggests knowingness and control (the judge's view). Yet invoking the idea of self-deception carries a high cost—the cost of contradicting ourselves. In using a self-contradictory expression, we bypass coherent description and explanation to adopt "a license to improvise" social verbiage in any way we like when we discuss puzzling conduct.[54]

Haight's primary sympathies lay with the social worker because she believed that the free choice presupposed in holding people responsible may not exist: "Free choice (and so responsibility too) may be a chimera. I suspect that it is."[55] Even if freedom does exist, we have no way of telling where and when it is found. In particular, we can say nothing about the responsibility of self-deceivers: "For the same reason that we have chosen a paradox to name them, we have no obvious way to judge them."[56]

But matters are really even worse for human minds if Haight's analysis is right. Not only is it doubtful that free choice exists, it is doubtful that the concepts of free choice and moral responsibility are even coherent. To be sure, there is one clear notion of free choice that refers to actions not causally determined (if such there are). But free choice in the sense of absence of causation is not a prerequisite for holding people responsible. On the contrary, it would destroy responsibility because we are not responsible for actions we do not cause. Responsibility requires the impossibility that actions be both caused and uncaused: "We may feel that there *must* be a third possible relation between events, neither cause nor its mere absence, because . . . responsibility demands it. So it does, and so responsibility may be an illusion: I am bound to say that I think it probably is."[57]

Haight's argument is not without force, but I think it does not succeed. To begin with, it is false that responsibility requires some "third possible relation"—neither causation nor its absence—between human actions and their antecedents. The ordinary concept of free choice that is presupposed in holding people responsible does not require that actions be totally uncaused, even by the person. On the contrary, our concept of responsibility requires that persons have a significant degree of causal control over their conduct. That control is exercised by acting on reasons (whether good or bad reasons) rather than by being pushed by external forces or internal compulsions which render reasons inefficacious.

The extent to which we are able to control our conduct guided by reasons is a matter for empirical investigation. Science has often corrected commonsense judgments about freedom by identifying hidden physiological and social causes. It shows that we are sometimes like the dupe who was confident he was tying his shoelaces because they were loose, when in fact he was caused to do so by a posthypnotic suggestion. It is logically possible that science might someday establish that human reason lacks any causal influence and is only an inefficacious epiphenomenon. That would indeed destroy moral responsibility. Yet it seems far more likely that science will only continue to identify causal factors that give us the capacity to control much of our conduct on the basis of reasons. Uncovering these factors is no more threatening to responsibility than noting that food and water are causal prerequisites for staying alive in order then to be able to act on reasons. In any case, it is not causal determinism per se that threatens moral responsibility but only the denial of any causal efficacy to human reasoning.

Furthermore, Haight's charge that we lack workable criteria for holding people responsible—that our criteria are a complete muddle—is unduly pessimistic. Very often we make reasonable judgments about blame and praise, guilt and innocence. Consider what Haight said about being free in the sense required for responsibility:

> For an act to be widely accepted as *free* without any question, it would probably have to be (1) not irrational (we often take irrationality to be a sign of compulsion), (2) not the *only* rational thing that can be done in the circumstances, (3) not something that the agent wants more than anything else, (4) not something that he does not want, (5) not something that clearly goes against his interests.[58]

Haight implied that paradigmatic free acts are those that most people agree without hesitation are free. Yet taking a vote only yields the lowest common denominator among the views of the inarticulate and articulate, the morally insensitive (including sociopaths) and the sensitive, the immature and the mature, the skeptics and nonskeptics about freedom, and so on. I believe that most sensitive observers would reject all of Haight's five restrictions as being unnecessary for an act to be free in a sense presupposed by moral accountability. Surely we have significant control over our actions, and are morally accountable for how we exercise that control, in many situations where we (1') act irrationally, (2') have only one rational option available to us, (3') act on the basis of our strongest want, (4') do something that in some respects we desire not to have to do, and (5') act against our own best interests.

Following the last passage cited, Haight linked the concept of freedom with the experience of feeling undetermined by anything— even one's own motives or reasons. She quoted from William Golding's novel, *Free Fall*, in which the protagonist reports this feeling:

> Free-will cannot be debated but only experienced, like a colour or the taste of potatoes. I remember one such experience. . . . The gravelled paths of the park radiated from me: and all at once I was overcome by a new knowledge. I could take whichever I would of these paths.

There was nothing to draw me down one rather than the other. I danced down one for joy in the taste of potatoes. I was free. I had chosen.[59]

Here it seems the protagonist's contemplated choice and act strike him as severed from his past and even his present motives. Which path is chosen is not a matter of reasoning on the basis of foreseeable effects, but instead whim decides the issue. Whimsical decisions, however, are the poorest candidates for a paradigm of freedom in a sense relevant to moral philosophy. The kind of free agency presupposed in holding people accountable is linked to the ability to control based on reasons, not to freedom from reasons.[60]

Responsibility presupposes control based on reasons in the sense that people are significantly able to guide their own conduct—to help themselves. In everyday discourse we often say the individuals who are irrational have lost control. If I habitually overeat because of strong urges to squelch my anxiety, I am losing control in this colloquial sense: I abandon my effort to guide my conduct in light of norms of rational conduct. But in another sense, the one relevant to moral responsibility, I retain control all the while because I could have avoided overeating by making a greater effort and showing greater concern. Also, we sometimes say of our reasonable actions that we had no choice: "I had to keep my promise" or "it was necessary to give the donation." Here we mean that we had no morally reasonable alternative, not that we were physically or psychologically unable to do otherwise.[61]

We can grant that our criteria for holding people morally accountable and for assessing blame and guilt are not crystal clear, any more than they are a complete muddle. Haight's skepticism is a healthy reminder of this. There are indeed many difficult and ambiguous cases in which those criteria are not straightforwardly applicable, one way or the other, whether we are talking about self-deceivers or anyone else. There are also novel kinds of moral situations that call for uncommon wisdom, for silence before the morally indecipherable, or even for moral improvisation. Nevertheless, even in these situations there remains a difference, as Haight herself allowed, between "sensitive and adroit" improvisation and insensitive improvisation performed by "the thick-skinned, the clumsy, the self-righteous."[62]

Finally, despite Haight's preference for the social worker's leniency, deriving from her suspicions that responsibility is an illusion, she confessed at the end of her book that she has never found "any moral or practical line that we take with self-deceivers" which takes account of the many contingencies and variations involved.[63] Veiled in these words seems to be the same longing for a simple moral view of all self-deception that we found in Collingwood and Fingarette. Such a view might be forthcoming, it is also hinted, if we were only clearer about human conduct.

In response, let us emphasize that ascriptions of moral responsibility are as complex as any other moral judgments. They involve moral interpretations of the facts about human behavior, especially about the capacity to act on reasons in particular situations. It is impossible to formulate any single line concerning all self-deception due to the very contingencies and variations to which Haight carefully directed our attention. Ultimately, our willingness to apply imperfectly precise moral criteria, always with the possibility of error, is itself based on our moral commitment, a commitment that cannot be proved to be justified solely by a recitation of the causal factors giving us the abilities and opportunities to control our lives in response to reasons.

DIMENSIONS OF RESPONSIBILITY

I rejected the view that responsibility for self-deception is always vague, ambiguous, or uncertain. I also argued that Freud's theory of mental illness does not imply a view of all self-deceivers as victims of unconscious forces beyond their control. In a more constructive vein, I wish to draw together some distinctions and considerations relevant to assessing responsibility for self-deception, drawing on insights from the Moral Ambiguity Tradition.

Moral accountability, to begin with, should be distinguished from other senses of responsibility to which it is closely related.[64] *Responsibility-as-accountability* arises when an act or event is attributable to a person who is appropriately called to account morally for it. We might be called upon to answer for it in several ways: to explain why we acted as we did; to provide excuses or justification where relevant; and to be subject to praise or blame, credit or condemnation, reward or punishment, respect or the need for apology, forgiveness or the demand to make amends. We also hold ourselves to account when we respond with feelings of guilt or self-esteem, shame or pride, self-forgiveness or self-punishment. Where the context makes it clear that what is at issue is culpability for harm done, the question of accountability-responsibility becomes one of guilt *(responsibility-as-guiltiness)* and blame *(responsibility-as-blameworthiness)*.

By contrast, *responsibility-as-obligation* is the possession of moral obligations and duties or at least general areas of moral commitment. Some duties are attached to specific roles, such as the responsibilities of parenthood and those of defense attorneys, engineers, or doctors. Other obligations are role free, such as the general responsibilities to respect the rights of others, to keep promises, or to support just causes.

Responsibility-as-capacity is having the ability to meet moral obligations and be responsive to moral considerations. Young children, animals, and sociopaths are nonresponsible in this sense because they lack a sufficiently developed capacity to reason, control their conduct, and respond in morally sensitive ways.

Responsibility-as-virtue is displaying the virtue of conscientiousness in meeting moral obligations. Thus, when we speak of a responsible individual we refer to someone who not only has the capacity to meet obligations but is generally diligent in doing so.

Although the preceding senses of responsibility refer to aspects of moral responsibility, each has a legal analogue. The standards for *legal responsibility*, however, often differ somewhat from those for ascribing moral responsibility. They may be more stringent, such as manufacturers' "strict liability" for even unforeseeable harm resulting from their products, harm for which they are not morally culpable. Or they may be less stringent, as in areas of private morality where it would cause more harm than good for the law to intrude.

There is also a value-neutral concept of *causal responsibility*, as when we say, "The heavy winter snow and unusual spring heat were responsible for the Utah floods." In this sense an infant is responsible for starting a fire by knocking over a kerosene lamp, although moral and legal responsibility belong entirely to the careless parents who left the child unattended. Seriously mentally ill self-deceivers might be responsible for harm in this causal sense even though they are not morally responsible.

Focusing now on responsibility-as-accountability, there are four main aspects of self-deception for which a person might be responsible: (1) the entrance into self-deception, (2) remaining in self-deception, (3) actions and omitted actions based on or influenced by the self-deception, and (4) the effects of those actions.[65] Sometimes it is not particularly important to take these distinctions into account. For example, Clifford's shipowner (mentioned in Chapter 3), who deceived himself about the safety of his passenger ship, is accountable for getting into his state of self-deception, for remaining in it, for actions based on it (such as sending the unsound ship to sea), and for the deaths this caused.

At other times, however, the distinctions are important. A person may have very little responsibility for having entered into self-deception and yet be responsible for remaining in it. Consider a man who as a child refused to admit to himself that his father was a vicious criminal, even though he had ample evidence showing he was. We understand this self-deception as entirely natural and probably not an object of moral scrutiny. But when as a young man he continues to refuse to recognize the hard evidence concerning his father's crimes and thereby disrupts the lives of other family members who are seeking to deal realistically with the father, we might hold him fully accountable if he is psychologically able to deal with the truth. Conversely, a father may be responsible for initially deceiving himself about the criminal activities of his son. But the self-deception might develop into a seriously neurotic state over which he loses substantial control, thereby lessening his responsibility for remaining in and acting from self-deception.

Furthermore, there are also different types of judgments that may come into play in holding self-deceivers accountable for any of these aspects of self-deception, judgments related to some of the other senses of "responsibility." There are judgments about: (1) the appropriateness of ascribing an act or its effects to individuals and calling them to account for it, (2) guilt or innocence, and (3) blameworthiness, the justifiability of acts of blame, forgiveness, or praiseworthiness. These judgments, in turn, presuppose judgments about the extent of moral obligations, and they are typically subject to considerable disagreement among reasonable moral agents. A philosophical account of responsibility for self-deception cannot settle these disagreements. Yet it should identify the main variables in assessing moral accountability in these three directions. Let us indicate some of these variables and in doing so comment on how differing views about moral obligations complicate the assessment of the variables.

First, the question of accountability begins with the question: To whom should an act or effect be ascribed? A ship goes down. Should the event be dismissed as no one's fault, as due instead to unfortunate weather conditions or unforeseeable anomalies in an aging hull? Or is it the effect of something done by the manufacturer, the government, a terrorist, a less-than-superior captain, or a self-deceiving owner? In deciding who is to be held accountable we must uncover the facts about causes preceding the event, but we must also resolve an evaluative question about which cause ought to be singled out for moral purposes. We hold the shipowner responsible because he has an obligation to keep the ship in adequate repair. In general, singling out one person as *the* cause of something requires us to adopt attitudes, frequently controversial ones, about both the person's obligations and the standards of reasonable care in meeting those obligations.

Second, judgments about obligations obviously enter into judgments of guilt or innocence. Guilt (in the relevant sense) is the state of having violated an obligation or duty. As we saw in Chapter 3, self-deceivers may be guilty of distorting their own understanding of their obligations. Or they may culpably ignore, stay ignorant of, or rationalize away facts relevant to meeting their obligations. Self-deception about the mechanical condition of the brakes on one's car can be immoral because driving with defective brakes could cause serious harm to others. But there will be many disagreements about just how far our obligations extend and just how much it is reasonable to expect in meeting them.

Third, judgments of blame can be equally complicated in further ways. Guiltiness should not be confused with blameworthiness; nor should blameworthiness be confused with justifiable acts of blaming. Blame is having or expressing a strongly negative attitude toward someone and for a certain thing, but any number of mitigating circumstances might make it best to forgive and forget the offense of a guilty person. Sometimes it is best for our own well-being not to adopt this attitude in order to prevent anger and hate from disrupting our lives and our relationships with others. (Perhaps "Judge not that ye be not judged" should be read as "Blame not that ye be not blamed.") Even where we cannot help but adopt an attitude that a person is blameworthy, it may be wrong for us to engage in acts of blaming. The severity of the individual's own self-blame and suffering may warrant withholding further acts of blaming.[66] The Reverend Dimmesdale, discussed in Chapter 3, is one example. Or we may be in a pitifully weak moral position to engage in acts of blaming because we are personally guilty of similar or worse wrongs. We may not be worthy to blame the blameworthy.

Finally, whereas guilt and blameworthiness are distinct, many of the considerations used in assessing them are the same. Let us list some of them.

(1) The content or target of the self-deception; that is, what the self-deception is about. Much self-deception has nothing to do with morality, such as self-deception about how many books are in my home. And we may tragically deceive ourselves about the good in us (often owing to a regrettable sense of inferiority).[67]

(2) The importance of the obligations that are threatened by the self-deception. If, for example, the lives of others are at stake, as they were in the case of Clifford's shipowner, we demand especially high standards for avoiding self-deception. We are less demanding about negligence in failing to guard against self-deception about more minor commitments.

(3) The actual degree of harm done. This includes harm to others and the warping of one's own moral understanding.

(4) The degree to which there is harm to one's own interests. Some self-deceivers suffer dearly, far more than anyone they might harm, and this may temper our condemnations.

(5) The extent to which it is reasonable to expect people to understand the possible impact of the self-deception in meeting the relevant obligations. How much do they know, and how much should they have known given their intelligence and access to information, as well as given our sense of how much can be expected of people in such situations? If the self-deception leads to wrongdoing in a largely unforeseeable way, we temper or withhold judgments of blame.

(6) The degree of control in entering into, remaining in, acting out of, and preventing bad effects of self-deception. In measuring control, several things need to be considered: the extent to which they were aware or could reasonably be expected to be aware of what they are deceived about; how easily they could have avoided the specific acts of ignoring, self-pretense, emotional detachment, and so on involved in the self-deception; and what psychological cost would be involved in avoiding the self-deception and actions following from it. If unconscious motivations are present, how difficult would it be for the person to identify and modify them? Where compulsions are involved, either as contributing causes or as effects, what ordeal would be required to resist them?

(7) The specific motives for entering into, remaining in, and acting out of self-deception. If psychological survival or stability is at stake or if the motives are mainly altruistic, we usually temper attitudes of blame for harm caused. We also should consider (looking ahead to the next chapter) whether deep-seated needs are being expressed, such as the fundamental need for self-esteem, which could not easily be satisfied in other ways. Are there lingering effects of abuse or deprivation in childhood that weaken an otherwise normal rationality? Is the family or work environment unusually hostile in a way bearing on the self-deception? To the extent, however, that cowardice, greed, self-seeking, or cruelty are motives, blame is increased.

(8) The availability or unavailability of help and the individual's responsiveness to it. It is one thing to lack any constructive support from friends or advisors in seeing through the deception and the harm it causes. It is something else if there is readily available support that is disregarded.

Moral responsibility for self-deception reflects the complexity of moral responsibility in general. Assessing it can involve the consideration of many factors. It is hoped that we often manage to make these assessments with reasonable insight after being presented with the details about a situation. Sometimes, however, relevant factors cannot be identified or weighed with any precision. To that extent responsibility for self-deception is vague, uncertain, or ambiguous by being open to alternative interpretations. Yet these difficulties pertain to specific individuals in particular situations, not to self-deceivers in general. In thinking about self-deception we should balance our "craving for generality" (to borrow Wittgenstein's phrase) with a heightened sensitivity to differences.

6
Vital Lies

With the truth, one cannot live. To be able to live one needs illusions. . . . This constantly effective process of self-deceiving, pretending and blundering, is no psychopathological mechanism, but the essence of reality.

—Otto Rank, *Truth and Reality*

The Vital Lie Tradition confronts us with the possible good of self-deception and the possible harm in seeking to eliminate it from ourselves and others. It portrays self-deception as frequently beneficial and healthy, and often benign. And it emphasizes the role of self-deception as a valuable coping technique promoting vital human needs such as self-respect, self-improvement, hope, friendship, love, and viable community.

Rarely do thinkers in the Vital Lie Tradition offer sweeping defenses of self-deception such as that suggested by Otto Rank in the epigraph. In fact, some of the writers discussed in this chapter, especially Eugene O'Neill and Henrik Ibsen were also concerned to unmask harmful forms of hyocritical self-pretense. Perhaps the Vital Lie Tradition is best viewed as a tradition of themes that artists, philosophers, psychologists, and others have developed in opposition to excessively moralistic condemnations of self-deceivers. Yet taken together these themes do suggest a general perspective on much self-deception that sharply contrasts with that found in the other traditions, especially the Authenticity Tradition.

In the first section of this chapter, I sample representative literary works in the Vital Lie Tradition. Some philosophical theses in this tradition and the conception of rationality accompanying many of them are discussed in the second section. In the third section, I explore the possibility that non–self-deceiving forms of faith, hope, and imaginative expression can fulfill most vital needs without violating a commitment to live by confronting even painful truths. In the concluding section, based on themes from the entire book, I outline a conception of being honest with oneself.

BENEFICIAL ILLUSIONS
AND DESTRUCTIVE DISILLUSIONERS

Ignorance can be invigorating, knowledge enervating, and disillusionment destructive. These are time-honored themes in literature. They are given biblical expression in Ecclesiastes: "For in much wisdom is much grief: and he that increaseth knowledge increaseth sorrow."[1] *Oedipus Rex* shows us how even a little knowledge (of awful truths) can be demoralizing. Witness Teiresias's opening lines, "How dreadful knowledge of the truth can be / When there's no help in truth!"[2] Physically blind but spiritually sighted, Teiresias is portrayed as sensible and humane for his reluctance to reveal to Oedipus his patricide and incest. In contrast, Oedipus is portrayed as manifesting intemperance and hubris in pursuing the truth at any cost.

In a less somber vein, Jonathan Swift is one of many comic writers who have explored the contribution of self-imposed illusions to happiness. In *A Tale of a Tub*, he wryly remarks that "when a man's fancy gets astride of his reason; when imagination is at cuffs with the senses, and common understanding, as well as common sense, is kicked out of doors; the first proselyte he makes is himself. . . . If we take an examination of what is generally understood by happiness," he continues, "as it has respect either to the understanding or the senses, we shall find all its properties and adjuncts will herd under this short definition, that it is a perpetual possession of being well deceived."[3]

Two works of drama that have special importance for understanding the beneficial aspects of self-deception and the possibly tragic effects of removing it, Henrik Ibsen's *The Wild Duck* and Eugene O'Neill's *The Iceman Cometh*, will be the focus of this section.

In *The Wild Duck*, Hjalmar Ekdal is a ludicrous self-deceiver who blinds himself to his failures as a professional photographer as well as to his complete dependence on others. Hjalmar believes he is the sole source of income for his family when in fact his wife receives large subsidies from his father's previous business partner. Only his wife's management of his money and time enables him to conduct even the most trivial matters of everyday life. His greatest joy is the veritable worship he receives from his teenage daughter, Hedvig, and yet he fails to reciprocate her love with even minimal courtesy. Hjalmar's self-deception enables him to disregard his failures and dependency while sustaining a pompously inflated self-image. He believes he is on the verge of making a brilliant discovery that will revolutionize photography and bring his family prosperity. In fact, he has merely assembled a pile of useless gadgets whose purpose remains a mystery. Yet he tinkers with the obscure device whenever he needs to bolster his self-confidence, daydreaming about it as a means of escaping a pitiably trivial life.

Hjalmar did not initiate the belief in his nascent creativeness; for that he lacked the requisite degree of imagination. It was his physician, Dr. Relling, who suggested and helped cultivate his illusion. Relling is a benevolent cynic who prescribes remedies for both the physical and psychological ailments of his patients. He encourages them to embrace false hopes and rationalizations—"life-lies"—designed to bring peace and happiness. In Relling's view, most people need fundamental illusions about their lives to provide "the stimulating principle" for effective coping. Without self-deception they would be reduced to despair, self-contempt, and unhappiness: "Take away the life-lie from the average person, and you take his happiness along with it."[4]

Relling's antagonist, Gregers Werle, is a former schoolmate of Hjalmar's and also the son of the former business partner of Hjalmar's father. Gregers speaks on behalf of "the claim of the ideal," insisting on the unqualified pursuit of virtue. In doing so he exaggerates both the human capacity for goodness and the average person's devotion to truth. In particular, he naïvely views Hjalmar as a noble soul capable of living honestly and magnanimously. The culminating events in the play are initiated when Gregers informs Hjalmar that Hedvig is not his (biological) daughter, that she is in fact the offspring of Gregers's own father (who for that reason has been subsidizing Hjalmar's family). Gregers is confident that his "mission" to inform Hjalmar of these truths will enable him to create a "true marriage" based on complete candor, forgiveness, and trust.

Instead, Hjalmar shuns his wife, destroys the harmony of the household, and grows completely indifferent to Hedvig, leaving her despondent. Confused by the failure of his mission, Gregers attempts a new remedy. He suggests to Hedvig that she can regain Hjalmar's love through an act of personal sacrifice: destroying the pet wild duck that had been a gift from Gregers's father (and her own biological father). But by the time Hedvig prepares to shoot her pet, her dearest possession, she grows convinced that Hjalmar's increasing coldness means he has permanently disowned her. Thrown into despair, and in a dazed identification with the wild duck that is to be the sacrifice, she goes to the attic and shoots herself.

Gregers's fanaticism and moral obtusity, or what Relling calls his "severe case of inflamed integrity," is born of hatred for his father and guilt concerning some of his father's wrongs. He is not fully aware of these motives, however, and self-deceivingly uses Hjalmar and Hedvig to salve his uneasy conscience. His motives for preaching virtue are profoundly selfish, and he is even incapable of feeling any genuine sadness or remorse for the tragedy he causes.

Despite his cynicism, Relling has a basic concern for others that Gregers lacks. When Gregers complains that without the noble pursuit of high ideals life would lack meaning, Relling rejoins: "Oh, life wouldn't be too bad if it weren't for these blessed bill collectors who come pestering us poor folk with their claims of the ideal."[5] Human decency, the play suggests, opposes stringent idealistic demands to abandon life-giving self-deceptions. Not only can such demands lead to tragedy; usually they are also motivated by self-deception.

O'Neill's *The Iceman Cometh* bears striking resemblances in theme and plot to *The Wild Duck*. In this play the setting is Harry Hope's gin-mill saloon and hotel on the West Side of New York in 1912. A group of down-and-out patrons of the bar are preparing for one of their biannual binges. Larry, the rough analogue of Dr. Relling, defends life-lies or "pipe dreams" as vitally necessary: "To hell with the truth! As the history of the world proves, the truth has no bearing on anything. It's irrelevant and immaterial, as the lawyers say. The lie of a pipe dream is what gives life to the whole misbegotten mad lot of us, drunk or sober."[6] Larry purports to be a hardened cynic. In fact, he is the most compassionate character in the play. Compassion prompts him to encourage pipe dreams in others, and he is himself self-deceived when he pretends to be indifferent and philosophically aloof. In this respect he differs from the clinically detached Dr. Relling.

Within the play the expression *pipe dreams* retains its original reference to the fantasies and hallucinations induced by smoking opium pipes, with alcohol replacing opium as the favored drug. Yet O'Neill also uses the expression to refer to self-deceptions that generate self-esteem and the vitality based on it. The dwellers at Harry Hope's hotel sustain a viable community made possible by the mutual encouragement of self-deception. Refusing to acknowledge their own self-pretense, they are nevertheless readily able to see through everyone else's dissimulation. They tacitly agree to support the others' pipe dreams as a requirement for membership in the community, and in return they benefit from the community's willingness not to demand honesty from them about their pipe dreams.

Hickey is a traveling salesman who in the past has visited the bar twice a year to lead the group on their most memorable binges. But when he arrives this time, he brings a disturbing new gospel, one akin to that of Gregers Werle. He proclaims that he has come to save his friends from their pipe dreams: "I know from my own experience, they're the things that really poison and ruin a guy's life and keep him from finding any peace."[7] Pipe dreams, he insists, cause guilt and self-hatred. Happiness is possible only by embracing "the old dope of honesty is the best policy—honesty with yourself." Only later do we learn that Hickey's gospel, like that of Gregers, is grounded in self-deception and motivated by guilt. Several hours before arriving at the bar, Hickey had killed his wife under the self-deceiving illusion that he was bringing peace both to her and to himself.

The ensuing double plot involves both pathos and tragedy. Pathos develops as Hickey disillusions one after another of his friends by encouraging them to act on their pipe dreams. He gets Harry Hope, for example, to pursue his dream of leaving the bar to revive old friendships he neglected during twenty years of alleged mourning for his wife. After walking halfway across the street in front of his bar, Hope runs back, insisting that a car almost hit him. As Hickey foresaw, the others also fail to act on their dreams, and each returns too shaken to continue believing his or her own lies. Moreover, no one wishes any longer to indulge the others in the protection of their pipe dreams. Hickey's prediction is quite false: disillusionment does not bring peace to the drinkers. Instead, it reduces them to despair and shatters their community with fighting and insults.

Hickey is perplexed. In order to unravel what went wrong, he begins a long confession about the origin of his gospel of honesty. He explains how he and his wife, Evelyn, had based their marriage on the shared pipe dream that Hickey would one day become faithful to her and abandon periodic visits to prostitutes. Hickey's years of infidelity never altered her easy forgiveness of him, and this he came to despise: "Sometimes I couldn't forgive her for forgiving me. I even caught myself hating her for making me hate myself so much. There's a limit to the guilt you can feel and the forgiveness and the pity you can take! You have to begin blaming someone else, too."[8]

Yet he does not realize the extent of his *ressentiment* until during a trance-like confession he blurts out what he had said to himself immediately after killing Evelyn: "Well, you know what you can do with your pipe dream now, you damned bitch!"[9] Horrified by this self-revelation, he quickly denies having uttered the words. Then, rather than acknowledge (to himself and his listeners) his real motives for killing Evelyn, he seizes a new pipe dream suggested by Harry Hope: he must have been insane when he killed Evelyn and remained so since then.

If experiencing tragedy requires acknowledgment and understanding, then Larry and Parritt are the only tragic characters in the play. Parritt is the son of Rosa Parritt, who was Larry's former lover when he participated in the anarchist movement. Arriving at the bar the night before Hickey arrives, Parritt seeks in Larry a father figure (indeed, possibly his real father) who will help him deal with his guilt for having turned in his mother to the police. Rosa Parritt based her life on the fanatical pursuit of freedom, and hence Parritt's betrayal condemned her to a spiritual death in prison worse than the physical death of Evelyn. Yet he acknowledges this to himself only after he is mesmerized by Hickey's confession into identifying with Hickey's act of murder.

Larry still loves Rosa Parritt, and hearing Paritt admit his spiritual matricide shatters his posture of detachment. He commands Parritt to ''Get the hell out of life, God damn you, before I choke it out of you!''[10] Interpreting this as a paternal confirmation of his own tortured need for retribution, Parritt climbs to the hotel roof and jumps to his death. As the play ends, most of the regular patrons of Hope's hotel begin to rebuild their community based on pipe dreams. Larry, however, cannot conceal from himself the horror of what he has witnessed and participated in. He sits apart, wishing for death, no longer able to make use of the opiate of self-deception.

Despite numerous parallels with *The Wild Duck*, *The Iceman Cometh* is a richer exploration of self-deception. Ibsen provided only one major example of how life-lies can be beneficial, whereas O'Neill packed the stage with nearly twenty pipe dreamers. They represent illusions of all varieties: political, marital, sexual, educational, professional, religious, philosophical.[11] Thus we are confronted with a microcosm of our world in which ubiquitous self-deception helps foster vitality, hope, and community in all areas of life.

This enables O'Neill to identify more realistically the interpersonal dynamics of self-deception. In place of the melodramatic image of Dr. Relling planting illusions in his patients, we are shown a world where self-chosen illusions are sustained by spontaneous support from other self-deceivers. O'Neill showed us how different people's pipe dreams can be complementary, interlocking, and mutually supportive. Harry Hope, for example, could not pretend to himself that he is still in mourning for his wife (whom he hated while she was alive) were it not for all his friends encouraging his self-pretense. We are also shown how commitment to a pipe dream can be intensified by sharing it with others—witness the bonding of Hickey and Evelyn through their belief in his eventual reform.

Another example is the interplay between the illusions of Rocky, the night bartender, and Margie and Pearl, two hookers who work for him. Rocky refuses to admit he is a pimp and instead regards himself as a business manager generously helping Margie and Pearl avoid squandering their money. In turn, the women draw a somewhat mysterious distinction between themselves and other hookers. Margie says at one point, "We wouldn't keep no pimp, like we was reg'lar old whores. We ain't dat bad." Pearl echoes, "No, We're tarts, but dat's all."[12] In this case affirming each other's pipe dreams not only provides mutual psychological support but is necessary for sustaining the logical coherence of the interwoven pipe dreams.

Much the same is true for Chuck and Cora, whose pipe dream is that they will later be married. Here the illusion also fosters deeper affection, while serving (ironically) to prevent a disastrous marriage. Because they keep their romantic plans at the level of flirtation and kidding, a buffer is provided to prevent serious movement toward a marriage as ill-fated as Hickey and Evelyn's. Their pipe dream protects them from a harsh truth and shields them from pursuing an ideal that could bring disaster to themselves and others.

Finally, O'Neill's play offers some important caveats missing in Ibsen's more one-dimensional play. Even though *The Iceman Cometh* dramatizes Vital Lie themes, it also implies rational limits to those themes. In particular, it does not offer an unqualified endorsement of Larry's claim that the lie of the pipe dream gives life to all of us. His claim is true with respect to most of the residents at Harry Hope's hotel, but that is because their pipe dreams represent a balm for lost self-respect, a desperate last resort to sustain self-esteem, the only basis left for genuine community, and a way of enriching and elevating personal relationships. We admire Larry more than the other characters precisely because of the greater honesty and compassion that make him vulnerable to tragic despair. He is ennobled, not degraded, in overcoming self-deception, even though he is tragically unable to rekindle hope at the end of the play.

The Iceman Cometh portrays several instances in which pipe dreams ultimately foster death, not life. The dream shared by Hickey and Evelyn generates enormous guilt. It also encourages Hickey's deranged illusion that killing her was the best thing he could do. No doubt all this occurs because Hickey and Evelyn refuse to submit their ideal of purity to criticism, both from themselves and others. Greater openness, rather than clinging persistence, might have tempered their unrealistic demands. Also Rosa Parritt's illusions about the anarchist movement contribute to her neglect of Parritt, which in turn help cause his alienation and betrayal. It could even be argued that Larry's unwillingness to acknowledge his love for Rosa Parritt contributes to his inability to envisage a more creative solution for Parritt than suicide.

It is worth mentioning the nonfictional tragedy of Charles Chapin, a prominent newspaper executive who inspired O'Neill's creation of Hickey. After surrendering to the police for shooting his wife as she slept, Chapin insisted he had idolized her and had acted solely to give her peace. When questioned he insisted, "There was really nothing else to do. I'm quite satisfied I took the only course for an honorable man to take."[13] Written in 1939 on the eve of the full fury of modern fascism, *The Iceman Cometh* stands as a somber warning against the honor of distorted zealots whose ideals have been nurtured in self-deception. Balancing its insight into the possible good in self-deception, it offers a warning that fanatics like Stalin, Hitler, the Ayatollah Khomeini, and even Joseph McCarthy can be far more dangerous than conscious hypocrites.

Neither Hickey nor Gregers set out with self-conscious deliberation to purge others of so many daydreams and illusions that they would be reduced to utter despair. Let us take a glance at someone who did have such a plan.

The protagonist of Albert Camus's *The Fall*, Jean-Baptiste Clamence, is by his own account a thoroughgoing egotist preoccupied with maintaining a sense of superiority over others. He confesses that during his earlier career as a lawyer he had deceived himself about this fact. Without admitting it to himself, he had sought clients whose defense would bring him notoriety and public praise. By representing widows and orphans, he appeared to be motivated by a zeal for justice; in fact, he sought glory in being perceived as a champion of justice.

Clamence's self-satisfaction is ruined, however, following an episode in which he hears laughter coming from the direction of the water as he walks along the Seine. The event evokes the repressed memory of his cowardice several years earlier when he had passively witnessed a woman commit suicide by jumping into the Seine. The emotionally reverberating, haunting laughter prompts him to explore his other memories. In doing so he gradually comes to acknowledge that his guiding passion has always been to dominate and manipulate other people, especially the weak, for whom he has a hidden contempt. As he falls from innocence about his former self-deception, his egotism remains intact, and he becomes obsessed with how all of us use the appearance of ethical conduct as a ruse for oppression. Seized by a cruel urge to force this revelation on others, he nevertheless continues to base his self-esteem on admiration from others. He knows that direct criticism and disillusionment will provoke other people to reciprocate with spiteful condemnations of him. Thus, his problem is how to elude judgment while retaining social esteem.

His clever solution is to abandon his career as a lawyer and embrace a new vocation of "judge-penitent." Instead of directly condemning his targeted victims, he first confesses to them his past phoniness and even his present vocation. Having picked victims of some discernment, he thereby creates an impersonal mirror that forces them to see through their own self-deception and moral duplicity. Indirectly he prompts them to judge themselves without judging him. He is so successful that his victims regard him as a prophet who facilitates their self-revelations. Clamence can think of himself as a God, judging others while remaining aloof from judgment, even admired: "How intoxicating to feel like God the Father. . . . I pity without absolving, I understand without forgiving, and above all, I feel at last that I am being adored!"[14]

If we imagine ourselves as Clamence's clients as he pursues his role as judge-penitent, we must conclude that he is only partially successful. He succeeds, as Camus intended, in puncturing our moral hypocrisy by preying on our self-doubts about how egotism pollutes our moral commitments. But we reject his cynical claim to have "brought out the fundamental duplicity of the human being" in having vanity as the sole motive behind apparent morality.[15] We are double, but in the different sense of being condemned to having mixed motives for most of our endeavors. We pity Clamence for being unable to accept this fact, and we blame him for the sadistic enjoyment he takes in unmasking self-deceivers and observing their suffering.

RATIONALITY

Recently several philosophers have called attention to the beneficial aspects of some self-deception. D. W. Hamlyn, for example, observed that "there is a sense in which self-deception may sometimes be the right policy, in that it may be the only way of maintaining a viable human life."[16] A concern for truth, he suggested, is not of paramount importance in all situations. In fact, a preoccupation with truth and with avoiding self-deception can inhibit the spontaneous emotions on which important personal relationships depend, emotions like love and compassion.

In a similar vein Amélie Rorty described a dying doctor who deceives himself about his illness and thereby prevents himself from collapsing into despair. The doctor's self-deception seems to nurture fresh capacities for love, optimism, and humor in dealing with his ordeal and responding to the people who care for him. This illustration shows how "individual instances of self-deception can be beneficial and perhaps in some sense rational or at least canny."[17] Elsewhere, Rorty proffers a stronger generalization:

> Like programs for eradicating the vices, attempts at doing away with self-deception would damage habits that are highly adaptive. Those incapable of self-deception are probably also incapable of romantic love, certain sorts of loyalty, and dedication to causes that require acting slightly larger than life. While these gifts have their dangers, they have on occasion served us well. What we need is not the wholesale substitution of self-knowledge for self-deception, but the gifts of timing and tact required to emphasize the right one in the appropriate place.[18]

Other philosophers have contended that self-deception can be admirable when its motives and results are good. Béla Szabados, for example, described a father confronting his dying son. The father manages to hold himself together by a self-deceiving denial that the son's illness is incurable.[19] His primary motives are love and hope. Earlier, John King-Farlow drew attention to such cases. He described a father who deceives himself about the damage to his health caused by extra night work taken on to help support his family. His self-pretense prevents subtle behavioral giveaways to members of his family who would suffer if they learned of his sacrifice. King-Farlow portrayed the self-deception as a morally heroic response to a difficult situation. Generalizing, he remarked that "often there can be wisdom, and even a great moral strength associated with this strange business of 'conning' oneself for a good purpose."[20]

Frequently accompanying such claims is the suggestion that when self-deception is morally permissible, it is rational and reasonable to engage in it. This view deserves to be developed because it sharply conflicts with an influential conception of rationality. This conception, which might be called *evidence-centered rationality*, makes all evasion of evidence (as in the preceding examples) irrational by definition. According to it, rational persons form beliefs in strict accord with the best available evidence and then shape their conduct, emotions, and attitudes consistently with those beliefs.[21] Rational persons also adopt the most effective means for meeting their goals, but it is assumed that the calculation of these means should be based on beliefs warranted by available evidence. Self-deception is in this view a clear-cut case of irrationality because it constitutes an evasion of evidence or apparent truths.

From this perspective the Vital Lie Tradition represents a major heresy and implies a competing conception of rationality centered on usefulness in serving at least legitimate (i.e., not harmful) desires, wants, needs, and values other than those involved in a concern for truth. Let us call this the will-centered conception of rationality or, more simply, *will-centered rationality*. Will-centered rationality is a standard for beliefs as well as actions: a belief is rational if it best serves the believer's needs and values, and an action is rational if there is no more efficient way to meet the agent's goals given what it is rational for the agent to believe. Such a conception was developed and applied to self-deception early in this century by the British pragmatist F. C. S. Schiller.

In *Problems of Belief*, Schiller proposed that truth can be viewed as a general type of value. It is the primary "cognitive value" that is the object of attempts to know and understand, and it contrasts with noncognitive generic values like goodness, beauty, and pleasure. Schiller insisted that it is proper to use these noncognitive values in assessing whether beliefs are rational: "We must allow that it is possible, legitimate, and, in point of fact, universal, for mixtures of values, variously compounded of truth, beauty, goodness and even of pleasure, to determine our systems of belief."[22] In particular, the desire to have a simple, elegant, and pleasing picture of ourselves and our world inevitably influences belief formation, and this influence should be accepted as legitimate and reasonable.

"Even (and perhaps especially!) among philosophers," Schiller continued, "the 'rationality' of a theory, when honestly examined, is found to consist largely in the appeal it makes to their taste, their sense of fitness and harmony, and in its consonance with their convictions about the non-cognitive values."[23] Philosophical standards of rational belief are themselves the outgrowth of the value judgments and desires of the people who formulate them. Philosophers who bemoan the influence of noncognitive values in evaluating beliefs are excessively "intellectualistic," "rationalistic," and blind to how beliefs express human needs, for beliefs "must be conceived in their biological setting as vital reactions and means of adjustment to the conditions of life."[24]

Furthermore, truth is not a supreme value that should always have priority when it conflicts with these other values. All values, including truth, are subordinate to the paramount good of survival. Indeed, all values derive from their conduciveness to life;[25] hence ultimately beliefs should be assessed as rational or unreasonable by reference to the standard of survival.

On this basis Schiller found much self-deception fully warranted. To the extent that it makes an important contribution to survival, it is a positive good. And it frequently does make a contribution as "an essential requisite of human life": "The ordinary man could hardly carry on, could he not delude himself into the belief that, in some ways at least, he was more than ordinary. A certain amount of self-deception, therefore, is universal and salutary."[26] Schiller added that we tend to overlook the extent of our self-deception because society encourages us not to express our inflated views of ourselves: "If a belief is vitally necessary, but its avowal is socially *tabu*, the only thing to do is to act on it, but to leave it unstated. It would be socially intolerable, for example, if every one inflicted on every one else his candid opinion of himself."[27]

Of course, not all self-deception is salutary. Where it threatens or handicaps life, it should be rejected. Many self-deceiving religious and political ideologies, for example, are an "unprofitable waste of energy and time" because they are merely paid lip service and not acted on.[28] Moreover, where self-deception lacks survival value it may be criticized on the basis of general values that are conducive to life. Here Schiller, like Bishop Butler, condemned as dishonest pharisaical beliefs about oneself and others.[29]

Unfortunately, Schiller's ethics of survival is too vague to provide much guidance for when self-deception should be criticized or condoned. It is often unclear whether "survival" means mere continued existence or whether it means effective functioning in life. The notion of effective functioning tacitly refers to some standard specifying the goals that ought to be sought, presumably goals transcending mere biological survival. Yet Schiller had little to say about the precise values that should have priority in assessing beliefs.

This difficulty was in part confronted and in part sidestepped by Jack Meiland in a provocative essay, "What Ought We to Believe? or The Ethics of Belief Revisited." While Meiland did not take himself to be defending self-deception, his conception of rationality implied conclusions about the reasonableness of self-deception that are even more striking than those of Schiller. Meiland made no attempt to establish any one value as ultimate and insisted that all of a person's values should be taken into account in assessing the rationality of his or her beliefs. When the person's concern for truth conflicts with other values, it is rational to let the concern for truth give way if the person values something else more. In fact, he contended that it is sometimes both rational and morally obligatory to form beliefs that fly in the face of evidence.

Meiland explained his view with two examples. The first concerned two business partners, Jones and Smith. Jones discovers hard evidence "which is sufficient (in anyone's eyes) to justify the belief" that Smith has been stealing money from their firm. He finds himself in the following dilemma:

> He is, and knows that he is, the type of person who is unable to conceal his feelings and beliefs from others. He thus knows that if he

decides that Smith has indeed been stealing money from the firm, it will definitely affect his behavior toward Smith. Even if Jones tries to conceal his belief, he knows that he will inevitably act in a remote, cold, censorious and captious manner toward Smith and that eventually both the friendship and the business partnership will break up.[30]

Jones hopes that his partner will voluntarily stop the thefts. But above all, he wants to sustain their close friendship. His solution is to get himself to believe that his partner is innocent and has never stolen money from the firm. The second example concerns a married couple:

Take the classical case in which a wife finds a blonde hair on her husband's coat, a handkerchief with lipstick on it in his pocket, a scrap of paper with a phone number scrawled on it, and so on until everyone would agree that the evidence is sufficient that the husband has been seeing another woman. However, the wife believes that their marriage is basically sound and can weather this storm. Like Jones, she knows that she cannot conceal her suspicions and hence decides to believe that her husband is not being unfaithful to her.[31]

Meiland said that both Jones and the wife were reasonable and fully justified in believing the opposite of what an impartial observer would have sufficient and compelling evidence to believe. Because their personalities rule out conscious pretense as an effective means of preserving their relationships and because they deeply value those relationships, it is rational for them flagrantly to disregard evidence. In general, individuals' values and personalities should be consulted in determining the amount and kinds of evidence needed to make their beliefs rational. This means that the relationship between beliefs and the evidence that warrants them is not a purely factual matter about what the data show to be true or probable. Instead, it is a normative relationship in which many values—not just a commitment to truth—should play an important role.

Therefore, Meiland concluded, if there is a "behavior which one ought to prevent oneself from engaging in," such as breaking up a friendship or love relationship, "and if one can . . . prevent this behavior by adopting a certain belief, then one ought to adopt that belief, apart from the epistemic warrant or lack thereof for that belief."[32] This holds for all kinds of "oughts," including "ethically ought" (for the sake of doing what is morally good or right) and "prudentially ought" (for the sake of one's own well-being).

At one point Meiland suggested that Jones and the wife are not self-deceivers because they do not conceal from themselves that they are forming beliefs contrary to what the evidence shows.[33] Yet our account of self-deception dictates otherwise. They are self-deceivers because they evade acknowledging to themselves what the evidence plainly establishes as true. This remains so even if they do not deceive themselves about their evasion of truth. Furthermore, Meiland implausibly portrayed Jones and the wife as simply "deciding" by fiat what they will believe. Even if that is possible in unusual cases, the vast majority of us could create the requisite belief only by engaging in self-deceiving tactics such as distracting attention from the evidence or rationalizing away its full import, as well as deceiving ourselves about our use of these tactics. In any case, Meiland suggested that his general argument remained unchanged even if self-deception is ascribed to Jones and the wife, and he implied that self-deception is justified and rational in such situations. This places him squarely in the Vital Lie Tradition.

One additional writer should be mentioned here because of his explicit and careful defense of the rationality of some self-deception that serves good ends. According to Robert Audi, self-deception is rational whenever "it advances, better than readily available alternatives, the person's rational wants; does not embody or produce irrational beliefs, wants, or actions, at least not in a way that outweighs its contribution to realization of the person's rational wants; and does not have an excessively high threshold of evidential eradication."[34] The last clause suggests that self-deception is not rational when it is so entrenched that presenting compelling evidence will not uproot it. Also, it suggests that self-deception is not rational insofar as it lowers responsiveness to evidence in general. Audi's main idea is that self-deception may be the best way to satisfy rational wants without generating irrational beliefs or producing bad side-effects concerning how we respond to evidence.

Audi offered the example of a woman who overcomes a paralyzing fear of public speaking by systematically putting the thought of the fear out of mind and replacing it with positive thoughts about her skills in speaking. Eventually she avows only confident thoughts about her speaking abilities. These avowals are sincere in that they do not involve intentional deceit, but they need not express genuine conviction or belief. Her fear remains, as does her knowledge of it, but both are largely kept unconscious. Her avowals are rational if they are motivated by the reasonable desire to view herself as competent and if the self-deception provides the most effective way of developing that sense of competency, given her personality and situation.

We have now covered enough ground to be able to summarize the central themes in the Vital Lie Tradition. They can be expressed in a list of nine theses.

(1) Because it is inevitable that factors other than evidence influence belief formation and because vital human needs are frequently served by self-deception, much self-deception is inescapable.

(2) People who are incapable of self-deception are probably incapable of romantic love and certain other forms of loyalty and dedication, or at least substantially less capable than they otherwise would be.

(3) The degree to which people ought to be guided by evidence and truth-centered desires (i.e., desires to obtain, acknowledge, and live by the truth) is not a purely factual matter. It can be decided only by a value judgment. Even if some people consistently choose to base their beliefs rigorously on the available evidence, they are still doing so because of a value commitment about what ought to guide belief formation.

(4) A good deal of self-deception is morally permissible, especially when its motives are morally permissible, its foreseeable consequences are not harmful, and no moral obligations are violated.

(5) Self-deception can be a morally admirable response, even a heroic response, to a difficult or tragic situation. Clearly this is so where altruism is the motive, other options are more undesirable, and an intended good is achieved through the self-deception.

(6) Occasionally people morally ought to engage in self-deception if there is no other realistic way for them to meet important moral obligations.

(7) Attacking or trying to remove the self-deceptions of other people can sometimes be mischievous, immoral, self-righteously hypocritical, or disastrous.

(8) It is often permissible and occasionally morally obligatory to encourage, support, or foster self-deception in other people, especially where the self-deception is a desperate last resort in coping with difficult situations or a stopgap in dealing with a crisis.

(9) It is reasonable to engage in self-deception when it provides the most effective way to avoid actions that morally ought not to be done. More generally, when self-deception is morally permissible and serves rational desires or needs, it is rational to engage in it so long as there are no overriding bad consequences in doing so and as long as no better options are available.

These theses fall into several different categories. (1) and (2) are psychological assertions, that is, claims about human minds and behavior. (3) is a conceptual claim about the relationship between beliefs and the evidence that warrants them. (4), (5), and (6) are moral evaluations of self-deceivers. (7) and (8) are moral evaluations of responses to other people's self-deception. And (9) is an evaluation of the rationality of self-deception. Most of these theses are plausible and insightful responses to excessively moralistic condemnations of self-deceivers. Yet a few caveats are needed.

First, concerning (6), I think it is extremely rare that morality actually obligates us to engage in self-deception. Reconsider in this connection Meiland's examples of the wife and business partner who he says ought to form beliefs that fly in the face of evidence sufficient to refute them. Allowing that their self-deception is morally permissible, it is too much to claim that they morally ought to deceive themselves. There is no general obligation for spouses to blind themselves to a partner's infidelity or betrayal, even in order to sustain a basically good marriage. If they do, they are making a special self-sacrifice—sometimes an admirable one, sometimes a foolish one—that goes beyond the requirements of duty. Similarly, the self-deception of the business partner who tries to protect his dishonest associate is at best super-erogatory, at worst a naïve effort to create good by shielding personal betrayal. There is also the question of just how much worth there can be in friendships and loves founded on deception about matters central to the relationship. Certainly there is a substantial good in trying to avoid self-deception in such matters.

Second, as concerns (8), it is a short step from justifying the indulgence of some self-deceptions in others to becoming complacent, indifferent, or patronizing. None of us is flattered to be regarded as unworthy of being presented with the truth (tactfully) as others see it. And most of the time there are reasonable and non–self-deceiving hopes that it would be preferable to support in others. Perhaps too often we support others' self-deception in order to avoid the difficulty in providing more substantial help that the truth, offered in the right way, would bring.

Third, I am unhappy with the suggestion in (9) that self-deception, understood as evading truth, is rational and fully reasonable without qualification. Granted, it can be reasonable according to the will-centered conception of rationality that stresses the satisfaction of legiti-mate desires and needs. Yet there remains the nagging sense that it is better if we do not need to engage in evading truth in order to satisfy legitimate desires.[35] By *better*, I do not mean morally better but only more rational. It would be more rational according to a richer ideal of a rational person than either the will-centered or the evidence-centered conceptions of rationality captured. What is this ideal?

It would complement and restrict will-centered rationality with what might be called *truth-centered rationality*. Truth-centered rationality is the ideal of forming true and justified beliefs and acknowledging truths relevant to one's endeavors. Unlike evidence-centered rationality, it does not go to the extreme of rejecting all faith and hope that leaps beyond the available evidence (as I shall discuss more fully in the next section). Moreover, the value of this ideal is distinct from morality per se, although its demands often overlap with the requirements of morality. (We could hardly meet our moral obligations without having considerable concern for truth!) Even though it may be morally permissible to sometimes evade the truth and even rational in the one limited respect of satisfying a need or legitimate desire in an efficient way, the evasion remains imperfectly rational, by definition, because it shows an imperfect commitment to acknowledging relevant truths.

What is the basis or justification for prizing truth-centered rationality? Some philosophers would locate it in the inherent worth of all truth or knowledge. Yet does all truth and knowledge have inherent worth? Much of it does, such as when it constitutes fundamental understanding or immediate delight—these things are worth having for their own sake. But I see no sense in saying it is intrinsically worthwhile for me to know that my pencil needs sharpening or that it is inherently good that it is true that whales are mammals. Knowing that my pencil needs sharpening is only instrumentally good because it enables me to sharpen it in order to continue writing. Truth-centered rationality does not require us to prize knowledge and truth per se but instead certain attitudes, commitments, and standards concerning truth.

These attitudes, commitments, and standards can be cited and elucidated but not reduced in meaning or importance to any more fundamental norms. Like moral, aesthetic, and other fundamental types of values, they make their own valid claims on us. Truth-centered rationality encompasses the values of clarity of thought, nonarbitrariness of belief, impartiality, relevance, consistency, respect for evidence, and rigor in argument. It also encompasses the intellectual virtues: intellectual honesty, intellectual courage, integrity of mind, devotion to living in light of the truth. These "values of reason," as R. S. Peters referred to them, make demands on us as rational beings that are not justifiable solely by reference to moral or other values.[36]

To say that the values of truth-centered rationality are in this sense fundamental is not, of course, to say that they are paramount or overriding in all situations. We have admitted that moral values sometimes make it morally permissible or even admirable to disregard their claims. Yet even when truth-centered rationality is legitimately sacrificed for other values, something significant is lost. There may be a fault or weakness in being unable to find a (nonmorally) better way to act which is consistent with the ideals of truth-centered rationality. But all this means is that we may have to be imperfectly (nonideally) rational on some occasions when morality conflicts with and is more pressing than an ideally perfect devotion to truth.

A similar response can be made with respect to what might be called the Paradox of Truth-Centered Rationality. Suppose that our desire is to obtain truth in a given area of inquiry but that the best way to satisfy this desire (given our psychological makeup and the situation) involves a self-deceiving evasion of certain other truths? For example, we might be more creative in our inquiries if we were to evade acknowledging some of our limitations or some of the difficulties in conducting the inquiries. For if we were fully aware of these limitations and difficulties then we would be discouraged from beginning the inquiries or sustaining them with vigor.[37] Here, ironically, a desire for truth is best served by evading truth, and it seems rational to be irrational. Does this mean that an unqualified commitment to truth-centered rationality is self-defeating or paradoxical in some self-contra-dictory way?

I think we must grant that occasionally there are truth-generating self-deceptions that are useful to the person dedicated to truth-centered rationality. Nothing is deeply puzzling, however, in admitting that a concern for obtaining some truths is at times best served by evasion of other truths. Nor is there a contradiction in recognizing that a person is in some ways rational and some respects not rational. In order to retain truth-centered rationality as a coherent ideal we need only insist that such truth-producing self-deceptions are still irrational in one respect. The Paradox of Truth-Centered Rationality merely forces us to acknowl-edge humbly our inability to pursue consistently this fundamental ideal. This attitude is, after all, in the spirit of the Vital Lie Tradition, which underscores the psychological limits on the pursuit of all ideals and insists that excessively idealistic demands are an evil against which we must guard ourselves.

FAITH, HOPE, AND IMAGINATION

I rejected the claim that self-deception is in all respects rational simply because it is morally permissible and serves human needs. I also mentioned the possibility that non–self-deceiving hope can often serve vital needs as effectively as self-deception while not conflicting with the ideal of truth-centered rationality (which is based on the commitment to acknowledge truth and refrain from evasion of it). But is truth-centered rationality a viable ideal that could generate vitality in most of us? Doesn't it encourage an overintellectualistic life devoid of vigor and the satisfaction of many important needs and desires? Would not trying to live by it render most of us emotionally impoverished by constraining us always to submit to hard facts? Would it not necessarily subvert love and enriching loyalties that seem to thrive when there is a willingness to leap beyond evidence?

Nothing in the ideal of truth-centered rationality forbids a variety of reasonable ways of transcending available evidence in forming beliefs, attitudes, and emotions. Three such avenues for fulfilling vital needs without having to engage in self-deception are especially significant: faith, hope, and imaginative expression.

Faith, as understood here, refers to a belief not based on evidence establishing it as true or even on a belief contrary to the main direction of evidence available to a person. In addition, the belief must be "active" in the sense of being expressed in behavior, statements, or emotions revealing trust in what is believed. When faith is *in* someone or something (its object), the object must be regarded as good in some respect. In this sense we have faith in the future success of a friend, the worth of our achievements and prospects, and the possibilities for world peace but not in the worthlessness of the present prison system. Faith, in short, is an active belief that goes beyond the evidence and is directed toward something perceived as good.

Clearly, faith can be formed and held in self-deception, that is, on the basis of evading truth or refusing to acknowledge to oneself what one knows or should know. It can also be grounded in unintentional wishful thinking, bias, fear, hate, or naïveté. Yet it is equally clear that faith need not involve self-deception at all, even where it leads to false beliefs. For although it entails going beyond the evidence in forming beliefs, it does not necessarily involve evasion of evidence, truth, or self-acknowledgment of how things appear to be.

In order to develop this point, let us consider William James's famous defense of faith in "The Will to Believe." With one qualification, I believe that James successfully defended the moral permissibility and reasonableness of some faith in a manner consistent with truth-centered rationality. His thesis was that individuals are warranted in believing what best expresses their vital needs or "passional nature" when they are confronted with a "genuine option" between propositions that cannot be decided by the available evidence. A genuine option has three features. It is forced in that upon confronting it one must pick one of the alternatives involved in the option ("Believe this proposition or go without it by disbelieving it or withholding judgment"). It is momentous in that something important turns on the decision. And it is composed of live options in that the person finds each alternative proposition somewhat tempting or possibly true. All of us confront many genuine options that cannot be resolved solely by the evidence, especially those involving moral and religious issues.

James first pointed out that it is a logical truth that such options must be resolved by factors other than evidence. By definition, the evidence is not decisive, and hence our "passional" nature must decide the matter, for it includes our desires, emotions, standards of rationality, and virtually all psychological influences on beliefs other than evidence. Whether we withhold judgment or adopt a faith in such situations is decided on the basis of these influences:

> Our passional nature not only lawfully may, but must, decide an option between propositions, whenever it is a genuine option that cannot by its nature be decided on intellectual grounds; for to say, under such circumstances, "Do not decide, but leave the question open," is itself a passional decision,—just like deciding yes or no,— and is attended with the same risk of losing the truth.[38]

Thus, if we always choose to avoid erroneous beliefs by forsaking faith, we are expressing a deep need not to be caught in error. If instead we adopt a faith, we may be expressing the desire to obtain the truth even at the risk of embracing error.

Which is the more reasonable belief policy: always avoid error at any cost by shunning faith or sometimes seek truth and risk error by adopting faith commitments? The latter policy is more reasonable, for without faith we lose too many goods worth having. Moral and religious beliefs offer rewarding possibilities for the human personality, even though evidence cannot prove them to be true. Equally important are some self-confirming or self-verifying faiths—beliefs that if acted upon make it more likely that they will become true. In particular, friendships and loves are generally initiated when one or both parties are willing to trust in the possibility of reciprocation of caring and affection. Doubting this from the outset will make us hesitant to offer appropriate overtures of warmth and kindness or make us unreceptive to offers of friendship. Again, most group endeavors presuppose a shared trust that others will keep their commitments, even though this trust is not warranted by hard evidence. And faith in our own abilities and commitments provides the confidence needed to invigorate the pursuit of our goals. In all these situations, acting on faith helps bring about the good we seek.

Unfortunately, James failed to add an important qualification at this point. He placed no restrictions on how faith should be formed and held. As a result, he left too much room for disregarding evidence and for using other self-deceiving evasions once one decides to pursue a faith commitment in response to a genuine option. This opens the door for his popularizers—the Dale Carnegies and Norman Vincent Peales— to encourage inflated self-confidence and vanity formed through self-indoctrination, self-hypnotism, naïveté, and blindness to the significant truths that are available to us.

Yet James's essential position can easily accommodate a strong caveat against these abuses of truth-centered rationality. After all, his central argument was inspired by his profound respect for truth. The rationale he gave for adopting faith expressing vital needs was to obtain important truths. In all of his writings, James stressed the importance of restraining faith with the virtues of an open mind, tolerance, and receptiveness to new evidence. He opposed dogmatism and cheap faith adopted for material benefit rather than concern for truth. With this in mind, "The Will to Believe" can be viewed as presenting a compelling defense of non–self-deceiving forms of faith that serve vital needs.

Hope is a second attitude that can serve vital needs without self-deception. It is a mark of hope that we are not certain that what we hope for will occur; nor are we certain it will not occur. We must, however, believe it is possible—not just logically possible but feasible or practicable (even though we do not understand how it is practicable). Like wishing, hope involves a desire for something, but only wishes can be for things believed to be impossible. I can wish, though not reasonably hope, that the people I love will not grow old and die, but I can hope that they will have long lives and die without suffering.

Yet there is more to hope than a desire for something believed to be possible. We must also be willing to live as if what we hope for will occur (or has occurred or is occurring). Unlike mere wishing, hope requires a kind of risk taking, whether expressed through actions, reasoning, emotions, or anticipation. The sincerity and intensity of hopes are measured by how much they enter into our lives. In fact, a person acting on the basis of hope may display exactly the same behavioral tendencies as someone who is fully convinced and has firm faith. For this reason entire religious perspectives can be founded on hope, rather than faith, even though for most believers the two are intertwined.[39]

Hope, then, is desiring something believed to be possible though not certain and living as if it will occur. A hope can be self-deceptive in three ways. It might be (1) based on self-deceptive beliefs about what is possible or probable (e.g., Pollyanna-like hopes); (2) based on self-deception about desires for what is hoped for (especially when we do not really want what we hope for); and (3) based on self-deception about the degree of our willingness to risk living as someone who has genuinely pinned hope on something (e.g., insincere hopes). The last form shades into self-deceiving beliefs that we have genuine hope rather than mere wishes (or, alternatively, full conviction).

Yet hope need not and commonly does not involve self-deception. It can serve essential needs in ways consistent with the commitment to truth at the heart of truth-centered rationality. Even though evidence does not establish the feasibility of what is hoped for or establish the truth of beliefs about its likelihood, rational hope does not contradict any warranted beliefs. And the rationality of hope is increased when evidence supports accompanying beliefs.

Hopes are appraised more in terms of the desires they embody than by reference to evidence. The hope to murder someone is an immoral hope; the hope to succeed in one's legitimate endeavors is morally permissible; and the hope that good people will receive their just rewards is morally admirable. In general it is immoral to sustain hopes that deflect us from meeting our obligations. It is also imprudent to maintain hopes that thwart self-fulfillment and to fail to hope for things more central to our basic needs.

Sustaining a capacity for reasonable hope enables us to fulfill vital needs without blinding ourselves to evidence or to the risks we take in transcending evidence. It provides an inexhaustible resource for attaching our lives to perceived goods. Hopes enliven us, give us reasons for living, bestow promise on our lives, and mobilize our energies. Perhaps there is even a duty to nurture hope when it is a prerequisite for evoking our moral commitment.

Imaginative expression is a third way to serve vital needs without self-deceptive evasions of evidence. This includes aesthetic experiences in response to art and nature, as well as daydreams, playful pretense, humor, and vicarious participation (as with fans who play out their athletic fantasies by identifying with their heroes).

Of special interest are the fantasies and aesthetic experiences in response to works of art that evoke our emotions.[40] These might be called *imaginative emotions*; that is, emotions whose objects (people, events, situations, and so on) are believed to be imaginary. Examples are the terror we feel while watching a Hitchcock movie, sadness in reading a Dickens novel, and hearty amusement in response to a Shakespearean comedy.

Imaginative emotions have at times puzzled philosophers. Some philosophers have denied the existence of such emotions on the ground that genuine emotions require a belief in the reality of the object of the emotion—for example, that to be afraid requires believing there is a real danger.[41] Because we know that the Hitchcock movie involves no real danger to us, we do not really feel fear as we watch it. Other philosophers have granted that we can experience fear and other emotions in response to fictional things but have contended that at the time we must temporarily believe, or half-believe (possibly through self-deception), that the object of the emotion exists.[42]

Both views seem to me mistaken. We are perfectly able to experience emotions by attending to an idea, imagined scene, or hypothesized event that we know (and fully believe) does not exist. Indeed, many of our most intense emotions have as their cognitive core imaginative attention rather than belief. Hitchcock's murder scenes are frightening to see and frightening to anticipate seeing, even though we know that our attention is gripped by the portrayal of a purely imaginary event.

Imaginative expression also includes fantasy, pretense, and non–self-deceptive self-pretense. For most of us, these forms of expression are occasional and episodic, but they can be ritualized and lasting. Consider in this connection Erie Smith in O'Neill's play *Hughie*.[43] Erie is a "teller of tales." Night after night he enjoys recounting fictitious stories about himself to a night clerk at a hotel. The clerk listens eagerly to Erie's boasting about being a big-time gambler, a ladies' man, and someone with ties to organized crime. Both Erie and the clerk know the stories are pretense, but the ritual helps bolster Erie's self-confidence and enlivens both of their nights. In general, all of us rely to some extent on daydreams, fantasies, pretense, and jokes to provide a healthy and non–self-deceptive expression of desires—desires for self-esteem, respect from others, comradeship, sex, and so on.

Some people are able to integrate their conscious self-pretense more fully into their lives than Erie Smith managed to do. They seem capable of guiding their lives by ideals they know are unattainable, all the while acting *as if* they were attainable. Friedrich Nietzsche emphasized this possibility with his doctrine of "conscious illusions." He suggested, for example, that acting as if we have free will (in a sense that places us outside the causal nexus) might inspire us to more vigorous action, even though we believe we are causally determined.[44] A more plausible example is that some individuals might pursue ideal visions of themselves, acting as if they could really attain their ideals, while knowing they cannot.[45] This knowledge precludes both faith and hope in achieving their ideals, but for these individuals imaginatively envisioning their ideal selves may carry the same inspirational force as faith and hope.[46]

HONESTY WITH ONESELF

Self-understanding makes possible meaningful life, especially morally significant life. At least that was the conviction of thinkers from Socrates to Butler and from Nietzsche and Kierkegaard to Sartre. Self-deception does not always undermine meaningful life, because imperfect self-understanding can be enough to make a life worth living and because self-deception occasionally adds zest to such a life. Morally significant life, however, does require us to make a large commitment to being honest with ourselves, for only self-honesty can overcome our self-made obstacles to self-understanding. In addition, devotion to self-honesty is itself one fundamental concern that bestows significance on life.

In this section I shall comment briefly on self-honesty and its relationship to self-understanding. In doing so, I will review some of the main themes from previous chapters.

Being honest with ourselves is difficult because evading truth is often attractive and easy. It is also difficult because it requires clarity about what self-deception is and about why, how, and when we engage in it. This study suggests that the relationship between self-deception and self-honesty is complex and is itself an ideal target for self-deception. Self-honesty has special importance in meeting moral obligations, in developing authenticity, and in attempting to explore the shadowy areas of our lives. Yet it needs to be balanced with other values, such as kindness and self-respect. With this in mind, what could be simpler than to adopt self-serving attitudes concerning self-deception: for example, to stress its role in serving legitimate needs in order to disguise the harm it supports; or to be lackadaisical about it in order to sustain inner hypocrisy; or to engage in self-righteous condemnations of it in others as a way of bolstering self-esteem?

Avoiding dishonesty with ourselves demands both more and less than avoiding all self-deception. It demands more because it also includes being loyal to oneself, not cheating or degrading oneself, and not betraying one's most significant aspirations and talents.[47] It demands less because it only requires avoiding unjustified instances of self-deception. Dishonest or morally unjustified self-deception undermines moral conscientiousness. In that sense it is a derivative wrong, that is, dishonest self-deception is wrong because it contributes to some particular fault: an immoral act, a bad habit or character trait, a morally unwarranted attitude or emotion. This was the ground explored by the Inner Hypocrisy Tradition. Members of that tradition also showed how self-deception can be inherently hypocritical because it inflates what a candid self-appraisal would reveal about one's character. In addition, when the fault involved is an instance of acting against one's better moral judgment, self-deception helps explain moral weakness. At the same time, self-deception can itself be viewed as moral weakness insofar as it constitutes a failure to act on one's capacity for honesty.

As the Authenticity Tradition showed, an expanded view of dishonest self-deception emerges if we adopt the ideal of authenticity. This ideal requires that we shape our character and lives autonomously on the basis of confronting significant truths and avoid passively modeling ourselves on social conventions or limiting ourselves to what we have been in the past. Because the significant truths emphasized in this tradition tend to be related to all aspects of life, more self-deception becomes suspect. Avoiding self-deception then becomes the key to achieving the primary goals of autonomy, such as developing individuality, employing one's talents, courageously affirming freedom, or fully accepting death.

Much self-deception, however, is neither dishonest nor otherwise immoral. The Vital Lie Traditon showed that it may be a necessary or expedient way of serving needs and important interests without harming anyone. In this role it is neither a paradigm of honesty or truth-centered rationality. Nor, however, is it necessarily dishonesty, for that term carries connotations of blameworthiness that are inappropriate here. Moreover, even when self-deception leads to harm and dishonesty, it might be the best compromise available in the situation and, therefore, excusable in whole or in part.

Some self-deception combines with neurosis and other mental illness to lessen capacities for honesty and effective moral agency. In extreme cases there is a drastically lessened ability to acknowledge evaded truths and to use them in practical reasoning. Once again, moral criticism needs to be tempered in light of mitigating factors. Special relationships of friendship or therapy can also make it appropriate to set aside moral evaluations, at least temporarily, in order to place us in a position to help. The Moral Ambiguity Tradition uncovered the complexity of these assessments of responsibility.

Each of the four traditions, then, conveys insights into when self-deceivers are or are not dishonest in morally culpable ways. Yet we also have rejected something in each tradition. A few writers in the Inner Hypocrisy Tradition, especially Kant and Clifford, exaggerated when they claimed that all self-deception is immoral. Similarly, some members of the Authenticity Tradition, notably Sartre, were intolerant when they condemned all self-deceivers on the basis of controversial claims about the significant truths and appropriate goals of autonomy. They also failed to establish authenticity as the sole or supreme value or even in all respects as a distinctively moral requirement (as opposed to a more inclusive ideal involving morality and other values). The Moral Ambiguity Tradition erred in viewing responsibility for self-deception as inherently ambiguous or opaque. And contrary to the Vital Lie Tradition, even useful self-deception remains a failure of rationality in a sense centered on the commitment to truth.

If deceiving ourselves is not always dishonest, can we at least say that avoiding self-deception is a mark of honesty? Granted, as the Vital

Lie Tradition showed, in a few situations it is morally best to deceive oneself. But even then, is it nevertheless a sign of honesty to avoid self-deception and, in that one respect, is it morally virtuous? Not necessarily. Avoiding or overcoming self-deception can be the direct means for achieving deeply immoral goals. Picture Hitler making a special effort not to deceive himself about the efficiency of his extermination camps. Perhaps he is tempted by other pressing war needs to cut corners, but he makes a special effort to be exceptionally rigorous about not evading any relevant truths concerning the means to achieving his fanatically anti-Semitic ends. Would that make him exceptionally honest in that one respect? Calling him honest would express approval or praise, and nothing about his conduct was praiseworthy. His avoidance of self-deception would only have accented the horror of what he was doing.

I do not mean to imply that honesty must actually serve morally acceptable ends. The world is such that honesty may inadvertently bring about more harm than would dishonesty. But the unproblematic labeling of individuals as honest for avoiding self-deception requires that they not have immoral motives for avoiding self-deception. Honest avoidance of self-deception can thus be thought of as a "dependent virtue"[48]—a virtue only when it is displayed in a context in which other virtues are present or at least certain vices are absent.

Where good motives are present, we might be willing to praise a person as honest even though the avoidance of self-deception contributes to beliefs or conduct of which we disapprove. For example, I am certain that some Jehovah's Witnesses display agonizing self-honesty in deciding that they and their children should die rather than accept blood transfusions, which are prohibited by their religion. In my view their decision is morally and tragically mistaken, and I support laws to protect their children. Yet they may be honest about relevant facts and honest in the way they form their convictions.

Moreover, even when the avoidance of self-deception can be called honest, such honesty need not be a specifically moral virtue. Consider artists who avoid self-deception about the quality of the ingredients for their pottery and do so for aesthetic reasons, such as to maximize the beauty or perceptual worth of their products. They are honest in that respect, but why consider that kind of honesty a morally admirable trait? It seems enough to say that they display craftsmanship or artistic integrity, which is admirable according to values other than specifically moral ones. Again, we take pains to avoid self-deception while making career choices because we know our personal happiness depends on it. Prudence requires it, and that is why we do it. We are honest, but not necessarily in a morally admirable way. Avoiding self-deception, in short, is neither always honest nor, when it is honest, always morally admirable.

At this point it is perhaps tempting to follow Aristotle in distinguishing between two kinds of virtue or human excellences: moral and intellectual.[49] The latter might include intellectual honesty, intellectual courage, and perhaps craftsmanship. Yet this simple dichotomy blurs as much as it clarifies. Surely intellectual honesty and courage—that is, honesty and courage about truth—are moral virtues when they serve to sharpen moral understanding and to provide strength in confronting onerous moral requirements. As often as not, honesty functions simultaneously as a moral virtue and an intellectual virtue of reason, and there is usually no need to segregate them into two categories of value.

This study allows that beyond the duty incumbent on us all to avoid dishonest self-deception, there is a highly personal dimension to honesty in avoiding self-deception. Individuals are free to commit themselves to self-honesty to a degree surpassing minimal moral requirements. Doing so may be highly admirable (morally or otherwise), assuming it does not cause overshadowing faults. It may even be a supererogatory achievement, producing good beyond the demands of common duty.

As an example, consider the life of Ludwig Wittgenstein, whose revolutionary contributions to philosophy emerged from his single-minded devotion to truth.[50] This devotion led him to give away his inherited fortune, resign a distinguished professorship at Cambridge, shun the artificial constraints of conventional society, and lead an austere life devoid of distractions from this writing. Everyday self-pretense, especially that based on the human "edifice of pride" that pollutes openness to love and fresh ideas,[51] undermined (in his view) honesty in writing philosophy: "If you are *unwilling* to know what you are, your writing is a form of deceit";[52] "you cannot write anything about yourself that is more truthful than you yourself are."[53] But self-honesty can also require testing ourselves in action to see whether we are living a lie. This requirement led Wittgenstein to volunteer to be a soldier in order to confront death and thereby gain a perspective on what truly makes life worthwhile. In general, his conduct and attitudes transcended whatever minimal requirements of self-honesty are incumbent on all of us.

In the last section, I mentioned three resources for promoting vital needs without self-deception: faith, hope, and imaginative expression. Reflection on Wittgenstein, and others like him, suggests an even more direct resource: the capacity for basing self-esteem on a commitment to self-honesty. Self-esteem is a fundamental need in reflective beings, because without it there may be little concern for satisfying other vital

needs. Fortunately, it is also highly malleable in that the basis for it can
be shaped in many ways. One way is to base self-esteem on a quest for
self-honesty and the will to avoid dishonest forms of self-deception.
After all, the need for self-esteem usually generates a desire to value
ourselves for what we really are. We want our characters and lives to
have genuine significance, not a mere shadowy illusion of worth.
Placing a commitment to self-honesty at the heart of our self-esteem
assures us of a sense of self-worth and serves as a way to increase self-
understanding.

Self-understanding is not the possession of a handful of doctrines
and maxims. Much less is it a process of amassing more and more facts.
Mere snippets of information contribute little to self-understanding, and
accumulating such snippets can (as Kierkegaard warned) create a rubble
that conceals our true selves. To understand ourselves morally is in part
to discern significant truths from appropriate moral perspectives without distortion by self-deception and in part to make appropriate adjustments in character.

Self-understanding involves self-acknowledgment of our motives in
important areas of our lives (for example, in personal relationships,
career choices, religion), as well as acknowledgment of our primary
commitments, our main faults and strengths, and our status as biological and social creatures. These things have special significance in
increasing the meaning we find in life. In fact, just as self-understanding
is a prerequisite for a worthwhile life, our vision of a worthwhile life
shapes our conception of self-understanding.

In order to be fully acknowledged, as we noted in Chapter 2,
significant facts must be integrated into how we respond to ourselves
and the world. Kierkegaard had this in mind in commenting on the
Socratic faith that moral knowledge and virtue go together: " 'If they
truly had understood, their lives would have expressed it, they would
have done what they understood.' To understand/and to understand
are therefore two things? Certainly they are."[54] Psychological integration leads to increased inner unity not in the sense of removing all inner
conflicts but in providing a general continuity within a personality
whose various aspects have been thoroughly interrelated in consciousness and action.

The need for these adjustments partially explains why self-understanding cannot be produced solely by introspective peering into one's
stream of consciousness. In addition, the raw data uncovered by
introspection have no special status by themselves because they must be
actively interpreted in light of significant truths. Insight comes only as
we look outward to the full social context that gives meaning to both our
inner states and our outward behavior.[55] And rather than simply

peering into the shadowy areas of immediate consciousness, we would do best to integrate into our lives the insights from science, philosophy, art, literature, religious thought, and other disciplines.

Hence there is no easy path to achieving self-understanding. Nor is there a sure test for when we are being honest with ourselves, although habits of disciplined and imaginative thought certainly help. T. S. Eliot was exaggerating when he wrote,

> We are only undeceived
> Of that which, deceiving, could no longer harm.[56]

Yet it is virtually impossible not to be sometimes self-deceived in ways that cause harm to ourselves or to others. At the same time, as Eliot also reminded us, cynical musing on our inevitable failures carries its own brand of self-deceit about the good that can be achieved:

> Disillusion can become itself an illusion
> If we rest in it.[57]

Epilogue

In theory the appeal to universal truth is an appeal to common principles that all men [and women] can understand on equal terms. *In practice,* it is a divisive instrument for exacerbating conflict and arbitrarily restricting the range of action in which there can, among men [and women] of diverse faiths and loyalties, be shared understanding and mutual respect.

        —Arthur E. Murphy, *The Theory of Practical Reason*

We ensnare ourselves in paradox when we focus on the expression *self-deception* in abstraction from the practical contexts in which it functions and while gripped by the model of deceiving other people. This paradox, in turn, inspires skepticism about the coherence and importance of the concept of deceiving oneself. I have tried to dispel this paradox and skepticism by exploring the natural habitat in which the concept evokes our practical interests. That habitat is not the den of the logician, the epistemologist, or even the philosopher of mind. Instead, it comprises several rich moral traditions wherein self-deception is understood to be a major thread in unraveling what it is to be a responsible human being. I have also resisted other forms of skepticism: for example, skepticism about the possibilities of holding self-deceivers responsible, of meeting vital needs without sacrificing concern for truth, and of objective reasons in morality.

Nevertheless, renouncing theoretical, skeptical doubts does not dispel inevitable practical doubts. As with all fundamental modes of human behavior, uncertainty often arises concerning our motives for engaging in self-deception, our motives for criticizing others for it, the extent of our responsibility for the harm it causes, and the appropriate occasions and means for surmounting it. In this concluding note, I wish to comment on another source of practical doubt: uncertainty about the moral values that form the basis for judgments about self-deception.

It is a truism, first stated by Aristotle,[1] that morality cannot be expressed with mathematical precision and certainty. The complexity of human personalities, the diversity of situations, and the multitude of moral values combine to make it inevitable that values will come into conflict, creating dilemmas that lack clear solutions. In fact, two millennia of philosophical discussion suggest that matters are worse than Aristotle envisioned. Not only are values imprecise and subject to tragic conflicts, they also enter into morally coherent systems among which there are sometimes irresolvable differences.[2] Disputes among ethicists over fundamental moral principles are not temporary stages on the road to some grand theory that any rational person would have to accept. Instead they reflect ultimate differences in how reasonable and responsible persons might balance valid moral claims. This diversity of moral perspective does not preclude fruitful dialogue and reason-giving across perspectives.[3] But it does foreclose anything like complete moral agreement among all morally sensitive people. It also has implications for applying the concept of self-deception within moral disputes.

The Inner Hypocrisy Tradition presupposed considerable agreement about the values used in criticizing self-deceivers. It assumed a set of moral truths that all of us would acknowledge insofar as we are not biased and evasive. But to the extent that there is reasonable doubt about these values, there is uncertainty about when self-deceivers ought to be condemned. Moreover, there is a deeper problem. Uncertainty about specific values may make it questionable whether people are even self-deceived about them in the first place (let alone whether the people should be morally criticized).

As an illustration, consider the accusation made by the anti-abortionist: "You are committing or supporting murder, and deep in your heart you know it. You are willfully deceiving yourself about truths that any sensitive person must appreciate." Likewise, consider the pro-abortionist's rejoinder: "It is you who are self-deceived about your cruelty in violating the freedom of women to control their bodies and lives and in adding to their suffering over what is already a sufficiently difficult decision. Your alleged concern for human life masks a misogyny that you are unwilling to acknowledge to yourself."

Emotionally charged accusations like these, made in the midst of heated moral controversy, carry considerable rhetorical force. They assert a double condemnation: moral insensitivity and dishonest self-deception about that insensitivity. Yet the accusations are often doubly inappropriate. They deflect attention from serious argument concerning the primary moral issues, and they also erode any hope for mutual understanding and tolerance. The primary issues in the abortion controversy center on how to weigh the conflicting values involved, especially the values of respect for human life and respect for women's freedom.[4] Accusations of self-deception in this context usually presuppose that the opponents would understand and weigh the relevant values in precisely the same manner if they were being fully honest. Yet deeply honest and reflective individuals do differ—this is a stubborn fact that honesty requires us to admit. Over-eagerness to invoke the notion of self-deception may be little more than a symptom of our frustration over being unable to persuade others to agree with us, or it may be a sign of insensitivity to their genuine moral concern.

Much the same can be said about more far-reaching differences among moral and religious interpretations of life. Recall from Chapter 3, for example, the clash between Nietzsche's and Scheler's attitudes toward Christianity. Nietzsche held that it is grounded in self-deceiving *ressentiment* by the weak. Scheler denied this, contending that Christian virtues are an expression of moral and psychological strength. Recall also the enduring disputes concerning the rationality of belief in God: some theists charge that atheists are guilty of hubris in self-deceivingly refusing to humble themselves before God, and some atheists (such as Freud, Marx, and Sartre) charge that theists self-deceivingly embrace comforting illusions. Such sweeping analyses of motives are outrageous, even though of course *some* Christians, theists, and atheists are correctly analyzed by each party to these disputes. Accuracy is possible only by moving from general claims about collective self-deception to the examination of specific individuals. More important, these disputes set up barriers of prejudice that undermine tolerance—a primary virtue within morally pluralistic societies—and also prevent the enrichment of appreciating alternative religious and cultural traditions.

The Authenticity Tradition generated a related difficulty. At first glance it seemed to bypass such disputes by moving away from an emphasis on objective moral values. Yet most members of this tradition proceeded to build into their concepts of authenticity certain "significant truths" that they felt had to be acknowledged by all reasonable and honest individuals. Almost always the alleged truths turned out to be highly controversial assumptions that could not be established by evidence convincing to all reasonable people. Furthermore, even if they could have been established as true, the insistence that they were so significant that all honest people had to acknowledge them and that failure to do so was the height of immorality expressed a dubious value judgment. As a result, *authenticity* became a weapon of intolerant moral condemnation, if not flagrant moral presumption. For this reason I recommended an alternative conception of authenticity that did not require acknowledging any specific philosophical theses but instead advocated the autonomous confrontation of important topics and issues.

It might seem that matters should improve when we diagnose self-deception in ourselves about our own moral values, for here we need not grapple with the special difficulties in bridging the chasm between two personalities. Unfortunately, however, new difficulties arise. In identifying self-deception in ourselves we can be even more biased, and we lose the advantages in identifying bias provided by psychological distance. Worse yet, we have to deal more intimately with conflicts within our own value perspectives, especially at times when we undergo changes in our values.

Value changes deserve emphasis. Nowhere is honesty with ourselves more important than in revising our values. It is precisely then that we may have the greatest difficulty in diagnosing our self-deception. Most of us learned this while making the treacherous transition from youth to early adulthood. While doing so, we had to modify the ideals instilled in us by parents and peers. Some of us had to substantially modify or outgrow faith in a religion that had become intellectually and morally crippling.

These changes were at times overwhelming. In modifying inherited beliefs and attitudes, we retained our need for the emotional moorings they supplied. There were moments when we seemed to ourselves to be dishonestly evading appropriate new commitments and other moments when we felt dishonest in rebelling against people and relationships worth preserving. All the while, feelings of guilt played havoc: irrational guilt deriving from attitudes that we were right to outgrow, and warranted guilt for genuine failings. Our recurring sense of lying to ourselves was in part appropriate, but in part it was a symptom of irrational guilt based on childhood influences. Perhaps overall we did our honest best to reshape attitudes and commitments into a mature value perspective. But how were we to know this at the time? Accurately diagnosing our honesty and our dishonesty required a background of stable values that could serve as a'target for self-acknowledgment and evasion. But it was precisely such stability that was in the process of being established.

These difficulties are not unique to moral and religious values. They pertain as well to personal tastes and attitudes. When we fall in love, to use a singularly important example, we seem to others, or even to ourselves (at moments),[5] to misunderstand the beloved: to exaggerate virtues, downplay vices, bestow a degree of attention out of proportion to what the person seems objectively to deserve. To be sure, love is notoriously fertile ground for both willful self-deception and unintentional bias. Much of love's vision, however, has nothing to do with self-deception or bias about the beloved's "true" worth—whatever that may be. Love is a value-bestowing passion.[6] It can be blind, but it is more often a transforming creative vision. Still, it can be virtually impossible at times for us as lovers to sort out the elements of willful self-deception and unintentional bias from the heightened evaluation inherent in love.

Whether uncertainty and conflict pertain to diverse moralities within a community or to the commitments of an individual, they should caution us about hasty ascriptions of self-deception (to others or to ourselves). They should also remind us again of the importance of social tolerance and self-acceptance. When values are indeterminate in ways that make it uncertain whether acknowledgment of them is being evaded, we had best remain focused on the difficult task of reasoning about those values themselves and restrain our eagerness to attack one another (or ourselves).

These considerations, however, should not serve as an occasion for easing once more into the quagmire of skepticism. For there remain at least four areas in which ascriptions of self-deception about moral requirements retain firm footing, even when the precise extent of the requirements is in doubt.

First, doubt about how to balance conflicting values should not extend to uncertainty about whether any relevant moral considerations exist. After all, the very possibility of moral dilemmas arising through the clash of values presupposes that there are such values. And "before our reasons can conflict, there must first of all *be* reasons."[7] Often there is little difficulty in identifying how an individual's obvious biases form the basis for an evasion of attention to one set of valid moral considerations or to one side of an issue.

Second, in our discussion of authenticity we distinguished self-deception about specific propositions (including those about values) from self-deception about topics and issues. Whereas there may be enormous doubt about who has the correctly reasoned judgment on a particular issue, there may be little doubt about who lacks any reasoned judgment at all or about who is evading entire topics. One of the greatest frustrations of the applied ethicist is dealing with people who shut their minds to entire areas of moral concern or who refuse to acknowledge to themselves that there is a major issue that ought to evoke their attention. This includes glaring contemporary moral issues ranging from world hunger to women's rights to the dangers of nuclear deterrence, to give but a few examples.

Third, usually we can distinguish values from the facts relevant to applying them. It may be doubtful whether a person is self-deceived directly about values but clear that the person is evading the facts or related evidence.

Fourth, whereas accusations of self-deception often imply that the accused holds a false belief, when suitably qualified they need not. They may only imply that individuals are evading the views they would acknowledge if they were considering an issue fairly and honestly. Sometimes we can discern this evasion without having to establish whether what is being evaded is the moral truth.

These four areas suffice to ensure the cogent application of the concept of self-deception to morality. There is no need to postulate a universal consensus among ideally rational and morally responsible individuals about all fundamental principles. Faith in that consensus has motivated the development of many insightful ethical theories, even though none of them has fully succeeded. It has also been used to support a terrifying history of dogmatism and cruelty. The concept of self-deception has a similarly mixed record. It has been used irresponsibly as both a weapon and an obfuscating device. It has also been used as a constructive tool for understanding moral responsibility. Exploring *self-deception* in both these roles deepens our grasp of moral complexity and enriches our appreciation of moral diversity.

Notes

CHAPTER 2. EVADING SELF-ACKNOWLEDGMENT

1. Gilbert Geis, "The Heavy Electrical Equipment Antitrust Cases of 1961," in *White Collar Crime*, ed. Gilbert Geis and Robert F. Meier (New York: Free Press, 1977), 117–132; John Herling, *The Great Price Conspiracy* (Washington, D.C.: Robert B. Luce, 1962).

2. Leo Tolstoy, *Anna Karenina*, trans. David Magarshack (New York: New American Library, 1961). Quotations are from pages 154–161, 211–223, and 286–290.

3. Raphael Demos, "Lying to Oneself," *Journal of Philosophy* 57 (1960): 588–595.

4. John Turk Saunders, "The Paradox of Self-Deception," *Philosophy and Phenomenological Research* 35 (1975): 559–570. Cf. Ruben C. Gur and Harold A. Sackeim, "Self-Deception: A Concept in Search of a Phenomenon," *Journal of Personality and Social Psychology* 37 (1979): 147–169. Two writers, however, have appealed to unconscious beliefs while denying that self-deceivers must also hold a conflicting conscious belief: Robert Audi, "The Epistemic Authority of the First Person," *Personalist* 56 (1975): 5–15; "Self-Deception, Action, and Will," *Erkenntnis* 18 (1982): 133–158; "Self-Deception and Rationality," in *Self-Deception and Self-Understanding*, ed. Mike W. Martin (Lawrence: University Press of Kansas, 1985), 169–194; and D. W. Hamlyn, "Self-Deception," *Proceedings of the Aristotelian Society* 45 (1971): 45–60.

5. Ronald B. De Sousa, review of *Self-Deception* by Herbert Fingarette, *Inquiry* 13 (1970): 308–321.

6. Jeffrey Foss, "Rethinking Self-Deception," *American Philosophical Quarterly* 17 (1980): 237–243.

7. Amélie Oksenberg Rorty, "Belief and Self-Deception," *Inquiry* 15 (1972): 387–410.

8. David Pugmire, " 'Strong' Self-Deception," *Inquiry* 12 (1969): 339–346.

9. John V. Canfield and Don F. Gustavson, "Self-Deception," *Analysis* 23 (1962): 32–36.

10. Béla Szabados, "Self-Deception," *Canadian Journal of Philosophy* 4 (1974): 51-68; "The Self, Its Passions and Self-Deception," in Martin, *Self-Deception and Self-Understanding*, 143-168; and R. Lance Factor, "Self-Deception and the Functionalist Theory of Mental Processes," *Personalist* 58 (1977): 115-123. Also see Charles B. Daniels, "Self-Deception and Interpersonal Deception," *Personalist* 55 (1974): 244-252.

11. Stanley Paluch, "Self-Deception," *Inquiry* 10 (1967): 268-278.

12. Frederick A. Siegler, "An Analysis of Self-Deception," *Noûs* 2 (1968): 147-164.

13. Terence Penelhum, "Pleasure and Falsity, " *American Philosophical Quarterly* 1 (1964): 81-91.

14. H. O. Mounce, "Self-Deception," *Proceedings of the Aristotelian Society* 45 (1971): 61-72.

15. Other writers who departed from an exclusive emphasis on "belief" include Herbert Fingarette, *Self-Deception* (Atlantic Highlands, N.J.: Humanities Press, 1969); M. R. Haight, *A Study of Self-Deception* (Sussex: Harvester Press; and Atlantic Highlands, N.J.: Humanities Press, 1980); Kent Bach, "An Analysis of Self-Deception," *Philosophy and Phenomenological Research* 41 (1981): 351-370; and John King-Farlow, "Self-Deceivers and Sartrian Seducers," *Analysis* 23 (1963): 131-136. As will be seen in Chapter 5, Herbert Fingarette was the primary influence on my conception of self-deception.

16. Cf. Stanley Cavell, "Knowing and Acknowledging," in *Must We Mean What We Say?* (New York: Charles Scribner's Sons, 1969), 257; and *The Claim of Reason* (New York: Oxford University Press, 1982), 428.

17. George Eliot, *Middlemarch* (New York: New American Library, 1964), 413.

18. Cf. Richard S. Lazarus, "Cognitive and Coping Processes in Emotion," in *Stress and Coping*, ed. Alan Monat and Richard S. Lazarus (New York: Columbia University Press, 1977), 150.

19. Cf. Patrick Gardiner, "Error, Faith and Self-Deception," *Proceedings of the Aristotelian Society* 70 (1969-70): 239.

20. Cf. Hamlyn, "Self-Deception," 52; Alan R. Drengson, Critical Notice of H. Fingarette's *Self-Deception, Dialogue: Canadian Journal of Philosophy* 12 (1973): 146; and Robert Brown, "Integrity and Self-Deception," *Critical Review* 25 (1983): 126.

21. Cf. C. D. Broad, *The Mind and Its Place in Nature* (London: Routledge and Kegan Paul, 1925), 367.

22. Haight, *A Study of Self-Deception*, 8-9, 35-36, 73. Also see her "Tales from a Black Box," in Martin, *Self-Deception and Self-Understanding*, 244-260.

23. Cf. T. S. Champlin, "Double Deception," *Mind* 85 (1976): 102.

24. Cf. Gardiner, "Error, Faith and Self-Deception," 243.

25. Cf. Ludwig Wittgenstein: "A picture held us captive. And we could not get outside it, for it lay in our language and language seemed to repeat it to us inexorably." *Philosophical Investigations*, 3rd edition, trans. G. E. M. Anscombe (New York: Macmillan, 1953), Remark 115.

26. John Canfield and Patrick McNally, "Paradoxes of Self-Deception," *Analysis* 21 (1961): 140-144.

27. George Orwell, *1984* (New York: New American Library, 1961), 32-33. Cf. p. 176. Amélie Rorty's application of the idea of referential opacity can be used to elucidate doublethink, although I think not to understand most self-deception as she suggests in "Belief and Self-Deception." Also see Mike W.

Martin, "Demystifying Doublethink: Self-Deception, Truth, and Freedom in *1984*," *Social Theory and Practice* 10 (1984): 319–331.

28. H. H. Price, *Belief* (New York: Humanities Press, 1969), 299–301.

29. Cf. Price, *Belief*, 302–314; and Benzion Chanowitz and Ellen Langer, "Self-Protection and Self-Inception," in Martin, *Self-Deception and Self-Understanding*, 117–135. Chanowitz and Langer expressed skepticism about the presence of purposefulness in such cases.

30. Theodor Reik, *Listening with the Third Ear* (New York: Arena Books, 1972).

31. Alfred Adler, *The Individual Psychology of Alfred Adler*, ed. Heinz L. Ansbacher and Rowena R. Ansbacher (New York: Harper and Row, 1964), 260. Also see Karen Horney's *Neurosis and Human Growth* (New York: W. W. Norton, 1950).

32. Cf. Stuart Hampshire, Critical Review of *The Concept of Mind*, in *Ryle*, ed. Oscar P. Wood and George Pitcher (Garden City, N.Y.: Anchor Books, 1970), 39.

33. David Hume, *A Treatise of Human Nature*, ed. L. A. Selby-Bigge (Oxford: Clarendon Press, 1968), 636. Cf. D. M. Armstrong, *Belief, Truth and Knowledge* (Cambridge: Cambridge University Press, 1973), 105.

34. William Shakespeare, *Othello, The Moor of Venice*, act 3, sc. 3.

35. John C. Nemiah, *Foundations of Psychopathology* (New York: Jason Aronson, 1973), 21, 169.

36. R. D. Laing, *The Divided Self* (Baltimore: Penguin Books, 1973).

37. Jean-Paul Sartre, *Being and Nothingness*, trans. Hazel E. Barnes (New York: Washington Square Press, 1966), 89.

38. Ibid.

39. Ibid., 83.

40. Richard Reilly, "Self-Deception: Resolving the Epistemological Paradox," *Personalist* 57 (1976): 393.

41. David Hume, *A Treatise of Human Nature*, 624. Cf. Bernard Mayo, "Belief and Constraint," in *Knowledge and Belief*, ed. A. Phillips Griffiths (Oxford: Oxford University Press, 1967), 153. Other philosophers have held that only rational beliefs are entirely nonvoluntary: e.g., H. H. Price, "Belief and Will," in *Philosophy of Mind*, ed. Stuart Hampshire (New York: Harper and Row, 1966), 106–111; Bernard Williams, "Deciding to Believe," in *Problems of the Self* (Cambridge: Cambridge University Press, 1973), 148; and C. K. Grant, *Belief and Action* (Durham: University of Durham, 1960), 15. The issues about willful belief were helpfully sorted by Robert Holyer, "Belief and Will Revisited," *Dialogue: The Canadian Philosophical Review* 22 (1983): 273–290.

42. Immanuel Kant, *The Doctrine of Virtue*, trans. Mary J. Gregor (Philadelphia: University of Pennsylvania Press, 1964), 94.

43. Ibid.

44. Ibid., 104.

45. E.g., King-Farlow, "Self-Deceivers and Sartrian Seducers," 131–136. Also see David Pears's discussion of Freud's and Donald Davidson's ways of distinguishing a "main" self from a subself in *Motivated Irrationality* (New York: Oxford University Press, 1984), 68ff. Davidson's view was akin to Fingarette's view. See Donald Davidson, "Paradoxes of Irrationality," in *Philosophical Essays on Freud*, ed. Richard Wollheim and James Hopkins (Cambridge: Cambridge University Press, 1982), 289–305.

46. David Kipp, "On Self-Deception," *Philosophical Quarterly* 30 (1980): 315. Also see his essay, "Self-Deception, Inauthenticity, and Weakness of Will," in Martin, *Self-Deception and Self-Understanding*, 261–283.

47. Cf. Szabados, "The Self, Its Passions and Self-Deception," in Martin, *Self-Deception and Self-Understanding*, 143–168.
48. Fingarette, *Self-Deception*, 1.
49. Ibid., 136.

CHAPTER 3. INNER HYPOCRISY

1. Plato, *Cratylus*, trans. Benjamin Jowett, in *The Collected Dialogues of Plato*, ed. Edith Hamilton and Huntington Cairns (Princeton, N.J.: Princeton University Press, 1961), 462. Also see *Republic*, op. cit., 629.
2. Aristotle, *Nicomachean Ethics*, trans. W. D. Ross, in *The Basic Works of Aristotle*, ed. Richard McKeon (New York: Random House, 1941), Book III, Ch. 5. For an insightful recent discussion see Holly Smith, "Culpable Ignorance," *Philosophical Review* 92 (1983): 543–571.
3. Reverend Daniel Dyke, *The Mystery of Selfe-Deceiving, or a Discourse and Discovery of the Deceitfulness of Man's Heart* (London, 1630), 8. A copy was kindly made available to me by the Department of Special Collections, A 1713 University Research Library, University of California, Los Angeles.
4. St. Thomas Aquinas, *Summa Theologiae* (New York: McGraw-Hill, 1964), vol. 25, 155. Cf. Obadiah 3, "The pride of thine heart hath deceived thee," and John 1:8, "If we say that we have no sin, we deceive ourselves, and the truth is not in us."
5. Joseph Butler, *The Works of Joseph Butler*, ed. W. E. Gladstone (Oxford: Clarendon Press, 1896), Vol. II, 19. Cf. Adam Smith: "This self-deceit, this fatal weakness of mankind, is the source of half the disorders of human life." (*The Theory of Moral Sentiments* [New York: Augustus M. Kelley, 1966], 223 [first published in 1759]).
6. Joseph Butler, "Upon the Character of Balaam," "Upon Self-Deceit," and the third of the *Six Sermons*, all in *The Works of Joseph Butler*. Part of what follows is taken from my essay, "Immorality and Self-Deception," *Dialogue: Canadian Philosophical Review* 16 (1977): 274–280.
7. Cognitive dissonance theory was developed in part to explain such tendencies. See Leon Festinger, *The Theory of Cognitive Dissonance* (Stanford, Calif.: Stanford University Press, 1957).
8. Max Scheler, *Ressentiment*, ed. Lewis A. Coser, trans. William W. Holdheim (New York: Schocken Books, 1972), 60.
9. Friedrich Nietzsche, *Genealogy of Morals*, in *Basic Writings of Nietzsche*, ed. and trans. Walter Kaufmann (New York: Modern Library), First Essay, Section 8, 470–471.
10. Scheler, *Ressentiment*, 83–113.
11. Butler, *Works*, 318–319; Reinhold Niebuhr, *The Nature and Destiny of Man*, Vol. 1: *Human Nature* (New York: Charles Scribner's Sons, 1961), 203–207. Cf. Philip Leon, *The Ethics of Power, or The Problem of Evil* (London: George Allen and Unwin), Chapter 9.
12. Albert Speer, *Inside the Third Reich*, trans. Richard Winston and Clara Winston (New York: Avon Books, 1971), 481. For a challenge to the trustworthiness of these memoirs, see Matthias Schmidt, *Albert Speer: The End of a Myth*, trans. Joachim Neugroschel (New York: St. Martin's Press, 1984).
13. Speer, *Inside the Third Reich*, 480–481. Cf. David Burrell and Stanley Hauerwas, "Self-Deception and Autobiography: Theological and Ethical Reflec-

tions on Speer's *Inside the Third Reich,*" *Journal of Religious Ethics* 2 (1974): 99–117; and Marcus K. Billson, "Inside Albert Speer: Secrets of Moral Evasion," *Antioch Review* (1979): 460–474.

14. Butler, *Works,* 177–178.

15. Kant, *The Doctrine of Virtue,* 94–95.

16. Ibid.

17. William Kingdon Clifford, "The Ethics of Belief," in *Lectures and Essays of W. K. Clifford,* ed. Leslie Stephen and Frederick Pollock, Vol. 2 (London: Macmillan, 1879), 186.

18. Ibid., 177–178.

19. Fyodor Dostoyevsky, *The Brothers Karamazov,* trans. Constance Garnett (New York: New American Library, 1957), 49.

20. Kant, *The Doctrine of Virtue,* 104.

21. Ibid., 94.

22. Ibid., 92–93.

23. Elsewhere Kant seemed aware of this. He restricted the term *self-deception* to culpable forms of evasion of self-acknowledgment, thereby making his negative view of self-deception true by definition. He suggested that a "blameless deluding of ourselves" sometimes serves virtue, such as when by pretending to be virtuous we inadvertently become virtuous and thereby "deceive the deceiver in ourselves" (*Anthropology from a Pragmatic Point of View,* ed. Hans H. Rudnick, trans. Victor Lyle Dowdell [Carbondale: Southern Illinois University Press, 1978], 37–38).

24. *The Doctrine of Virtue,* 93.

25. Wittgenstein, *Philosophical Investigations,* 90. Also see 11–12.

26. W. D. Falk, "Morality, Self, and Others," in *Morality and the Language of Conduct,* ed. Hector-Neri Castañeda and George Nakhnikian (Detroit: Wayne State University Press, 1965), 50.

27. Ibid., 51.

28. Cf. Ronald D. Milo, *Immorality* (Princeton, N.J.: Princeton University Press, 1984), 85, 98, 106–113.

29. Butler, *Works,* 318–319.

30. Cf. Marcel Eck, *Lies and Truth,* trans. Bernard Murchland (New York: Macmillan, 1970), 68.

31. Eva Feder Kittay disagrees and is willing to speak of blameless "victim hypocrites." See "On Hypocrisy," *Metaphilosophy* 13 (1982): 285–286.

32. Cf. Judith Shklar, "Let Us Not Be Hypocritical," *Daedalus* 108 (1979): 4. Reprinted in Shklar's *Ordinary Vices* (Cambridge: Belknap Press of Harvard University Press, 1984), 45–86.

33. Cf. Kittay, "On Hypocrisy," 285–286.

34. Cf. Adler, *The Individual Psychology of Alfred Adler,* 256–258; and Nathaniel Branden, *The Disowned Self* (New York: Bantam Books, 1973), 200.

35. Cf. Béla Szabados, "Hypocrisy," *Canadian Journal of Philosophy* 9 (1979): 204.

36. There is something to Gide's remark, at least in one respect, that self-deceived pretenders are the "true hypocrites," since their pretense is so successful that they are penetrated by their own facade (*Journal of "The Counterfeiters,"* in *The Counterfeiters,* trans. Justin O'Brien [New York: Modern Library, 1955], 427).

37. Nathaniel Hawthorne, *The House of the Seven Gables,* in *The Complete Novels and Selected Tales of Nathaniel Hawthorne,* ed. Norman Holmes Pearson (New York: Modern Library, 1937), 432.

38. Ibid., 382.

39. Hawthorne, *The Scarlet Letter,* in *The Complete Novels and Selected Tales of Nathaniel Hawthorne,* 169.

40. A variety of approaches to weakness of will were given in *Weakness of Will,* ed. G. W. Mortimore (New York: St. Martin's Press, 1971). Also see Donald Davidson, "How Is Weakness of the Will Possible?" in *Moral Concepts,* ed. Joel Feinberg (New York: Oxford University Press, 1970), 93–113. For an insightful comparative study of self-deception and weakness of will, see David Pears, *Motivated Irrationality.*

41. Cf. De Sousa, "Review of *Self-Deception,*" 316–317.

42. Cf. Gary Watson, "Skepticism about Weakness of Will," *Philosophical Review* 86 (1977): 326. At one point Milo came close to sharing my view of how self-deception and moral weakness are related, but he then refused to count self-deception about wrongdoing as a case of moral weakness. See *Immorality,* 112–113.

43. Demos, "Lying to Oneself," 594.

CHAPTER 4. AUTHENTICITY

1. Søren Kierkegaard, *Either/Or,* Vol. 2, trans. Walter Lowrie (Princeton, N.J.: Princeton University Press, 1959), 171.

2. Ibid., 268.

3. Ibid., 270.

4. Ibid., 267.

5. Ibid., 263.

6. Ibid., 228.

7. Ibid., 212.

8. Ibid., 220–221.

9. Ibid., 161, 230.

10. Ibid., 201–203.

11. Ibid., 216.

12. Ibid., 219–220.

13. Søren Kierkegaard, *Fear and Trembling* and *The Sickness unto Death,* trans. Walter Lowrie (Garden City, N.Y.: Doubleday Anchor Books, 1954), 162–207.

14. Ibid., 167.

15. Ibid., 225. Cf. *Either/Or,* 168. An interesting, though perhaps excessively judgmental, discussion of procrastination was given by John Sabini and Maury Silver in *Moralities of Everyday Life* (New York: Oxford University Press, 1982), 125–140. An insightful discussion of this passage was given by Arthur Edward Murphy, "The Moral Self in Sickness and in Health," in *The Theory of Practical Reason,* ed. A. I. Melden (La Salle, Ill.: Open Court, 1964), 134–161.

16. Kierkegaard, *Fear and Trembling,* 225.

17. Ibid., 232.

18. Sartre, *Being and Nothingness,* 76.

19. Ibid., 568.

20. Ibid., 621.

21. Ibid., 710.

22. Jean-Paul Sartre, *Anti-Semite and Jew,* trans. George J. Becker (New York: Schocken Books, 1965), 90.

23. Cf. Dagfinn Føllesdal, "Sartre on Freedom," in *The Philosophy of Jean-Paul Sartre*, ed. Paul Arthur Schilpp (La Salle, Ill.: Open Court, 1981), 392–407.

24. Sartre, *Being and Nothingness*, 566.

25. Ibid., 146, 729.

26. Ibid., 78.

27. Ibid., 707.

28. Ibid., 96–100. It seems clear that Sartre modeled his vignette on Lord Byron's portrayal of Julia's seduction of Juan, in *Don Juan*, CV–CXVII, reversing the female-male roles of seducer-seduced.

29. Sartre, *Being and Nothingness*, 100. Some interesting aspects of this game and social mirrors were explored by Daniel T. Gilbert and Joel Cooper in "Social Psychological Strategies of Self-Deception," in Martin, *Self-Deception and Self-Understanding*, 75–94.

30. Sartre, *Being and Nothingness*, 80.

31. Unfortunately, in the next two parts of his explanation Sartre used the expression *bad faith* in two different senses. In its wider sense, it is a synonym for *self-deception* and *inauthenticity*. In its second, narrower, sense, it refers to one of two main forms of self-deception, the other of which is *good faith* or *sincerity*. (See the third section of this chapter for a discussion of sincerity.) For clarity, I will continue to use *self-deception* for the wide sense and restrict *bad faith* to its narrower sense. For a fuller discussion of Sartre's views, see my essay, "Sartre on Lying to Oneself," *Philosophy Research Archives* 4 (1978): 1–26.

32. Sartre, *Being and Nothingness*, 113.

33. Ibid., 114–115.

34. Ibid., 79, 95.

35. Ibid., 78. For a recent psychological discussion see C. R. Snyder, "Collaborative Companions: The Relationship of Self-Deception and Excuse-Making," in Martin, *Self-Deception and Self-Understanding*, 35–51.

36. One equivocation emphasized by Sartre concerns the senses in which he thought characteristics are ascribed to nonconscious things and to conscious people. Nonconscious things are reducible to the sum of their characteristics, with each characteristic being a component of their complete identity. In this sense, a thing is what it is, or has being-in-itself. By contrast, conscious persons are never reducible to their characteristics of which they are conscious (whether reflectively or nonpositionally). They are responsible for their characteristics and the interpretations they give these characteristics, but they remain distinct from them. A conscious being exists "for itself" or has being-for-itself.

The "is" of predication has a corresponding ambiguity: is-reducible-to and is-conscious-of. People in bad faith equivocate on the senses in order to deny specific characteristics of themselves, others, or the world. For example, the woman on the date gets herself to believe that the man is-reducible-to his present polite behavior, regarding him as "sincere and respectful as the table is round or square" (*Being and Nothingness*, 97). In this way, "she has disarmed the actions of her companion by reducing them to being only what they are; that is, to existing in the mode of the in-itself," rather than recognizing his actions as emerging from his free consciousness. Such a recognition would be disturbing because it threatens to remind her that the man interprets his conduct as a preamble to sex.

Also, giving his philosophically Gothic imagination full play, Sartre applied this ambiguity to generate one of his favorite paradoxes: consciousness is what it is not, and is not what it is. That is, a conscious being is-conscious-of what it is-not-reducible-to, and is-not-reducible-to what it is-conscious-of.

37. Jean-Paul Sartre, "Existentialism Is a Humanism," trans. Philip Mairet, in *Existentialism from Dostoevsky to Sartre*, ed. Walter Kaufmann (New York: New American Library, 1975), 365.

38. Ibid., 365–366. The following steps in the argument are quoted from these pages. This sketchy argument is open to alternative interpretations. My interpretation differs from Thomas C. Anderson's in *Foundation and Structure of Sartrean Ethics* (Lawrence: Regents Press of Kansas, 1979), 43–65 and 82–85. I view authenticity, not freedom, as Sartre's ultimate value. Thomas contends that freedom is his ultimate value and that his argument is designed to show this, whereas I view the argument as defending the "will to freedom" understood as authenticity (and thereby justifying moral criticisms of inauthentic people who refuse to acknowledge to themselves their freedom).

39. "The other is indispensable to my existence, and equally so to any knowledge I can have of myself" ("Existentialism Is a Humanism," 361).

40. Sartre, *Anti-Semite and Jew*, 17–20.

41. Ibid., 21.

42. Sartre's main argument for complete causal indeterminism of consciousness is little more than an appeal to commonsense beliefs. He has no effective rejoinder to Spinoza's rejection of this appeal: "Experience teaches us no less clearly than reason, that men believe themselves to be free, simply because they are conscious of their actions, and unconscious of the causes whereby those actions are determined" (Baruch Spinoza, *Ethics*, trans. R. H. M. Elwes, in *Benedict De Spinoza*, ed. R. H. M. Elwes [New York: Dover Publications, 1955], Part III, Proof of Proposition II).

43. Cf. A. D. M. Walker, "The Ideal of Sincerity," *Mind* 87 (1978): 481–497.

44. Lionel Trilling, *Sincerity and Authenticity* (Cambridge, Mass.: Harvard University Press, 1971), 58.

45. Cf. Henri Peyre, *Literature and Sincerity* (New Haven, Conn.: Yale University Press, 1963), 241–242 and 323; and Marcel Eck, *Lies and Truth*, trans. Bernard Murchland (New York: Macmillan, 1970), 71–73.

46. Stuart Hampshire gave an insightful critique of Chamfort in "Sincerity and Single-Mindedness," in *Freedom of Mind and Other Essays by Stuart Hampshire*, ed. Stuart Hampshire (Princeton, N.J.: Princeton University Press, 1971), 232–256.

47. *Being and Nothingness*, 99. Here I am using Sartre's words from another context. David E. Cooper offers some insightful remarks concerning Sartre's claims about sincerity as well as about the concept of authenticity in *Authenticity and Learning: Nietzsche's Educational Philosophy* (Boston: Routledge and Kegan Paul, 1983), 8ff.

48. *Being and Nothingness*, 101.

49. Ibid., 110.

50. Ibid., 109.

51. Ibid.

52. Ibid., 108.

53. Ibid., 102.

54. Leo Tolstoy, *A Confession and What I Believe*, ed. and trans. Aylmer Maude (London: Oxford University Press, 1967), 24.

55. Ibid., 48.

56. Leo Tolstoy, *The Death of Ivan Ilych*, trans. Aylmer Maude, in *Great Short Works of Leo Tolstoy*, ed. John Bayley (New York: Harper and Row, 1967), 299. For a stimulating discussion see Ilham Dilman and D. Z. Phillips, *Sense and Delusion* (Atlantic Highlands, N.J.: Humanities Press, 1971).

57. *The Death of Ivan Ilych*, 299.

58. Martin Heidegger, *Being and Time*, trans. John Macquarrie and Edward Robinson (New York: Harper and Row, 1962), 307. David Kipp has defended a Heideggerian conception of authenticity, in opposition to that of Sartre, in "Self-Deception, Inauthenticity, and Weakness of Will," in Martin, *Self-Deception and Self-Understanding*, 261–283.

59. "Anticipation discloses to existence that its uttermost possibility lies in giving itself up, and thus it shatters all one's tenaciousness to whatever existence one has reached." *Being and Time*, 132–133.

60. Some examples from popular literature are the psychiatric perspective of R. D. Laing's *Divided Self*, the Marxist-Freudian perspective of Erich Fromm's *Beyond the Chains of Illusion*, the experimental psychology of Gardiner Murphy's *Outgrowing Self-Deception*, and more eclectic writings such as Nathaniel Branden's *The Disowned Self*, Sheldon Kopp's *An End to Innocence: Facing Life without Illusions*, and Daniel Goleman's *Vital Lies, Simple Truths: The Psychology of Self-Deception* (see the bibliography for complete publication information).

61. Karen Horney, *Neurosis and Human Growth: The Struggle toward Self Realization* (New York: W. W. Norton and Co., 1950), 178.

62. F. H. Bradley, *Ethical Studies* (Oxford: Oxford University Press, 1962), and *The Philosophy of Josiah Royce*, ed. John K. Roth (Indianapolis: Hackett Publishing Company, 1982).

63. Spinoza's response to Heidegger would be: "A free man thinks of death least of all things; and his wisdom is a meditation not of death but of life" (*Ethics*, Part IV, Proposition LXVII). Spinoza's value perspective may or may not be unsuitable on this point, but I find it unacceptable to accuse him of self-deception or inauthenticity.

64. The humanistic psychologist Carl Rogers set forth a compelling view of authenticity along these lines. See his essay, "'To Be That Self Which One Truly Is': A Therapist's View of Personal Goals," in *On Becoming a Person* (Boston: Houghton Mifflin Company, 1961), 163–196. In connection with Rogers's cautious optimism it is worth noting that the significant truths Sartre and some others identify offer little basis for human joy. Perhaps we can hope, with the Nobel laureate Saul Bellow, that "truth is not always so punitive. . . . There may be truths on the side of life. I am quite prepared to admit that being habitual liars and self-deluders, we have good cause to fear the truth, but I'm not at all ready to stop hoping. There may be some truths which are, after all, our friends in the universe" (*Writers at Work: The Paris Review Interviews*, 3rd series, ed. George Plimpton [New York: Penguin Books, 1967], 196).

CHAPTER 5. MORAL AMBIGUITY

1. R. G. Collingwood, *The Principles of Art* (New York: Oxford University Press, 1958), 217.

2. Ibid., 216.

3. Ibid., 282–283.

4. Ibid., 224.

5. Ibid., 284–285.

6. Ibid., 220.

7. Fingarette, *Self-Deception*, 18–20, 28, 34–35, 136.

8. Ibid., 138–140.

9. Another minor difference is that *disavowal*, by definition, always is about oneself—one's engagements—whereas we can be said to evade self-acknowledgment of virtually any feature of ourselves or the objective world existing independently of us. But the difference is mainly verbal: statements about self-deception concerning things in the objective world can be translated into Fingarette's terms as disavowal of our responses to that world as we "take account of" it.

10. Fingarette, *Self-Deception*, 35, 91. Fingarette's point was that "contrary to what others had argued, cognitive aspects [of self-deception] are not distinctive or crucial; the crucial occurrence in the move into self-deception is a 'volitional' one. Plainly there can be no volition without cognitive content. One cannot adopt and execute a policy, a commitment, without 'taking account' of the situation as one perceives it and believes it to be." (Quoted from personal correspondence from Herbert Fingarette, December 12, 1982.)

11. Cf. Saunders, "The Paradox of Self-Deception," 559–570; and Mrinal Miri, "Self-Deception," *Philosophy and Phenomenological Research* 34 (1974): 576–585.

12. Fingarette, *Self-Deception*, 42–43.

13. Cf. Hamlyn, "Self-Deception," 52.

14. Haight attempted to make consistency of action the generic aim in all self-deception, but I think that results in either overgeneralization or vacuous truth by definition. See *A Study of Self-Deception*, 82–86, 96.

15. Cf. John King-Farlow, Review of Herbert Fingarette's *Self-Deception*, *Metaphilosophy* 4 (1973): 82.

16. Fingarette, *Self-Deception*, 136.

17. Ibid., 1.

18. Ibid., 50–54.

19. Ibid., 138–140.

20. Mike W. Martin, "Morality and Self-Deception: Paradox, Ambiguity, or Vagueness?" *Man and World* 12 (1979): 47–60. I am grateful to Herbert Fingarette for the personal correspondence that led me to correct this misinterpretation.

21. Fingarette, *Self-Deception*, 101, 138.

22. Ibid., 140, 146.

23. Herbert Fingarette, "Alcoholism and Self-Deception," in *Self-Deception and Self-Understanding*, ed. Mike W. Martin (Lawrence: University Press of Kansas, 1985), 53.

24. Quoted from personal correspondence from Herbert Fingarette, April 26, 1982. In the same letter Fingarette used the expression "pre-moral condition."

25. Fingarette, *Self-Deception*, 141.

26. At one point Collingwood wrote, "The falsehoods which an untruthful consciousness imposes on the intellect are falsehoods which intellect can never correct for itself." (R. G. Collingwood, *The Principles of Art* [New York: Oxford University Press, 1958], 84.) But in the same connection, on p. 283, he emphasized the substantial ability of persons to purify their corrupt consciousness and correct the false beliefs imposed on the "intellect." On balance

his view seemed to be that self-deceivers have the capacity to correct the errors of the one part of them which he calls the intellect.

27. Fingarette, *Self-Deception*, 3-4. Fingarette took the example from Nemiah, *Foundations of Psychopathology*, 124-131.

28. Fingarette, *Self-Deception*, 87.

29. Ibid., 47-48.

30. Herbert Fingarette, *On Responsibility* (New York: Basic Books, 1967), 23.

31. Fingarette, *Self-Deception*, 146-147.

32. Fingarette, *On Responsibility*, 29 and 42.

33. Sigmund Freud, *The Standard Edition of the Complete Psychological Works*, trans. James Strachey (London: Hogarth Press, 1953-1966), Vol. 19, 13. Hereafter cited as *Works*.

34. Freud, *Works*, Vol. 29, 15-16.

35. Freud, *Works*, Vol. 16, 457. Cf. Vol. 15, 83.

36. Freud, *Works*, Vol. 16, 457.

37. Freud, *Works*, Vol. 19, 16.

38. Cf. Charles Brenner, *An Elementary Textbook of Psychoanalysis*, rev. ed. (Garden City, N.Y.: Anchor Books, 1974), 84-85.

39. Jonathan Glover, *Responsibility* (London: Routledge and Kegan Paul, 1970), 102-140. Glover provided an insightful overview of the moral implications of Freud's views in "Freud, Morality and Responsibility," in *Freud: The Man, His World, His Influence*, ed. Jonathan Miller (Boston: Little, Brown and Co., 1972), 151-163.

40. Fingarette, *Self-Deception*, 9, 111-135.

41. Cf. Berel Lang, "The Neurotic as Moral Agent," *Philosophy and Phenomenological Research* 29 (1968): 216-231.

42. Freud, *Works*, Vol. 19, 133.

43. Freud, *Works*, Vol. 21, 31-32, 37-38.

44. R. D. Laing, for example, portrayed schizophrenics as acting purposefully with respect to a hostile and horrifying environment. He claimed that their despair, isolation, and alienation are in part voluntary responses over which they have some control. In a manner reminiscent of Freud, he also insisted that various psychic splits in sane people—"schizoid states"—are closely akin to and shade into schizophrenic states. Psychotic and nonpsychotic states differ for him only in the degree of break with reality, not in the types of psychological evasions involved. See especially *The Divided Self* (Baltimore: Penguin Books, 1965).

45. See especially Jules Henry's analysis of much madness by reference to self-deceptive or self-directed sham (*Pathways to Madness* [New York: Vintage Books, 1973], 99-108; and *On Sham, Vulnerability and Other Forms of Self-Destruction* [New York: Vintage Books, 1973], 120-127).

46. Most notable is Erving Goffman's account of some schizophrenics as interpreting or "framing" their experience in a manner that is self-deceivingly purposeful and evasive (*Frame Analysis* [New York: Harper and Row, 1974], 112-115). Also see John M. Shlien, "A Client-Centered Approach to Schizophrenia: First Approximation," in *Psychotherapy of the Psychoses*, ed. A. Burton (New York: Basic Books, 1961), 285-317.

47. See, for example, John Hospers' essays, "Meaning and Free Will," *Philosophy and Phenomenological Research* 10 (1950); relevant sections reprinted as "Free-Will and Psychoanalysis" in *Readings in Ethical Theory*, 2nd ed., ed. Wilfrid Sellars and John Hospers (Englewood Cliffs, N.J.: Prentice-Hall, 1970),

633–645; and "What Means This Freedom?" in *Determinism and Freedom in the Age of Modern Science,* ed. Sidney Hook (New York: Collier Books, 1958), 126–142.

48. Haight, *A Study of Self-Deception,* 1–2, 13–14, 73–88, 106–107. Also see "Tales from a Black Box," in Martin, *Self-Deception and Self-Understanding,* 244–260.

49. Haight, *A Study of Self-Deception,* 120.

50. Ibid., 129.

51. Ibid., 124.

52. Ibid., 125.

53. Ibid.

54. Ibid., 129.

55. Ibid.

56. Ibid., 132.

57. Ibid., 149.

58. Ibid., 125.

59. William Golding, *Free Fall* (San Diego: Harcourt Brace Jovanovich, 1959), 1–2.

60. Cf. Murphy, *The Theory of Practical Reason.*

61. Cf. Herbert Fingarette, *The Meaning of Criminal Insanity* (Berkeley: University of California Press, 1974), 166.

62. Haight, *A Study of Self-Deception,* 129.

63. Ibid., 131.

64. Cf. Graham Haydon, "On Being Responsible," *Philosophical Quarterly* 28 (1978), 46–47. Also see H. L. A. Hart, *Punishment and Responsibility* (New York: Oxford University Press, 1968), Chapter 9; and Kurt Baier, "Guilt and Responsibility," in *Individual and Collective Responsibility,* ed. Peter A. French (Cambridge, Mass.: Schenkman Publishing Co., 1972), 35–61.

65. I am influenced in what follows by Robert Audi's essay, "Self-Deception, Action, and Will," 133–158.

66. Cf. Milo, *Immorality,* 220.

67. Cf. Haight, *A Study of Self-Deception,* 105.

CHAPTER 6. VITAL LIES

1. Ecclesiastes 1:18.

2. Sophocles, *Oedipus Rex,* in *The Oedipus Cycle,* trans. Dudley Fitts and Robert Fitzgerald (New York: Harcourt, Brace and World, 1949), 16.

3. Jonathan Swift, *A Tale of a Tub,* in *The Portable Swift,* ed. Carl Van Doren (New York: Viking Press, 1948), 66.

4. Henrik Ibsen, *The Wild Duck,* trans. and ed. Dounia B. Christiani (New York: W. W. Norton, 1968), 64.

5. Ibid., 74.

6. Eugene O'Neill, *The Iceman Cometh* (New York: Vintage Books, 1957), 9–10.

7. Ibid., 81.

8. Ibid., 239.

9. Ibid., 240.

10. Ibid., 248.

11. Cf. Robert Brustein, selections from *Theatre of Revolt*, in *Twentieth Century Interpretations of The Iceman Cometh*, ed. John Henry Raleigh (Englewood Cliffs, N.J.: Prentice-Hall, 1968), 96.

12. O'Neill, *The Iceman Cometh*, 67.

13. Quoted by Louis Sheaffer, *O'Neill: Son and Artist* (Boston: Little, Brown and Co., 1973), 494.

14. Albert Camus, *The Fall*, trans. Justin O'Brien (New York: Vintage Books, 1956), 143.

15. Ibid., 84.

16. Hamlyn, "Self-Deception," 59.

17. Rorty, "Belief and Self-Deception," 402.

18. Amélie Oksenberg Rorty, "Adaptivity and Self-Knowledge," *Inquiry* 18 (1975): 22.

19. Béla Szabados, "The Morality of Self-Deception," *Dialogue* 13 (1974): 26–29.

20. King-Farlow, "Review of Herbert Fingarette's *Self-Deception*," 82. King-Farlow's moral assessment of self-deception was more fully developed in "Self-Formation and the Mean (Programmatic Remarks of Self-Deception)," with Richard Bosley, in Martin, *Self-Deception and Self-Understanding*, 195–220.

21. Cf. John Passmore, *A Hundred Years of Philosophy* (Baltimore: Penguin Books, 1968), 95.

22. Ferdinand Canning Scott Schiller, *Problems of Belief* (New York: George H. Doran Company, 1924), 174.

23. Ibid., 171.

24. Ibid., 111–112.

25. Ibid., 179. Cf. 169–192.

26. Ibid., 124.

27. Ibid., 32.

28. Ibid., 86. Cf. 74–86, 124.

29. Ibid., 32.

30. Jack W. Meiland, "What Ought We to Believe? or The Ethics of Belief Revisited," *American Philosophical Quarterly* 17 (1980): 15.

31. Ibid., 16.

32. Ibid., 20.

33. Ibid., 17.

34. Robert Audi, "Self-Deception and Rationality," in Martin, *Self-Deception and Self-Understanding*, 182. Audi allowed that there may be degrees of rationality and irrationality.

35. H. O. Mounce, "Self-Deception," *Aristotelian Society Proceedings* 45 (1971): 71. Mounce suggested that it is generally better to avoid self-deception, although he does not explicitly say whether he means morally or nonmorally better.

36. R. S. Peters, "The Justification of Education," in *The Philosophy of Education*, ed. R. S. Peters (Oxford: Oxford University Press, 1973), 251–256.

37. Cf. Jon Elster on "the benefits of bias" in *Sour Grapes: Studies in the Subversion of Rationality* (Cambridge: Cambridge University Press, 1983), 157–166. Elster referred to the important psychological studies of R. Nisbett and L. Ross in *Human Inference* (Englewood Cliffs, N.J.: Prentice-Hall, 1980), 198–199, 271. Of course, self-deception can also be damaging to creativity when it belittles, denies, or handicaps our abilities to generate new ideas and valuable products. See Eliot Deutsch, *Personhood, Creativity and Freedom* (Honolulu:

University of Hawaii Press, 1982), and Carl R. Hausman, "Creativity and Self-Deception," *Journal of Existentialism* 7 (1967): 295–308.

38. William James, "The Will to Believe," in *Essays on Faith and Morals*, ed. Ralph Barton Perry (New York: Meridian Books, 1965), 42.

39. Cf. James L. Muyskens, *The Sufficiency of Hope* (Philadelphia: Temple University Press, 1979). Muyskens's analysis of hope also shaped my remarks here.

40. In her two-volume critique of intellectual dishonesty, *Vital Lies*, Vernon Lee emphasized the role of art in giving us emotional satisfactions that reality denies us. In doing so it is, she wrote, "the great hidden educator and moraliser" that helps us avoid self-deception by making us "distinguish between what *we want* and *what is*." (London: John Lane, 1912), Vol. II, 161–162. Cf. Vol. I, 108–109 and 151–153.

41. Cf. Kendall Walton, "Fearing Fictions," *Journal of Philosophy* 75 (1978): 5–27.

42. Jerry L. Guthrie has suggested that there is at least prima facie plausibility in viewing emotional responses to fiction as a species of self-deception ("Self-Deception and Emotional Response to Fiction," *British Journal of Aesthetics* 21 [1981]: 73).

43. Eugene O'Neill, *Hughie*, in *The Later Plays of Eugene O'Neill* (New York: Modern Library, 1967).

44. Friedrich Nietzsche, *The Gay Science*, trans. Walter Kaufmann (New York: Vintage Books, 1974), 169.

45. Nietzsche's views on self-deception and its contrast, conscious self-pretense, are complex. Sometimes he defended vital lie themes, as in his discussion of "pious illusions" in *On the Advantage and Disadvantage of History for Life*, trans. Peter Preuss (Indianapolis: Hackett Publishing Company, 1980), sec. 7; and in remarks like the following: "The falseness of a judgment is for us not necessarily an objection to a judgment. . . . The question is to what extent it is life-promoting, life-preserving, species-preserving, perhaps even species-cultivating" (*Beyond Good and Evil*, trans. Walter Kaufmann [New York: Vintage Books, 1966], 10–11). Yet he made far more remarks stressing intellectual honesty in overcoming self-deception. For example: "That it does not matter whether a thing is true, but only what effect it produces—absolute lack of intellectual integrity." (*The Will to Power*, ed. Walter Kaufmann, trans. Walter Kaufmann and R. J. Hollingdale [New York: Vintage Books, 1968]); "At every step, one has to wrestle for truth; one has had to surrender for it almost everything to which the heart, to which our love, our trust in life cling otherwise. That requires greatness of soul: the service of truth is the hardest service" (quoted by Walter Kaufmann from *The Antichrist*, in *Nietzsche: Philosopher, Psychologist, Antichrist*, 4th ed. [Princeton, N.J.: Princeton University Press, 1974], 356); and see the epigraph to Chapter 4 of this book. We might view his defense of conscious pretense and conscious illusion as an attempt to reconcile his emphasis on intellectual honesty (as part of the Authenticity Tradition) with his appreciation of the life-giving force of illusions (as part of the Vital Lie Tradition).

46. Related themes concerning conscious illusion have been developed by Hans Vaihinger and George Santayana. Vaihinger, who was influenced by Nietzsche, emphasized the usefulness of "fictions" or "hypotheses which are known to be false, but which are employed because of their utility," especially because of their heuristic role in generating new ideas and approaches (*The*

Philosophy of "As-If," 2nd ed. [New York: Barnes and Noble, 1952], xlii). Santayana regarded religious ideas about the supernatural as sheer myth, but that did not diminish their poetic power to inspire and to provide moral perspective. Regarded as fiction, they nevertheless inspire reverence and can unify the personality and elevate it to a higher degree of spirituality (*Reason in Religion*, Vol. 3 of *The Life of Reason* [New York: Dover Publications, 1982]).

47. Thus it is connected with all facets of Polonius's enticing injunction, "This above all, to thine own self be true." Shakespeare, *Hamlet*, I, iii.

48. The term and (roughly) the concept are Michael Slote's. See *Goods and Virtues* (Oxford: Clarendon Press, 1983), 61–75.

49. Aristotle, *Nicomachean Ethics*, in *The Basic Works of Aristotle*, ed. Richard McKeon (New York: Random House, 1968), Book 6.

50. See *Recollections of Wittgenstein*, ed. Rush Rhees (New York: Oxford University Press, 1984); Norman Malcolm, *Ludwig Wittgenstein: A Memoir* (New York: Oxford University Press, 1962); and *Ludwig Wittgenstein: The Man and His Philosophy*, ed. K. T. Fann (New York: Dell Publishing, 1967).

51. Ludwig Wittgenstein, *Culture and Value*, trans. Peter Winch (Chicago: University of Chicago Press, 1984), 26.

52. Quoted by Rush Rhees from Wittgenstein's unpublished manuscripts, *Recollections of Wittgenstein*, 174.

53. *Culture and Value*, 33.

54. Søren Kierkegaard, *Fear and Trembling and the Sickness unto Death*, trans. Walter Lowrie (New York: Doubleday Anchor Books, 1954), 221. Cf. Freud: "Knowledge is not always the same as knowledge: there are different sorts of knowledge, which are far from equivalent psychologically" (*The Complete Introductory Lectures on Psychoanalysis* [New York: W. W. Norton, 1966], Lecture 18).

55. Cf.: "Self-knowledge does not mean preoccupation with one's own thoughts; rather it means concern about the effects one creates. . . . The right sort of self-examination . . . consists not in idle brooding over oneself but in examining the effects one produces" (*The I Ching or Book of Changes*, trans. Richard Wilhelm and Cary F. Baynes [Princeton, N.J.: Princeton University Press, 1977], 85).

56. T. S. Eliot, "East Coker," in *The Complete Poems and Plays of T. S. Eliot* (New York: Harcourt, Brace and World, 1962), 125.

57. "The Cocktail Party," in *The Complete Poems and Plays of T. S. Eliot*, 363.

EPILOGUE

1. Aristotle, *Nicomachean Ethics*, trans. W. D. Ross, in *The Basic Works of Aristotle*, ed. Richard McKeon (New York: Random House, 1941), 936.

2. Cf. Stuart Hampshire, *Morality and Conflict* (Cambridge, Mass.: Harvard University Press, 1983), 151. Also see Alasdair MacIntyre, *After Virtue* (Notre Dame, Ind.: University of Notre Dame, 1981).

3. Sometimes the most we can hope for is mutual understanding of differences, but that in itself is of enormous—and generally unappreciated—importance. Stanley Cavell expressed this nicely: "[Morality provides] a way of encompassing conflict which allows the continuance of personal relationships against the hard and apparently inevitable fact of misunderstanding, mutually incompatible wishes, commitments, loyalties, interests and needs, a way of

mending relationships and maintaining the self in opposition to itself or others. . . . We do not have to agree with one another in order to live in the same moral world, but we do have to know and respect one another's differences" (*The Claim of Reason: Wittgenstein, Skepticism, Morality and Tragedy* [New York: Oxford University, 1979], 269).

4. These issues are extraordinarily complex and intractable. See *The Problem of Abortion*, 2nd ed., ed. Joel Feinberg (Belmont, Calif.: Wadsworth, 1984).

5. As Proust so insightfully illustrated in "Swann in Love," in *Swann's Way*, trans. C. K. Scott Moncrieff (New York: Vintage Books, 1970).

6. Cf. Irving Singer, *The Nature of Love*, Vol. 1, 2nd edition (Chicago: University of Chicago Press, 1984), 3-22.

7. Murphy, *The Theory of Practical Reason*, 414.

Bibliography

Adler, Alfred. *The Individual Psychology of Alfred Adler.* Edited by Heinz L. Ansbacher and Rowena R. Ansbacher. New York: Harper and Row, 1964.

Anderson, Thomas C. *The Foundation and Structure of Sartrean Ethics.* Lawrence: Regents Press of Kansas, 1979.

Aquinas, St. Thomas. *Summa Theologiae.* Vol. 25. New York: McGraw-Hill, 1969.

Aristotle. *Nicomachean Ethics.* Pp. 927–1112 in *The Basic Works of Aristotle,* edited by Richard McKeon. New York: Random House, 1941.

Armstrong, D. M. *Belief, Truth and Knowledge.* Cambridge: Cambridge University Press, 1973.

Audi, Robert. "The Epistemic Authority of the First Person." *Personalist* 56 (1975): 5–15.

———. "Self-Deception, Action, and Will. " *Erkenntnis* 18 (1982): 133–158.

———. "Self-Deception and Rationality." Pp. 169–194 in *Self-Deception and Self-Understanding: New Essays in Philosophy and Psychology,* edited by Mike W. Martin. Lawrence: University Press of Kansas, 1985.

Bach, Kent. "An Analysis of Self-Deception." *Philosophy and Phenomenological Research* 41 (1981): 351–370.

Baier, Kurt. "Guilt and Responsibility." Pp. 35–61 in *Individual and Collective Responsibility,* edited by Peter A. French. Cambridge, Mass.: Schenkman Publishing Co., 1972.

Becker, Ernest. *The Denial of Death.* New York: Free Press, 1975.

Beehler, Rodger. "Moral Delusion." *Philosophy* 56 (1981): 313–331.

Bellow, Saul. "Interview with Saul Bellow." Pp. 175–196 in *Writers at Work: The Paris Review Interviews,* 3rd series, edited by George Plimpton. New York: Penguin Books, 1967.

Billson, Marcus K. "Inside Albert Speer: Secrets of Moral Evasion." *Antioch Review* (1979): 460–474.

This bibliography is restricted to the sources cited and a few additional references. I give a more comprehensive bibliography in *Self-Deception and Self-Understanding: New Essays in Philosophy and Psychology* (Lawrence: University Press of Kansas, 1985).

Bok, Sissela. *Secrets*. New York: Pantheon Books, 1982.

Bradley, F. H. *Ethical Studies*. Oxford: Oxford University Press, 1962.

Branden, Nathaniel. *The Disowned Self*. New York: Bantam Books, 1973.

Brenner, Charles. *An Elementary Textbook of Psychoanalysis*. Garden City, N.Y.: Anchor Books, 1974.

Broad, C. D. *The Mind and Its Place in Nature*. London: Routledge and Kegan Paul, 1925.

Brown, Robert. "Integrity and Self-Deception." *Critical Review* 25 (1983): 115–131.

Brustein, Robert. Selections from *Theatre of Revolt*. Pp. 92–102 in *Twentieth Century Interpretations of The Iceman Cometh*, edited by John Henry Raleigh. Englewood Cliffs, N.J.: Prentice-Hall, 1968.

Burrell, David, and Stanley Hauerwas. "Self-Deception and Autobiography: Theological and Ethical Reflections on Speer's *Inside the Third Reich*." *Journal of Religious Ethics* 2 (1974): 99–117.

Butler, Joseph. "Upon the Character of Balaam," "Upon Self-Deceit," and Sermon 3 of the *Six Sermons*. Pp. 121–135, 168–184, 317–338 in *The Works of Joseph Butler*, edited by W. E. Gladstone. Vol. 2. Oxford: Clarendon Press, 1896.

Byron, Lord. *Don Juan*. Pp. 856–913 in *English Romantic Poetry and Prose*, edited by Russell Noyes. New York: Oxford University Press, 1956.

Camus, Albert. *The Fall*. Translated by Justin O'Brien. New York: Vintage Books, 1956.

Canfield, John V., and Don F. Gustavson. "Self-Deception." *Analysis* 23 (1962): 32–36.

Canfield, John, and Patrick McNally. "Paradoxes of Self-Deception." *Analysis* 21 (1961): 140–144.

Cavell, Stanley. "The Avoidance of Love: A Reading of King Lear." Pp. 267–353 in *Must We Mean What We Say?* New York: Charles Scribner's Sons, 1969.

———. *The Claim of Reason: Wittgenstein, Skepticism, Morality and Tragedy*. Oxford: Oxford University Press, 1982.

———. "Knowing and Acknowledging." Pp. 238–266 in *Must We Mean What We Say?* New York: Charles Scribner's Sons, 1969.

Champlin, T. S. "Double Deception." *Mind* 85 (1976): 100–102.

Chanowitz, Benzion, and Ellen Langer. "Self-Protection and Self-Inception." Pp. 117–135 in *Self-Deception and Self-Understanding: New Essays in Philosophy and Psychology*, edited by Mike W. Martin. Lawrence: University Press of Kansas, 1985.

Clifford, William Kingdon. "The Ethics of Belief." Pp. 177–211 in *Lectures and Essays of W. K. Clifford*, edited by Leslie Stephen and Frederick Pollock. Vol. 2. London: Macmillan, 1879.

Collingwood, R. G. *The Principles of Art*. New York: Oxford University Press, 1958.

Cooper, David E. *Authenticity and Learning: Nietzsche's Educational Philosophy*. Boston: Routledge and Kegan Paul, 1983.

Daniels, Charles B. "Self-Deception and Interpersonal Deception." *Personalist* 55 (1974): 244–252.

Davidson, Donald. "How Is Weakness of Will Possible?" Pp. 93–113 in *Moral Concepts*, edited by Joel Feinberg. New York: Oxford University Press, 1970.

———. "Paradoxes of Irrationality." Pp. 289–305 in *Philosophical Essays on Freud*, edited by Richard Wollheim and James Hopkins. Cambridge: Cambridge University Press, 1982.

Davis, Stephen T. "Wishful Thinking and 'The Will to Believe.' " *Transactions of the Peirce Society* (1972): 231–245.

De Beauvoir, Simone. *The Ethics of Ambiguity.* Translated by Bernard Frechtman. Secaucus, N.J.: Citadel Press, 1980.

Demos, Raphael. "Lying to Oneself." *Journal of Philosophy* 57 (1960): 588–595.

De Sousa, Ronald B. Review of *Self-Deception* by Herbert Fingarette. *Inquiry* 13 (1970): 308–321.

———. "Self-Deceptive Emotions." *Journal of Philosophy* 75 (1978): 684–697. Reprinted on pp. 283–297 in *Explaining Emotions,* edited by Amélie Oksenberg Rorty. Berkeley: University of California Press, 1980.

Deutsch, Eliot. "Personhood and Self-Deception." Chapter 1 (pp. 1–34) of *Personhood, Creativity and Freedom.* Honolulu: University of Hawaii Press, 1982.

Dilman, Ilham. *Freud and the Mind.* Oxford: Basil Blackwell, 1984.

Dilman, Ilham, and D. Z. Phillips. *Sense and Delusion.* Atlantic Highlands, N.J.: Humanities Press, 1971.

Dostoyevsky, Fyodor. *The Brothers Karamazov.* Translated by Constance Garnett. New York: New American Library, 1957.

Drengson, Alan R. Critical Notice of H. Fingarette, *Self-Deception. Dialogue: Canadian Journal of Philosophy* 12 (1973): 142–147.

Dyke, Daniel. *The Mystery of Selfe-Deceiving, or a Discourse and Discovery of the Deceitfulness of Man's Heart.* London, 1630. Department of Special Collections, University of California, Los Angeles, Library.

Eck, Marcel, *Lies and Truth.* Translated by Bernard Murchland. New York: Macmillan, 1970.

Edgley, Roy. *Reason in Theory and Practice.* London: Hutchinson University Library, 1969.

Eliot, George. *Middlemarch.* New York: New American Library, 1964.

Eliot, T. S. *The Complete Poems and Plays of T. S. Eliot.* New York: Harcourt, Brace and World, 1962.

Ellenberger, Henri F. *The Discovery of the Unconscious.* New York: Basic Books, 1970.

Elster, Jon. *Sour Grapes: Studies in the Subversion of Rationality.* Cambridge: Cambridge University Press, 1983.

Factor, R. Lance. "Self-Deception and the Functionalist Theory of Mental Processes." *Personalist* 58 (1977): 115–123.

Falk, W. D. "Morality, Self, and Others." Pp. 25–66 in *Morality and the Language of Conduct,* edited by Hector-Neri Castañeda and George Nakhnikian. Detroit: Wayne State University Press, 1965.

Fann, K. T., ed. *Ludwig Wittgenstein: The Man and His Philosophy.* New York: Dell Publishing, 1967.

Feinberg, Joel, ed. *The Problem of Abortion.* 2nd edition. Belmont, Calif.: Wadsworth, 1984.

Festinger, Leon. *The Theory of Cognitive Dissonance.* Stanford, Calif.: Stanford University Press, 1957.

Fingarette, Herbert. *The Meaning of Criminal Insanity.* Berkeley: University of California Press, 1974.

———. *On Responsibility.* New York: Basic Books, 1967.

———. *Self-Deception.* Atlantic Highlands, N.J.: Humanities Press, 1969.

Fingarette, Herbert, and Ann F. Hasse. *Mental Disabilities and Criminal Responsibility.* Berkeley: University of California Press, 1979.

Føllesdal, Dagfinn. "Sartre on Freedom." Pp. 392-407 in *The Philosophy of Jean-Paul Sartre*, edited by Paul Arthur Schilpp. La Salle, Ill.: Open Court, 1981.

Foss, Jeffrey. "Rethinking Self-Deception." *American Philosophical Quarterly* 17 (1980): 237-243.

Freud, Anna. *The Ego and the Mechanisms of Defense*. New York: International Universities Press, 1974.

Freud, Sigmund. *The Standard Edition of the Complete Psychological Works*. Translated by James Strachey. London: Hogarth Press, 1953-1966.

Gardiner, Patrick. "Error, Faith and Self-Deception." *Proceedings of the Aristotelian Society* 70 (1969-70): 221-243. Reprinted on pp. 35-52 in *The Philosophy of Mind*, edited by Jonathan Glover. New York: Oxford University Press, 1976.

Geis, Gilbert. "The Heavy Electrical Equipment Antitrust Cases of 1961." Pp. 117-132 in *White Collar Crime*, edited by Gilbert Geis and Robert F. Meier. New York: Free Press, 1977.

Gide, André. *The Counterfeiters, with Journal of "The Counterfeiters."* Novel translated by Dorothy Bussy, journal translated by Justin O'Brien. New York: Modern Library, 1955.

Gilbert, Daniel T., and Joel Cooper. "Social Psychological Strategies of Self-Deception." Pp. 75-94 in *Self-Deception and Self-Understanding*, edited by Mike W. Martin. Lawrence: University Press of Kansas, 1985.

Glover, Jonathan. "Freud, Morality and Responsibility." Pp. 152-163 in *Freud: The Man, His World, His Influence*, edited by Jonathan Miller. Boston: Little, Brown and Co., 1972.

————. *Responsibility*. London: Routledge and Kegan Paul, 1970.

Goffman, Erving. *Frame Analysis*. New York: Harper and Row, 1974.

Golding, William. *Free Fall*. San Diego: Harcourt Brace Jovanovich, 1959.

Goleman, Daniel. *Vital Lies, Simple Truths: The Psychology of Self-Deception*. New York: Simon and Schuster, 1985.

Grant, C. K. *Belief and Action*. Durham: University of Durham, 1960.

Grene, Marjorie. "Authenticity: An Existential Virtue." *Ethics* 62 (1952): 266-274.

Gur, Ruben C., and Harold A. Sackeim. "Self-Deception: A Concept in Search of a Phenomenon." *Journal of Personality and Social Psychology* 37 (1979): 147-169.

Guthrie, Jerry L. "Self-Deception and Emotional Response to Fiction." *British Journal of Aesthetics* 21 (1981): 65-75.

Haight, M. R. *A Study of Self-Deception*. Sussex: Harvester Press; Atlantic Highlands, N.J.: Humanities Press, 1980.

————. "Tales from a Black Box." Pp. 244-260 in *Self-Deception and Self-Understanding: New Essays in Philosophy and Psychology*, edited by Mike W. Martin. Lawrence: University Press of Kansas, 1985.

Hamlyn, D. W. "Self-Deception." *Proceedings of the Aristotelian Society* 45 (1971): 45-60.

Hampshire, Stuart. Critical Review of *The Concept of Mind*. Pp. 17-44 in *Ryle*, edited by Oscar P. Wood and George Pitcher. Garden City, N.Y.: Anchor Books, 1970.

————. *Morality and Conflict*. Cambridge, Mass.: Harvard University Press, 1983.

————. "Sincerity and Single-Mindedness." Pp. 232-256 in *Freedom of Mind and Other Essays by Stuart Hampshire*, edited by Stuart Hampshire. Princeton, N.J.: Princeton University Press, 1971.

Hart, H. L. A. *Punishment and Responsibility.* New York: Oxford University Press, 1968.

Harvey, Van A. "Is There an Ethics of Belief?" *Journal of Religion* 49 (1969): 41–58.

Hawthorne, Nathaniel. *The Complete Novels and Selected Tales of Nathaniel Hawthorne.* Edited by Norman Holmes Pearson. New York: Modern Library, 1937.

Haydon, Graham. "On Being Responsible." *Philosophical Quarterly* 28 (1978): 46–57.

Hegel, G. W. F. *The Phenomenology of Mind.* Translated by J. B. Baillie. New York: Harper Torchbooks, 1967.

Heidegger, Martin. *Being and Time.* Translated by John Macquarrie and Edward Robinson. New York: Harper and Row, 1962.

Hellman, Nathan. "Bach on Self-Deception." *Philosophy and Phenomenological Research* 44 (1983): 113–120.

Henry, Jules. *On Sham, Vulnerability, and Other Forms of Self-Destruction.* New York: Vintage Books, 1973.

———. *Pathways to Madness.* New York: Vintage Books, 1973.

Herling, John. *The Great Price Conspiracy.* Washington, D.C.: Robert B. Luce, 1962.

Holyer, Robert. "Belief and Will Revisited." *Dialogue: The Canadian Philosophical Review* 22 (1983): 273–290.

Horney, Karen. *Neurosis and Human Growth.* New York: W. W. Norton, 1950.

Hospers, John. "Free-Will and Psychoanalysis." Pp. 633–645 in *Readings in Ethical Theory*, 2nd ed., edited by Wilfrid Sellars and John Hospers. Englewood Cliffs, N.J.: Prentice-Hall, 1970.

———. "What Means This Freedom?" Pp. 126–142 in *Determinism and Freedom in the Age of Modern Science*, edited by Sidney Hook. New York: Collier Books, 1958.

Hume, David. *A Treatise of Human Nature.* Edited by L. A. Selby-Bigge. Oxford: Clarendon Press, 1968.

Ibsen, Henrik. *The Wild Duck.* Translated by Dounia B. Christiani. New York: W. W. Norton, 1968.

James, William. *Essays on Faith and Morals.* Edited by Ralph Barton Perry. New York: Meridian Books, 1965.

Johnson, Sonia. *From Housewife to Heretic.* New York: Anchor Books, 1983.

Kant, Immanuel. *Anthropology from a Pragmatic Point of View.* Translated by Victor Lyle Dowdell and edited by Hans H. Rudnick. Carbondale: Southern Illinois University Press, 1978.

———. *The Doctrine of Virtue.* Translated by Mary J. Gregor. Philadelphia: University of Pennsylvania Press, 1964.

———. *Foundations of the Metaphysics of Morals with Critical Essays.* Translated by Lewis White Beck and edited by Robert Paul Wolff. Indianapolis: Bobbs-Merrill, 1969.

Kauber, Peter, and Peter H. Hare. "The Right and Duty to Will to Believe." *Canadian Journal of Philosophy* 4 (1974): 327–343.

Kaufmann, Walter, ed. *Existentialism from Dostoevsky to Sartre.* New York: New American Library, 1975.

———. *The Faith of a Heretic.* Garden City, N.Y.: Anchor Books, 1963.

———. *Nietzsche: Philosopher, Psychologist, Antichrist.* 4th edition. Princeton, N.J.: Princeton University Press, 1974.

Kierkegaard, Søren. *Either/Or*. Translated by Walter Lowrie. 2 vols. Princeton, N.J.: Princeton University Press, 1959.

———. *Fear and Trembling* and *The Sickness unto Death*. Translated by Walter Lowrie. Garden City, N.Y.: Doubleday Anchor Books, 1954.

———. *Purity of Heart Is to Will One Thing*. Translated by Douglas Steere. New York: Harper Torchbooks, 1956.

King-Farlow, John. Review of Herbert Fingarette's *Self-Deception*. *Metaphilosophy* 4 (1973): 76–84.

———. "Self-Deceivers and Sartrian Seducers." *Analysis* 23 (1963): 131–136.

King-Farlow, John, and Richard Bosley. "Self-Formation and the Mean (Programmatic Remarks on Self-Deception)." Pp. 195–220 in *Self-Deception and Self-Understanding: New Essays in Philosophy and Psychology*, edited by Mike W. Martin. Lawrence: University Press of Kansas, 1985.

Kipp, David. "On Self-Deception." *Philosophical Quarterly* 30 (1980): 305–317.

———. "Self-Deception, Inauthenticity, and Weakness of Will." Pp. 261–283 in *Self-Deception and Self-Understanding: New Essays in Philosophy and Psychology*, edited by Mike W. Martin. Lawrence: University Press of Kansas, 1985.

Kittay, Eva Feder. "On Hypocrisy." *Metaphilosophy* 13 (1982): 277–289.

Laing, R. D. *The Divided Self*. Baltimore: Penguin, 1973.

Lang, Berel. "The Neurotic as Moral Agent." *Philosophy and Phenomenological Research* 29 (1968): 216–231.

Lazarus, Richard S. "Cognitive and Coping Processes in Emotion." Pp. 145–158 in *Stress and Coping*, edited by Alan Monat and Richard S. Lazarus. New York: Columbia University Press, 1977.

Lee, Vernon. *Vital Lies*. 2 vols. London: John Lane, 1912.

Leon, Philip. *The Ethics of Power, or the Problem of Evil*. London: George Allen and Unwin, 1935.

Linehan, Elizabeth A. "Ignorance, Self-Deception and Moral Accountability." *Journal of Value Inquiry* 16 (1982): 101–115.

Locke, John. "Of Enthusiasm." Pp. 428–441 in *An Essay on Human Understanding*, Vol. 2. New York: Dover, 1959.

Lovejoy, Arthur O. *Reflections on Human Nature*. Baltimore: Johns Hopkins University Press, 1961.

Malcolm, Norman. *Ludwig Wittgenstein: A Memoir*. New York: Oxford University Press, 1962.

Marcel, Gabriel. *Homo Viator: Introduction to a Metaphysic of Hope*. New York: Harper and Row, 1951.

Martin, Mike W. "Demystifying Doublethink: Self-Deception, Truth, and Freedom in *1984*." *Social Theory and Practice* 10 (1984): 319–331.

———. "Factor's Functionalist Account of Self-Deception." *Personalist* 60 (1979): 336–342.

———. "Immorality and Self-Deception." *Dialogue: Canadian Philosophical Review* 16 (1977): 274–280.

———. "*Invisible Man* and the Indictment of Innocence." *CLA Journal* 25 (1982): 288–302.

———. "Morality and Self-Deception: Paradox, Ambiguity, or Vagueness?" *Man and World* 12 (1979): 47–60.

———. "Sartre on Lying to Oneself." *Philosophy Research Archives* 4 (1978): 1–26.

———. "Self-Deception, Self-Pretence, and Emotional Detachment." *Mind* 88 (1979): 441–446.

————, ed. *Self-Deception and Self-Understanding: New Essays in Philosophy and Psychology.* Lawrence: University Press of Kansas, 1985.

Mayo, Bernard. "Belief and Constraint." Pp. 147–161 in *Knowledge and Belief,* edited by A. Phillips Griffiths. Oxford: Oxford University Press, 1967.

Meiland, Jack W. "What Ought We to Believe? or The Ethics of Belief Revisited." *American Philosophical Quarterly* 17 (1980): 15–24.

Melden, A. I. *Rights and Persons.* Berkeley: University of California Press, 1977.

Midgley, Mary. *Wickedness, A Philosophical Essay.* Boston: Routledge and Kegan Paul, 1984.

Milo, Ronald D. *Immorality.* Princeton, N.J.: Princeton University Press, 1984.

Miri, Mrinal. "Self-Deception." *Philosophy and Phenomenological Research* 34 (1974): 576–585.

Mortimore, G. W., ed. *Weakness of Will.* New York: St. Martin's Press, 1971.

Mounce, H. O. "Self-Deception." *Proceedings of the Aristotelian Society* 45 (1971): 61–72.

Murphy, Arthur Edward. *The Theory of Practical Reason,* edited by A. I. Melden. La Salle, Ill.: Open Court, 1964.

Murphy, Gardner. *Outgrowing Self-Deception.* New York: Basic Books, 1975.

Muyskens, James L. *The Sufficiency of Hope.* Philadelphia: Temple University Press, 1979.

Nemiah, John C. *Foundations of Psychopathology.* New York: Jason Aronson, 1973.

Neu, Jerome. *Emotion, Thought and Therapy.* Berkeley: University of California Press, 1977.

Niebuhr, Reinhold. *The Nature and Destiny of Man.* Vol. 1. *Human Nature.* New York: Charles Scribner's Sons, 1964.

Nietzsche, Friedrich. *Basic Writings of Nietzsche.* Edited and translated by Walter Kaufmann. New York: Modern Library, 1968.

————. *Beyond Good and Evil.* Translated by Walter Kaufmann. New York: Vintage Books, 1966.

————. *The Gay Science.* Translated by Walter Kaufmann. New York: Vintage Books, 1974.

————. *On the Advantage and Disadvantage of History for Life.* Translated by Peter Preuss. Indianapolis: Hackett, 1980.

————. *The Will to Power.* Edited by Walter Kaufmann. Translated by Walter Kaufmann and R. J. Hollingdale. New York: Vintage Books, 1968.

Nisbett, Richard, and L. Ross. *Human Inference: Strategies and Shortcomings of Social Judgment.* Englewood Cliffs, N.J.: Prentice-Hall, 1980.

Olafson, Frederick. *Principles and Persons: An Ethical Interpretation of Existentialism.* Baltimore: Johns Hopkins University Press, 1967.

O'Neill, Eugene. *The Iceman Cometh.* New York: Vintage Books, 1957.

————. *Hughie.* Pp. 259–293 in *The Later Plays of Eugene O'Neill.* New York: Modern Library, 1967.

Orwell, George. *1984.* New York: New American Library, 1961.

Paluch, Stanley. "Self-Deception." *Inquiry* 10 (1967): 268–278.

Pascal, Blaise. *Pensées.* Translated by A. J. Krailsheimer. Baltimore: Penguin Books, 1973.

Passmore, John. *A Hundred Years of Philosophy.* Baltimore: Penguin Books, 1968.

Pears, David. *Motivated Irrationality.* New York: Oxford University Press, 1984.

Penelhum, Terence, W. E. Kennick, and Arnold Isenberg. "Symposium: Pleasure and Falsity." *American Philosophical Quarterly* 1 (1964): 81–91.

Peterman, James F. "Self-Deception and the Problem of Avoidance." *Southern Journal of Philosophy* 21 (1983): 565–573.

Peters, R. S. "The Justification of Education." Pp. 239–267 in *The Philosophy of Education*, edited by R. S. Peters. Oxford: Oxford University Press, 1973.

Peyre, Henri. *Literature and Sincerity*. New Haven, Conn.: Yale University Press, 1963.

Phillips, D. Z. "Bad Faith and Sartre's Waiter." *Philosophy* 56 (1981): 23–31.

Plato. *The Collected Dialogues of Plato*, edited by Edith Hamilton and Huntington Cairns. Princeton, N.J.: Princeton University Press, 1961.

Pole, David. "Virtue and Reason." *Proceedings of the Aristotelian Society* 48 (1974): 43–62.

Price, H. H. *Belief*. New York: Humanities Press, 1969.

————. "Belief and Will." Pp. 91–116 in *Philosophy of Mind*, edited by Stuart Hampshire. New York: Harper and Row, 1966.

Proust, Marcel. *Swann's Way*. Translated by C. K. Scott Moncrieff. New York: Vintage Books, 1970.

Pugmire, David. " 'Strong' Self-Deception." *Inquiry* 12 (1969): 339–346.

Rank, Otto. *Truth and Reality*. Translated by Jessie Taft. New York: W. W. Norton, 1978.

Reid, Thomas. *Essays on the Active Powers of the Human Mind*. Essay 5, Chapter 4. Cambridge, Mass.: MIT Press, 1969.

Reik, Theodor. *Listening with the Third Ear*. New York: Arena Books, 1972.

Reilly, Richard. "Self-Deception: Resolving the Epistemological Paradox." *Personalist* 57 (1976): 391–394.

Rhees, Rush, ed. *Recollections of Wittgenstein*. New York: Oxford University Press, 1984.

Rogers, Carl. "A Theory of Therapy, Personality, and Interpersonal Relationships as Developed in the Client-Centered Framework." Pp. 184–256 in *Psychology: A Study of a Science*, Vol. 3, edited by S. Koch. New York: McGraw-Hill, 1959.

————. *On Becoming a Person*. Boston: Houghton Mifflin, 1961.

Rorty, Amélie Oksenberg. "Adaptivity and Self-Knowledge." *Inquiry* 18 (1975): 1–22.

————. "Belief and Self-Deception." *Inquiry* 15 (1972): 387–410.

————. "Self-Deception, Akrasia, and Irrationality." *Social Science Information* 19 (1980): 905–922.

Royce, Josiah. *The Philosophy of Josiah Royce*. Edited by John K. Roth. Indianapolis: Hackett Publishing, 1982.

Russell, J. Michael. "Saying, Feeling, and Self-Deception." *Behaviorism* 6 (1978): 27–43.

Sabini, John, and Maury Silver. *Moralities of Everyday Life*. New York: Oxford University Press, 1982.

Santayana, George. *Reason in Religion*. Vol. 3 of *The Life of Reason*. New York: Dover, 1982.

Sartre, Jean-Paul. *Anti-Semite and Jew*. Translated by George J. Becker. New York: Schocken Books, 1965.

————. *Being and Nothingness*. Translated by Hazel E. Barnes. New York: Washington Square Press, 1966.

————. "Existentialism Is a Humanism." Translated by Philip Mairet. Pp. 345–369 in *Existentialism from Dostoevsky to Sartre*, edited by Walter Kaufmann. New York: New American Library, 1975.

————. *No Exit and Three Other Plays*. Translated by Stuart Gilbert and Lionel Abel. New York: Vintage Books, 1949.

Saunders, John Turk. "The Paradox of Self-Deception." *Philosophy and Phenomenological Research* 35 (1975): 559–570.

Scheler, Max. *Ressentiment*. Edited by Lewis A. Coser and translated by William W. Holdheim. New York: Schocken Books, 1972.

Schiller, Ferdinand Canning Scott. *Problems of Belief*. New York: George H. Doran Co., 1924.

Schmidt, Matthias. *Albert Speer: The End of a Myth*. Translated by Joachim Neugroschel. New York: St. Martin's Press, 1984.

Schopenhauer, Arthur. *The World as Will and Representation*. Translated by E. F. J. Payne. Vol. 2, Chapter 19. New York: Dover, 1966.

Shafer, Roy. *A New Language for Psychoanalysis*. New Haven, Conn.: Yale University Press, 1976.

Shakespeare, William. *The Works of William Shakespeare*. New York: Oxford University Press.

Sheaffer, Louis. *O'Neill: Son and Artist*. Boston: Little, Brown and Co., 1973.

Shklar, Judith. "Let Us Not Be Hypocritical." *Daedalus* 108 (1979): 1–25. Reprinted on pp. 45–86 in Judith N. Shklar, *Ordinary Vices*. Cambridge, Mass.: Belknap Press of Harvard University Press, 1984.

Shlien, John M. "A Client-Centered Approach to Schizophrenia: First Approximation." In *Psychotherapy of the Psychoses*, edited by Arthur Burton. New York: Basic Books, 1961.

Sidgwick, Henry. "Unreasonable Action." *Mind* 11 (1893): 174–187.

Siegler, Frederick A. "An Analysis of Self-Deception." *Noûs* 2 (1968): 147–164.

————. "Self-Deception." *Australasian Journal of Philosophy* 41 (1963): 29–43.

Slote, Michael. *Goods and Virtues*. Oxford: Clarendon Press, 1983.

Smith, Adam. "Of the Nature of Self-Deceit." In *The Theory of Moral Sentiments*. New York: Kelley, 1966.

Smith, Holly. "Culpable Ignorance." *Philosophical Review* 92 (1983): 543–571.

Snyder, C. R. "Collaborative Companions: The Relationship of Self-Deception and Excuse-Making." Pp. 35–51 in *Self-Deception and Self-Understanding: New Essays in Philosophy and Psychology*, edited by Mike W. Martin. Lawrence: University Press of Kansas, 1985.

Solomon, Robert. *The Passions*. Notre Dame, Ind.: University of Notre Dame Press, 1983.

Sophocles. *Oedipus Rex*. Pp. 1–78 in *The Oedipus Cycle*, translated by Dudley Fitts and Robert Fitzgerald. New York: Harcourt, Brace and World, 1949.

Speer, Albert. *Inside the Third Reich*. Translated by Richard Winston and Clara Winston. New York: Avon Books, 1971.

Spinoza, Baruch. *Ethics*. Translated by R. H. M. Elwes. In *Benedict de Spinoza*, ed. R. H. M. Elwes. New York: Dover Publications, 1955.

Stendhal (Marie-Henri Beyle). *On Love*. Translated by H. B. V. under the direction of C. K. Scott-Moncrieff. New York: Da Capo Press, 1983.

Swift, Jonathan. *A Tale of a Tub*. Pp. 59–73 in *The Portable Swift*, edited by Carl Van Doren. New York: Viking Press, 1948.

Szabados, Béla. "Hypocrisy." *Canadian Journal of Philosophy* 9 (1979): 195–210.

————. "The Morality of Self-Deception." *Dialogue* 13 (1974): 24–34.

————. "Self-Deception." *Canadian Journal of Philosophy* 4 (1974): 51–68.

————. "The Self, Its Passions and Self-Deception." Pp. 143–168 in *Self-Deception and Self-Understanding: New Essays in Philosophy and Psychology*, edited by Mike W. Martin. Lawrence: University Press of Kansas, 1985.

Tolstoy, Leo. *Anna Karenina*. Translated by David Magarshack. New York: New American Library, 1961.

———. *A Confession and What I Believe*. Edited and translated by Aylmer Maude. London: Oxford University Press, 1967.

———. *The Death of Ivan Ilych*. Translated by Louise and Aylmer Maude. Pp. 245–302 in *Great Short Works of Leo Tolstoy*. Edited by John Bayley. New York: Harper and Row, 1967.

Trilling, Lionel. *Sincerity and Authenticity*. Cambridge, Mass.: Harvard University Press, 1971.

Vaihinger, Hans. *The Philosophy of "As-If."* 2nd edition. Translated by C. K. Ogden. New York: Barnes and Noble, 1952.

Walker, A. D. M. "The Ideal of Sincerity." *Mind* 87 (1978): 481–497.

Wallace, James D. *Virtues and Vices*. Ithaca, N.Y.: Cornell University Press, 1978.

Walton, Kendall. "Fearing Fictions." *Journal of Philosophy* 75 (1978): 5–27.

Watson, Gary. "Skepticism about Weakness of Will." *Philosophical Review* 86 (1977): 316–339.

Wild, John. "Authentic Existence." Pp. 356–366 in *Introductory Readings in Ethics*, edited by W. K. Frankena and J. T. Granrose. Englewood Cliffs, N.J.: Prentice-Hall, 1974.

Wilhelm, Richard, and Cary F. Baynes, trans. *The I Ching or Book of Changes*. Princeton, N.J.: Princeton University Press, 1977.

Williams, Bernard. *Problems of the Self*. Cambridge: Cambridge University Press, 1973.

Wittgenstein, Ludwig. *Culture and Value*. Translated by Peter Winch. New York: Blackwell, 1984.

———. *Philosophical Investigations*. Translated by G. E. M. Anscombe. 3rd edition. New York: Macmillan, 1953.

Wollheim, Richard, and James Hopkins, eds. *Philosophical Essays on Freud*. Cambridge: Cambridge University Press, 1982.

Index

171